endeavour

DIE
OLYMPISCHEN OLÍMPICOS
SPIELE ÁLBUM

THE OLYMPIC ALBUM

DE OLYMPISCHE SPELEN

O ÁLBUM OLÍMPICO

Endeavour London Ltd.
21–31 Woodfield Road
London W9 2BA
Fax +44 (0)20 3227 2432
info@endeavourlondon.com

ISBN 978-1-873913-40-6 (GB)
ISBN 978-1-873913-39-0 (D)
ISBN 978-1-873913-41-3 (NL)
ISBN 978-1-908271-16-7 (F)
ISBN 978-1-873913-80-2 (E)
ISBN 978-1-873913-42-0 (PORT)

Copyright © Endeavour London Ltd, 2011

No part of this book may be reproduced or transmitted in any form or by any other means without permission in writing from Endeavour London.

A catalogue record for the book is available from the British Library.

Printed in China

Created for Endeavour London Ltd by Windmill Books Ltd
First Floor, 9-17 St Albans Place, London N1 0NX

For Windmill Books Ltd
Art Director: Jeni Child
Managing Editor: Tim Cooke
Graphic Designer: Guy Callaby
Editorial Director: Lindsey Lowe

For Endeavour London Ltd
Picture Manager: Ben Bonarius
Production: Mary Osborne

Page 1: Michael Phelps (United States, 200 m individual medley
Page 3: Marion Jones (United States), 100 m; later stripped of medal for drug abuse

Contents

Introduction	008 – 009
1896 Athens, Greece	010 – 015
1900 Paris, France	016 – 023
1904 St. Louis, United States	024 – 031
1908 London, Great Britain	032 – 039
1912 Stockholm, Sweden	040 – 047
1920 Antwerp, Belgium	048 – 055

1924 Chamonix, France	056 – 061	
1924 Paris, France	062 – 069	
1928 Amsterdam, Netherlands	070 – 077	
1928 St Moritz, Switzerland	078 – 085	
1932 Lake Placid, United States	086 – 093	
1932 Los Angeles, United States	094 – 103	
1936 Garmisch-Partenkirchen, Germany	104 – 111	
1936 Berlin, Germany	112 – 123	
1948 St Moritz, Switzerland	124 – 131	
1948 London, Great Britain	132 – 143	
1952 Oslo, Norway	144 – 151	
1952 Helsinki, Finland	152 – 163	
1956 Cortina d'Ampezzo	164 – 173	
1956 Melbourne, Australia	174 – 187	

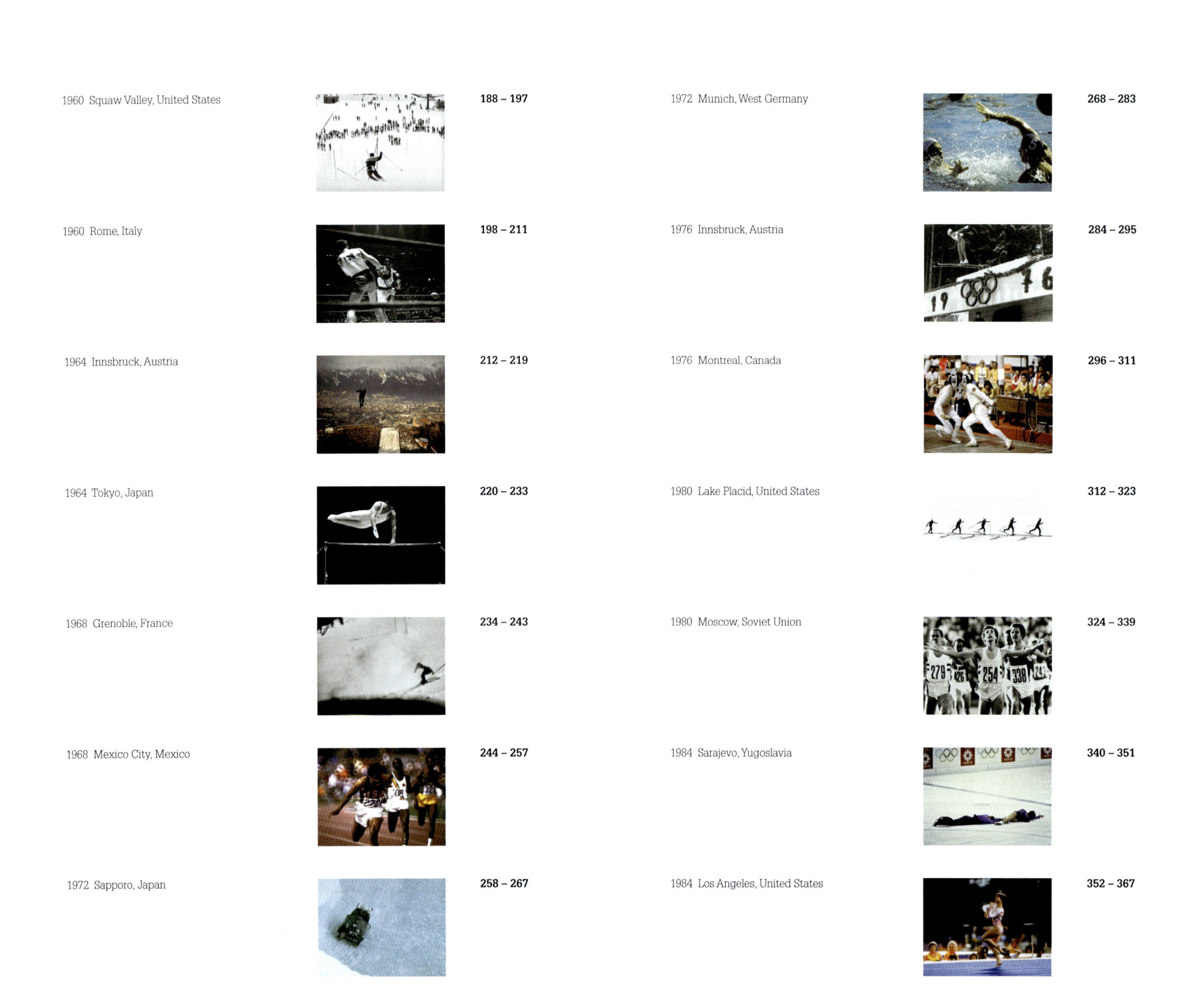

1960 Squaw Valley, United States	**188 – 197**
1960 Rome, Italy	**198 – 211**
1964 Innsbruck, Austria	**212 – 219**
1964 Tokyo, Japan	**220 – 233**
1968 Grenoble, France	**234 – 243**
1968 Mexico City, Mexico	**244 – 257**
1972 Sapporo, Japan	**258 – 267**
1972 Munich, West Germany	**268 – 283**
1976 Innsbruck, Austria	**284 – 295**
1976 Montreal, Canada	**296 – 311**
1980 Lake Placid, United States	**312 – 323**
1980 Moscow, Soviet Union	**324 – 339**
1984 Sarajevo, Yugoslavia	**340 – 351**
1984 Los Angeles, United States	**352 – 367**

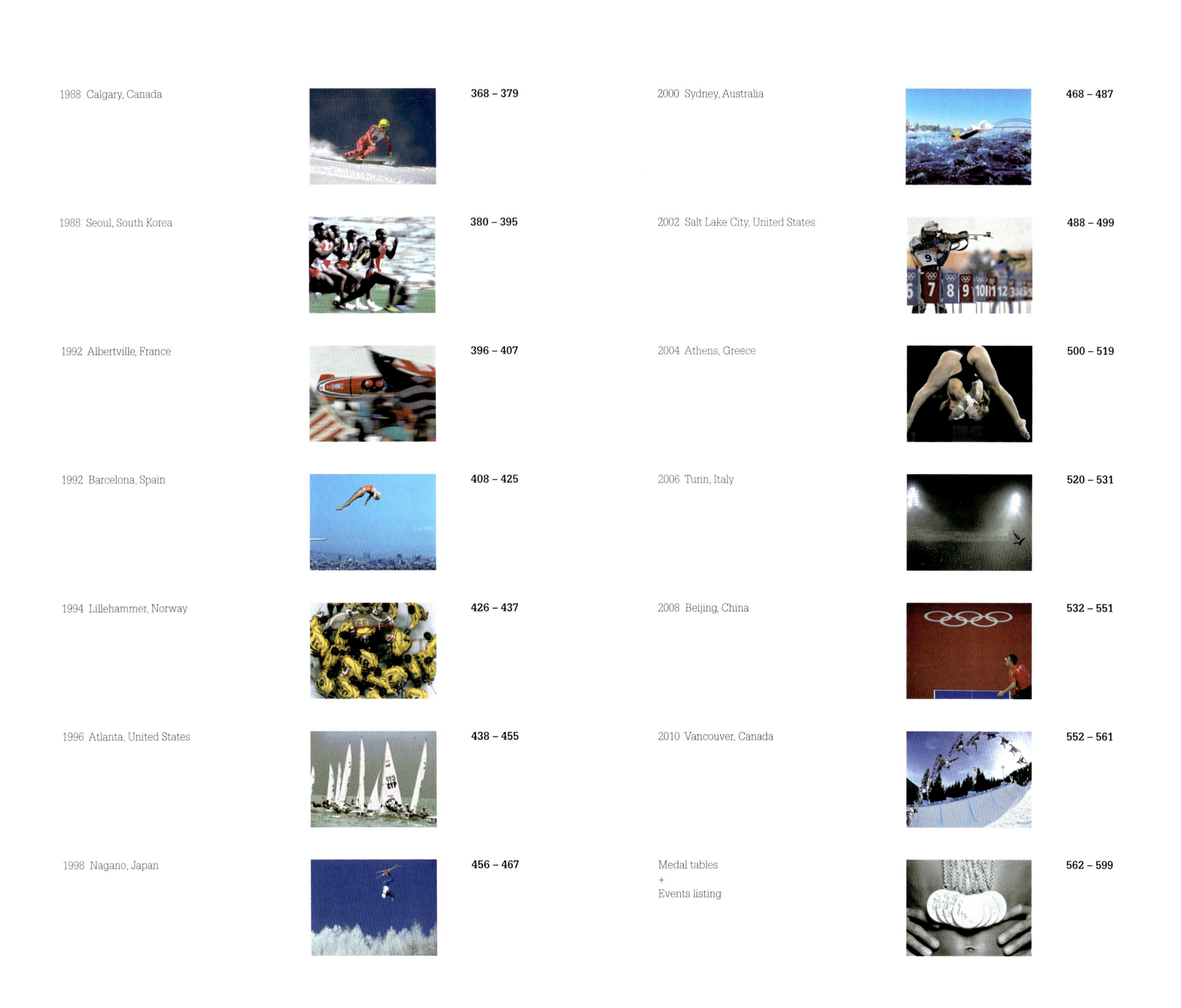

1988 Calgary, Canada	368 – 379
1988 Seoul, South Korea	380 – 395
1992 Albertville, France	396 – 407
1992 Barcelona, Spain	408 – 425
1994 Lillehammer, Norway	426 – 437
1996 Atlanta, United States	438 – 455
1998 Nagano, Japan	456 – 467
2000 Sydney, Australia	468 – 487
2002 Salt Lake City, United States	488 – 499
2004 Athens, Greece	500 – 519
2006 Turin, Italy	520 – 531
2008 Beijing, China	532 – 551
2010 Vancouver, Canada	552 – 561
Medal tables + Events listing	562 – 599

Introduction

The Olympic Games punctuate our lives, and have captured the world's imagination for over 110 years. From a small international sports meeting inspired by amateur ideals, the games have grown to become the largest single sporting event on earth. The first modern games, in 1896, had only 241 athletes from 14 nations; in Beijing in 2008, more than 11,000 athletes represented 204 countries.

The Olympic Album traces the history of this remarkable phenomenon in a series of stunning images that capture the spirit of the games' motto: 'Faster, Higher, Stronger'. It tracks not only the Olympic Games but also the Winter Olympics, first held in 1924. Many of the images celebrate outstanding athletes. Some have dominated a single games, winning a number of events; others are more notable for their longevity, competing in a series of games. Still others are associated with a single feat – a lightning sprint, a prodigious leap, a perfect score – that is etched on the memory of all those who witnessed it.

The games – 50 in all – are arranged in chronological order. Each games opens with a summary of its dates, location, sports and competitors. The images themselves provide a flavour of the particular games, with outstanding individuals, moments of drama or heartbreak, or breath-taking spectacle. At the back of the book the reference section presents the medal tables, listing the number of gold, silver and bronze medals won by each country in the order accepted by the International Olympics Committee. (The tables should be used with some caution: different methods of awarding medals were used for early games, and disqualifications sometimes take place years after the games concerned, and may affect the overall totals.)

Introduction Les Jeux Olympiques ponctuent nos vies et capturent l'imagination du monde entier depuis plus de 110 années. D'une petite réunion sportive internationale inspirée par des idées d'amateurs, les jeux ont évolué pour devenir le plus grand évènement sportif au monde. Les premiers jeux modernes, en 1896, ne comptaient que 241 athlètes de 14 nations différentes ; à Beijing en 2008, plus de 11000 athlètes ont représenté 204 pays.

L'Album Olympique retrace l'histoire de ce phénomène remarquable avec une série d'images capturant l'esprit de la devise des jeux : 'Plus vite, plus haut, plus fort'. Cet album ne retrace pas seulement l'histoire des Jeux Olympiques, mais aussi des Jeux Olympiques d'Hiver, organisés pour la première fois en 1924. De nombreuses images rendent hommage à des athlètes hors du commun. Certains ont dominé des jeux entiers en gagnant plusieurs épreuves ; d'autres sont surtout remarquables pour leur longue carrière, ayant participé à plusieurs éditions des Jeux. Quant à d'autres, ils sont restés et resteront dans les mémoires pour un exploit unique : un sprint à la vitesse de l'éclair, un bond prodigieux, un score parfait.

Les jeux (50 en tout) ont été rangés dans l'ordre chronologique. Chaque édition est introduite par un résumé de ses dates, de son lieu, de ses sports et de ses participants. Les images nous font goûter à l'ambiance même des jeux en question, avec des individus hors du commun, des instants de drame, ou encore des moments de spectacles à couper le souffle. A la fin du livre, la partie référence présente les tables des médailles, listant le nombre des médailles d'or, d'argent et de bronze gagnées par chaque pays dans l'ordre accepté par le Comité Olympique International. (Les tables doivent être utilisées avec une certaine précaution: des méthodes différentes de remise des médailles étaient en rigueur lors des premiers jeux, et des disqualifications peuvent parfois avoir lieu des années après les jeux concernés et peuvent alors influencer les résultats.)

Einleitung Die Olympischen Spiele unterbrechen unsere Leben und fesseln die Phantasie der Welt seit mehr als 110 Jahren. Die Spiele haben sich von einem kleinen internationalen, von amateurhaften Idealen inspirierten Sportfest zu einem der größten Sportevents der Welt entwickelt. An den ersten modernen Spielen 1896 nahmen nur 214 Athleten aus 14 Nationen teil. In Peking 2008 repräsentierten mehr als 11,000 Athleten 204 Länder.

Das Olympische Album begibt sich über eine Reihe phantastischer Bilder, die den Geist des Mottos der Spiele ‚Schneller, höher, stärker' einfangen, auf die Spur der Geschichte dieses außergewöhnlichen Phänomens. Es geht nicht nur den Olympischen Sommerspielen, sondern auch den Olympischen Winterspielen nach, die das erste Mal im Jahre 1924 abgehalten wurden. Viele der Bilder feiern hervorragende Athleten. Einige von ihnen haben nur einmal die Spiele dominiert, indem sie eine Reihe von Bewerben gewonnen haben; Andere haben sich durch ihre Langlebigkeit ausgezeichnet und nahmen an mehreren Spielen teil. Wieder Andere werden mit einem einzigen Event assoziiert – einem blitzschnellen Sprint, einem ungeheuren Sprung, einem perfekten Ergebnis – das sich in das Gedächtnis all jener eingebrannt hat, die Zeuge wurden.

Die Olympischen Spiele – 50 insgesamt – werden in chronologischer Abfolge angeführt. Die Darstellung jedes der einzelnen Spiele beginnt mit einer Zusammenfassung der Daten, dem Austragungsort, den Sportarten und den Teilnehmenden. Die Bilder selbst verleihen einen Eindruck der jeweiligen Spiele, mit herausragenden Individuen, dramatischen oder herzzerreißenden Momenten oder atemberaubenden Spektakeln. Im bibliographischen Teil am Ende des Buches werden die Medaillenspiegel präsentiert und die Gold-, Silber- und Bronzemedaillen pro Land in der vom Internationalen Olympischen Komitee genehmigten Reihenfolge aufgelistet. (Diese Listen sollten mit einiger Vorsicht genossen werden: verschiedene Methoden der Medaillenvergabe wurden in früheren Zeiten gebraucht, und Disqualifikationen werden manchmal erst Jahre nach den Spielen vorgenommen, was die Gesamtsumme an Medaillen beeinträchtigen könnte.)

Inleiding De Olympische Spelen vormen een constante in ons leven en spreken al meer dan 110 jaar tot de verbeelding. Van een klein internationaal sportevenement geïnspireerd op de idealen van amateurs zijn de Spelen uitgegroeid tot de grootste sportmanifestatie ter wereld. Aan de eerste moderne Spelen, gehouden in 1896, namen 241 atleten uit 14 landen deel; in Beijing, 2008, vertegenwoordigden 11.000 topsporters 204 landen.

In het Olympic Album wordt de geschiedenis van dit opmerkelijke verschijnsel gevolgd aan de hand van een reeks prachtige foto's waarop de geest van het Olympisch devies is vastgelegd: 'sneller, hoger, sterker'. Het boek beperkt zich niet tot de Olympische Zomerspelen, maar volgt ook de Winterspelen, die voor het eerst in 1924 werden gehouden. Veel van de afbeeldingen vormen een eerbetoon aan voortreffelijke atleten. Sommige van hen eisten een hoofdrol op bij één enkel Olympisch toernooi door meerdere onderdelen te winnen; anderen hebben geschiedenis geschreven door hun lange levensduur en streden in meerdere Olympische Spelen om de eerste plaats. Weer anderen worden met de Spelen geassocieerd door een enkel wapenfeit – een razendsnelle sprint, een buitengewone sprong, een perfecte score – dat in het geheugen is geëtst van allen die daarvan getuige waren.

De Spelen – vijftig in totaal – komen in chronologische volgorde aan bod. Elke editie van de Spelen begint met een opsomming van de data, de locatie, de sportonderdelen en de deelnemers. De afbeeldingen zelf laten de geest zien van de Spelen in kwestie met bijzondere sporters, momenten van tragedie of diepe teleurstelling, of adembenemende vertoningen. Achter in het boek kunt u de tabellen met de medailles vinden; een lijst toont het aantal gouden, zilveren en bronzen medailles dat door elk land werd gewonnen in de volgorde die is goedgekeurd door het Internationaal Olympisch Comité. (Bij de tabellen is een kanttekening op zijn plaats: bij de vroege Spelen werden verschillende methoden gebruikt bij het toekennen van de medailles, en soms vinden diskwalificaties plaats jaren na de Spelen in kwestie, wat invloed kan hebben op de totale uitkomst).

Introducción Los Juegos Olímpicos marcan nuestras vidas cada cuatro años y han acaparado la atención del mundo durante más de 110 años. Comenzaron como un pequeño acontecimiento deportivo a nivel internacional basado en ideales de aficionados y se han convertido en el evento deportivo más importante del mundo. La primera edición de los Juegos Olímpicos Modernos, que se celebró en 1896, contó solamente con 241 atletas de 14 países. En la edición de Pekín, en 2008, se presentaron más de 11.000 atletas provenientes de 204 países.

Olímpicos álbum examina la historia de este extraordinario fenómeno a través de numerosas y espectaculares imágenes que representan el espíritu del lema de los Juegos Olímpicos: "más rápido, más alto, más fuerte". Además, también analiza los Juegos Olímpicos de Invierno, que se celebraron por primera vez en 1924. Varias de las imágenes conmemoran atletas destacados: algunos de ellos han dominado una edición entera habiendo ganado numerosas pruebas; otros se destacan más por haber competido durante varios años, e incluso hay otros a los que se les asocia con alguna proeza que ha quedado grabada en la retina de los que la presenciaron: un sprint veloz como un rayo, un salto prodigioso o incluso un tanto perfecto.

Los Juegos Olímpicos, 50 en total, han sido clasificados en orden cronológico y cada uno cuenta con un resumen de las fechas, la ciudad, los deportes y sus participantes. Las mismas imágenes proporcionan un toque particular de los mismos: representan personajes destacados, momentos de tensión o de tristeza, además de momentos inolvidables. En el dorso del libro, la sección de referencias incluye las tablas de las medallas con la cantidad de oros, platas y bronces que ha ganado cada país en el orden establecido por el Comité Olímpico Internacional (las tablas deben tomarse como referencia general: en los primeros Juegos Olímpicos se emplearon métodos diferentes para otorgar las medallas y a veces algunos atletas han sido descalificados años después de haber participado. Estos factores podrían afectar la clasificación general).

Introdução Os Jogos Olímpicos assinalam as nossas vidas e têm captado a imaginação mundial há mais de 110 anos. Sendo a princípio um pequeno encontro desportivo internacional inspirado por ideais amadores, os jogos desenvolveram-se ao ponto de se tornarem no maior evento desportivo único à face da terra. Os primeiros jogos da era moderna, em 1896, contaram apenas com 241 atletas de 14 nações; em Pequim, em 2008, mais de 11 000 atletas representaram 204 países.

O Álbum Olímpico reconstitui a história deste notável fenómeno numa série de belíssimas imagens que captam o espírito da divisa dos jogos: "Mais rápido, mais alto, mais forte". O álbum acompanha não apenas os Jogos Olímpicos, mas também os Jogos de Inverno, que se realizaram pela primeira vez em 1924. Muitas das imagens glorificam atletas excepcionais. Alguns dominaram apenas nuns jogos, vencendo uma série de provas; outros são mais notáveis pela sua longevidade, competindo numa série de jogos. Outros ainda estão associados a uma única façanha – um sprint rapidíssimo, um salto prodigioso, um resultado perfeito – que está gravada na memória de todos aqueles que a testemunharam.

Os jogos – 50 no total – são dispostos por ordem cronológica. Cada um dos jogos abre com um resumo das datas, locais, modalidades e participantes. As próprias imagens proporcionam um sabor particular de cada um dos jogos, com individualidades proeminentes, momentos de drama ou de desgosto, ou de espectáculo deslumbrante. No verso do livro a secção de referência apresenta as tabelas das medalhas, indicando o número de medalhas de ouro, prata e bronze ganhas por cada país pela ordem aceite pelo Comité Olímpico Internacional. (As tabelas devem ser usadas com algum cuidado: nos jogos iniciais foram utilizados métodos diferentes de atribuição de medalhas e, por vezes, tiveram lugar desqualificações anos depois dos jogos em causa, que podem afectar os totais globais).

Prefazione I giochi olimpici segnano le nostre vite e catturano l'attenzione dell'immaginario mondiale da 110 anni. Da ristretto appuntamento sportivo internazionale ispirato da ideali amatoriali, i giochi si sono evoluti fino a diventare il maggior evento sportivo del pianeta. I primi giochi moderni, nel 1896, contavano soltanto 241 atleti provenienti da 14 nazioni; a Pechino nel 2008, oltre 11.000 atleti hanno rappresentato 204 Paesi.

Questo Album Olimpico traccia la storia di questo fenomeno degno di nota, in una serie di straordinarie immagini che catturano lo spirito del motto olimpico: "Citius, altius, fortius" (espressione latina che significa "Più veloce, più in alto, più forte"). Ripercorre le tappe non solo dei Giochi Olimpici, ma anche delle Olimpiadi Invernali, tenutesi la prima volta nel 1924. Molte delle immagini celebrano atleti d'eccezione. Alcuni di loro hanno dominato intere edizioni, vincendo in diversi eventi; altri invece sono famosi per aver partecipato a numerose edizioni, gareggiando in diversi giochi. Altri ancora hanno legato il loro nome per sempre a un qualche record, uno sprint fulmineo, una rimonta prodigiosa, un punteggio perfetto, impresso nella memoria di tutti coloro che ne sono stati testimoni.

I giochi, 50 in tutto, sono organizzati in ordine cronologico. Ciascun gioco è introdotto da una sintesi di date, luoghi, sport e partecipanti. Le immagini consentono di immergersi in questi speciali giochi, con i loro eccezionali personaggi, momenti di scalpore o drammatici, e anche attimi di spettacolo mozzafiato. Al termine del volume, un'appendice presenta l'Albo d'Oro, che elenca le quantità delle medaglie d'oro, d'argento e di bronzo vinte da ogni Paese, nell'ordine avallato dal Comitato Olimpico Internazionale (tali tabelle sono da usare con una certa cautela: nei primissimi giochi, sono stati usati metodi diversi per l'assegnazione delle medaglie, inoltre bisogna tenere conto che talvolta le squalifiche avvengono anni dopo che si è tenuto l'evento, falsando così le classifiche).

Foils

1896

Athens
Greece

Games of the I Olympiad

6 – 15 April 1896

43 events ▪ 9 sports

14 competing nations ▪ 241 athletes

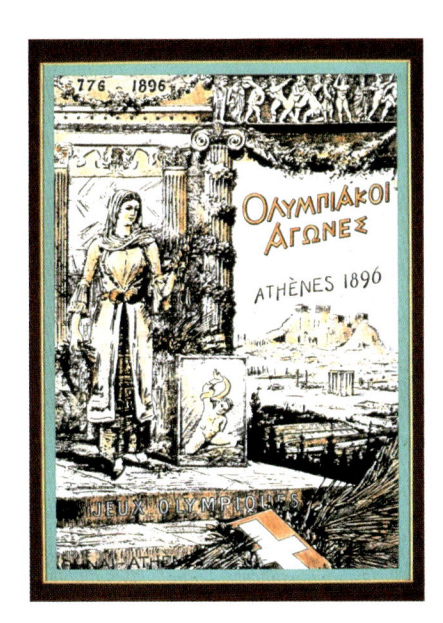

Coronation, Czar Nicholas II, Moscow

F.A. Lane, Herbert Jamison, Robert Garrett and Albert Taylor, U.S. athletics team

Leon Flemeng (France, left), gold, 100 km & Paul Masson (France), gold, 2,000 m & 10,000 m, cycling

100 m

Marathon training

Sweden/Denmark, gold, tug-of-war

1900

Paris
France

Games of the II Olympiad

15 May – 28 October 1900

95 events ▪ 18 sports

24 competing nations ▪ 997 athletes

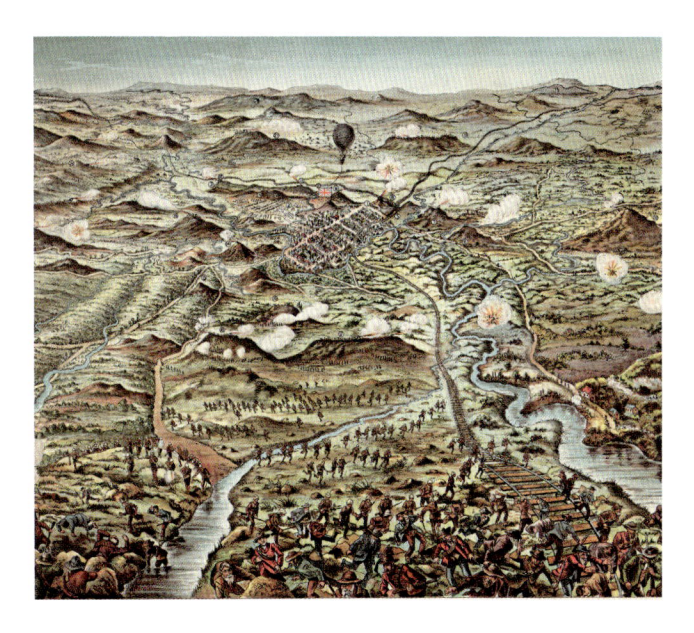

Siege of Ladysmith, Natal, Second Boer War

Charlotte Cooper (Great Britain), gold, singles & mixed doubles tennis

Reginald Frank Doherty (Great Britain), gold, men's doubles; bronze, men's singles tennis

Louis Prevel (France), sculls

Marathon

Léon de Lunden (Belgium), gold, pigeon shooting

Frantz Reichel (France), gold, rugby union

100 m freestyle swimming

1904

St Louis
United States

Games of the III Olympiad
1 July – 23 November 1904
91 events ▪ 17 sports
12 competing nations ▪ 651 athletes

Olympics and World's Fair, Festival Hall

Siege of Port Arthur, Manchuria, Russo–Japanese War

Frederick Winters (United States) silver, dumb-bell weightlifting

Martin Sheridan (United States), gold, discus throw

400 m, start

G.U. Smith (New Zealand), sprinter

Ralph Rose (United States), gold, shot put

Felix 'Andarín' Carvajal (Cuba), marathon

1904 St Louis

Dorando Pietri (Italy), marathon, disqualified

1908

London
Great Britain

Games of the IV Olympiad

27 April – 31 October 1908

22 sports ▪ 110 events

22 competing nations ▪ 2,008 athletes (1,971 men ▪ 37 women)

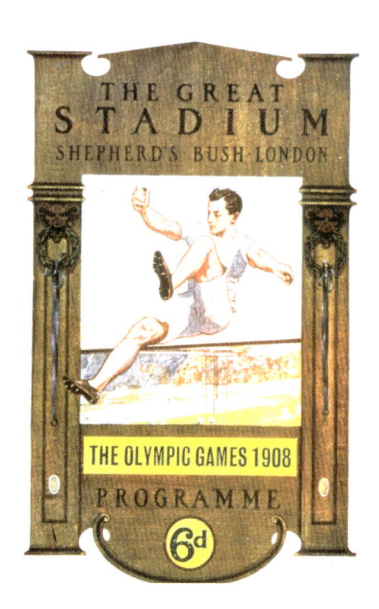

Spectators, marathon

▲ Women's archery
▶ Danish gymnast

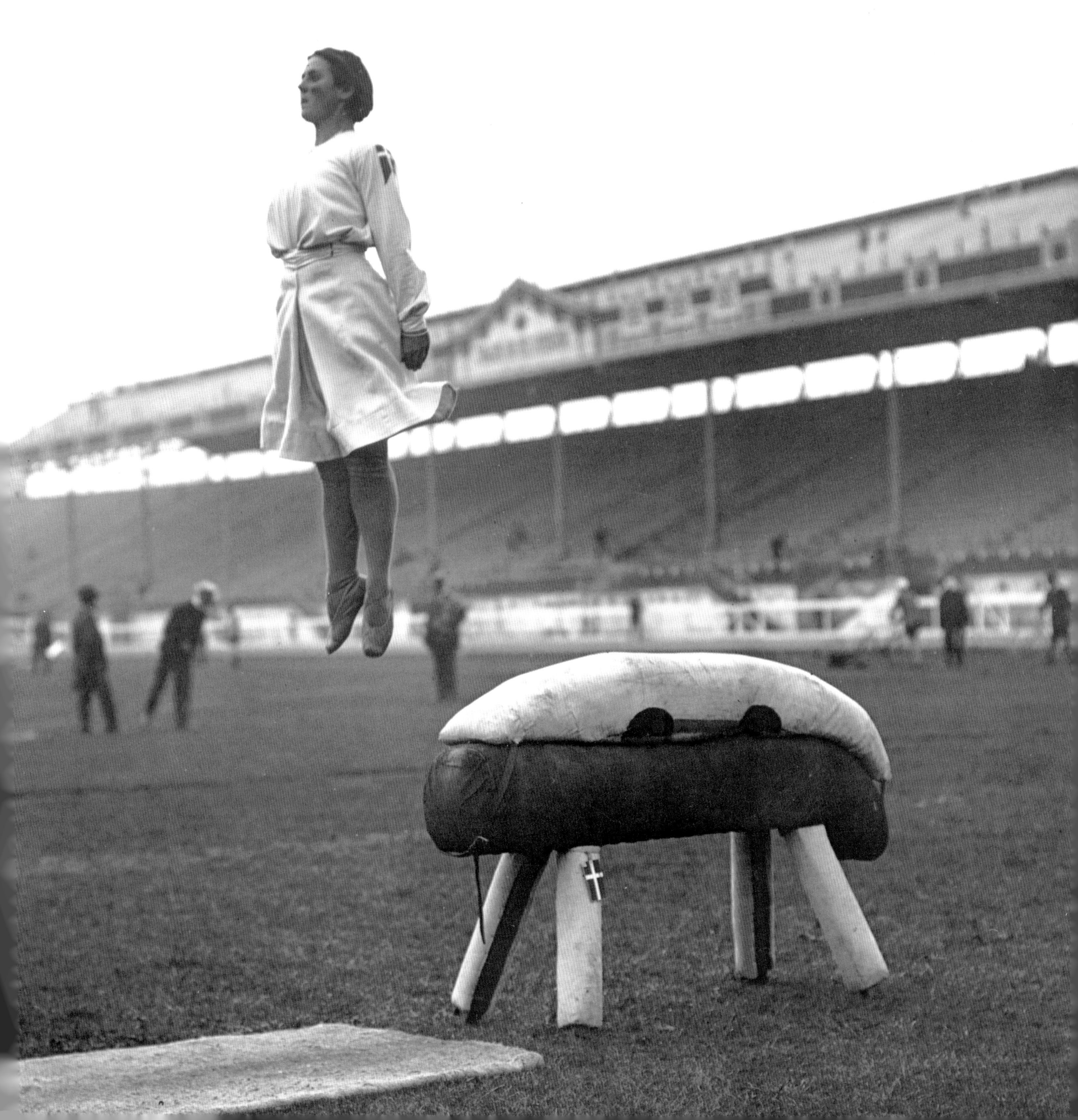

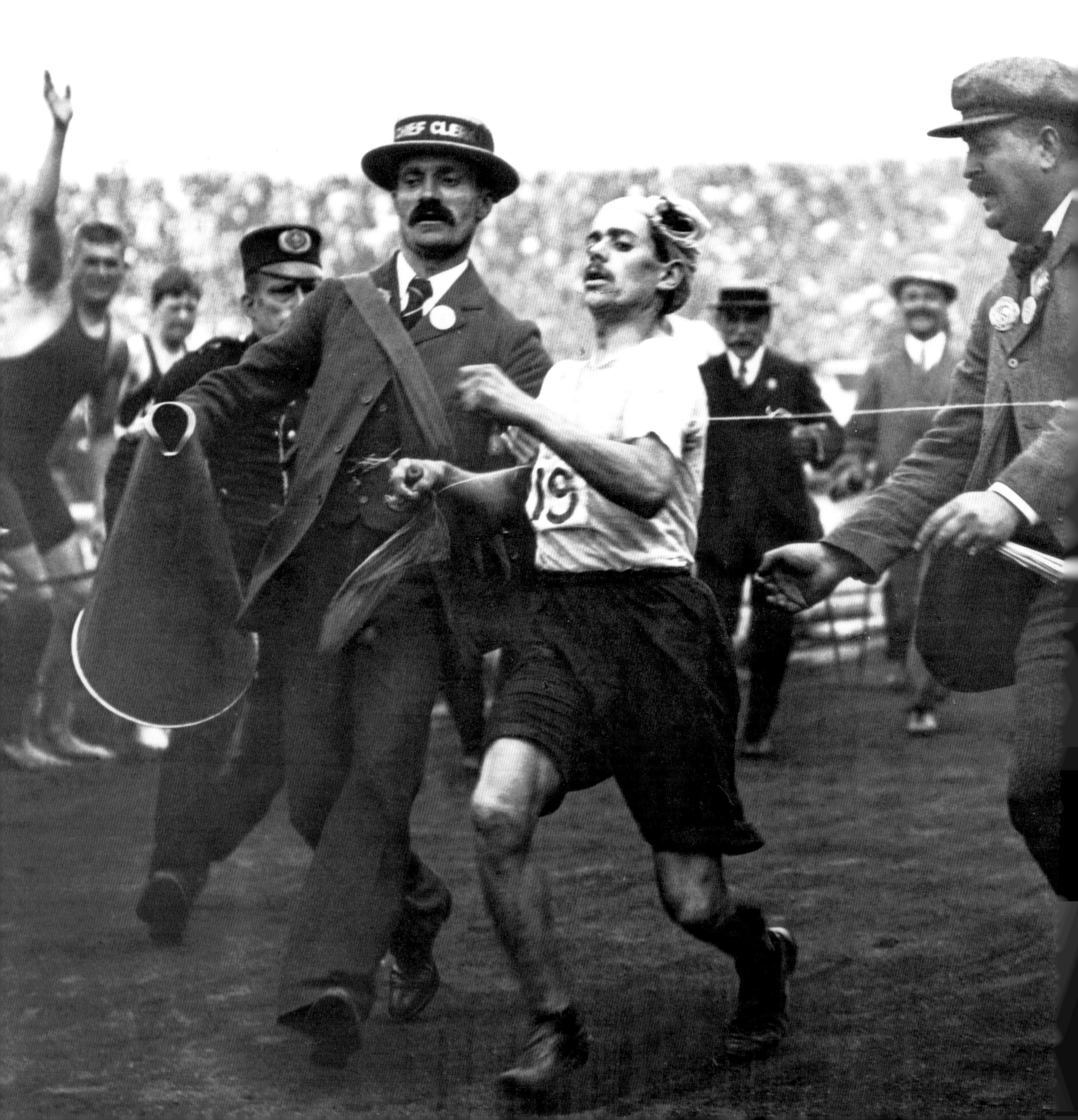
19

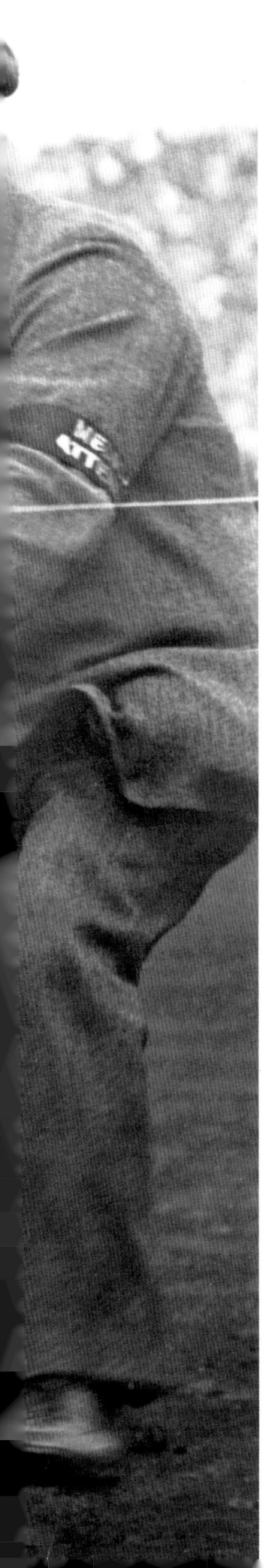

▲ Timothy Ahearne (Great Britain), gold, triple jump
◄ Dorando Pietri (Italy), marathon, disqualified

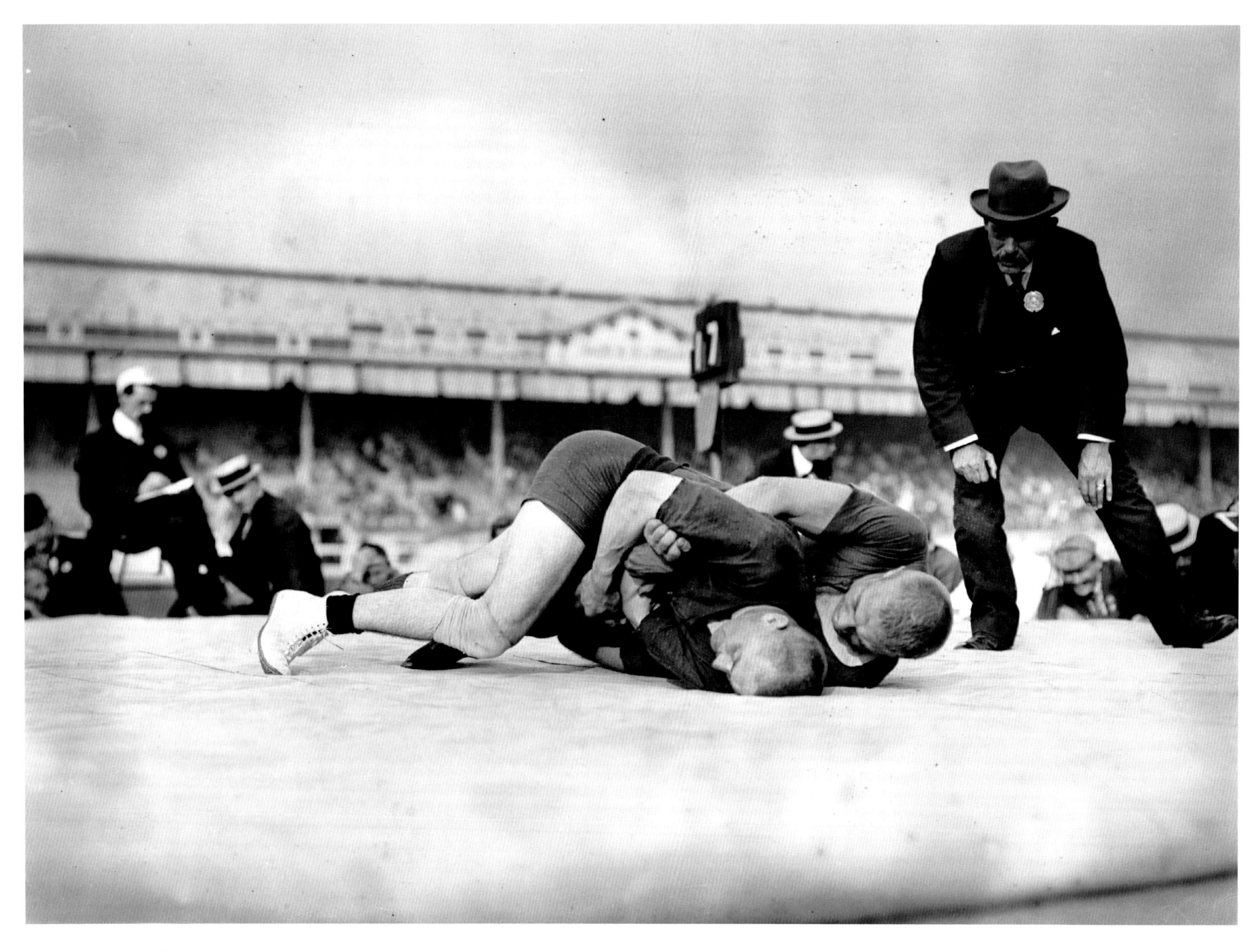

Greco-Roman wrestling

Medical checks, marathon

Richard Byrd (United States), silver, discus

1912

Stockholm Sweden

Games of the V Olympiad

5 May–27 July 1912

102 events ▪ 13 sports

28 competing nations ▪ 2,407 athletes

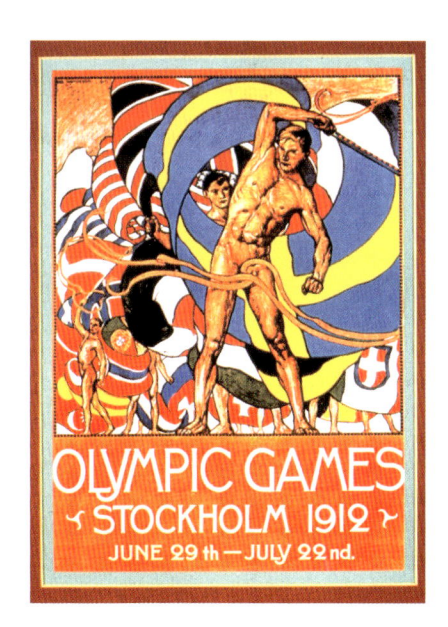

Titanic, 15 April, 1912

England (gold) vs Denmark (silver), football

Carl-Gustaf Lewenhaupt (Sweden), show jumping.

44   1912 Stockholm

▲ Jim Thorpe (United States), gold, pentathlon & decathlon
◀ Platform diving final

Swedish miniature rifle team

100 m, start

Belgium (gold) vs Czechoslovakia (silver), football

1920

Antwerp Belgium

Games of the VII Olympiad

20 April – 12 September 1920

154 events ▪ 22 sports

29 competing nations ▪ 2,626 athletes

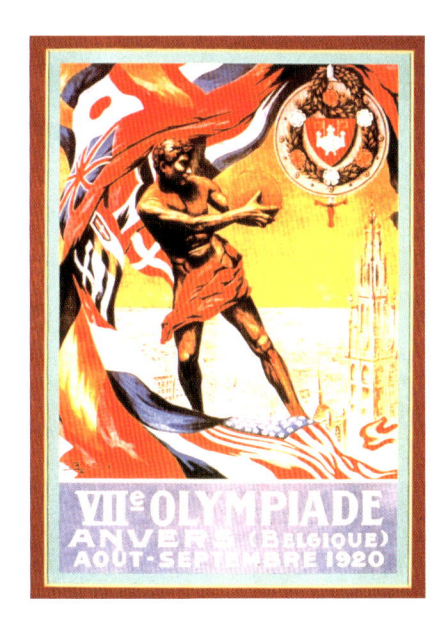

Prohibition, United States

Suzanne Lenglen & Max Decugis (France), gold, mixed doubles tennis

Harry Ryan & Thomas Lance (Great Britain), gold, 2,000 m tandem

Greco-Roman wrestlers, Sweden

Richmond Landon (United States), gold, high jump

Duke Kahanamoku (United States), gold, 100 m freestyle

Paavo Nurmi (Finland), gold, 10,000 m

Curling (Great Britain)

1924

Chamonix
France

1st Olympic Winter Games

25 January – 5 February 1924

16 events ▪ 6 sports

16 competing nations ▪ 258 athletes

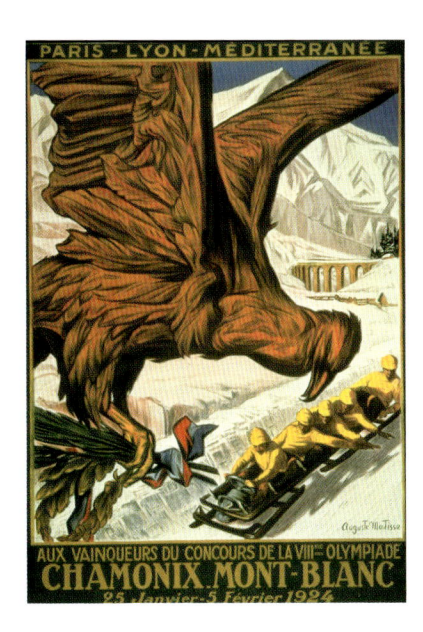

Lenin & Stalin, Soviet Union

Sonja Henie (Norway), figure skater aged 11

Medallists, women's figure skating

English speed skaters, training

1924 Chamonix

▲ United States vs Canada, ice hockey
▶ Great Britain (silver), bobsleigh

1924 Chamonix

Jackson Scholz (United States), gold, 200 m

1924
Paris
France

Games of the VIII Olympiad

4 May – 27 July 1924

126 events ▪ 17 sports

44 competing nations ▪ 3,089 athletes

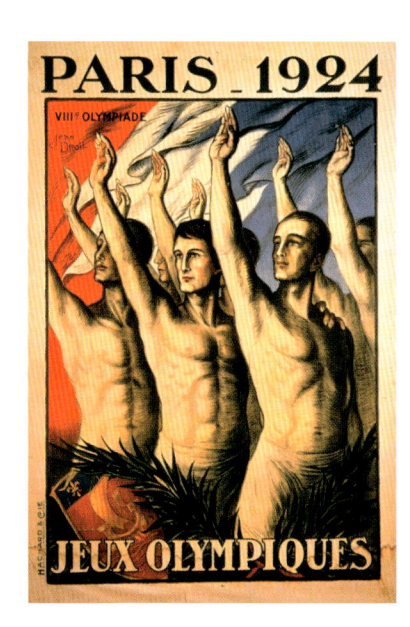

Mussolini, prime minister, Italy

Great Britain, bronze, polo

Uruguay, gold, football

▲ Lucy Mortons (Great Britain, right), gold, 200 m breaststroke & Ms. C. Jeans (Great Britain), swimming
▶ Johnny Weissmuller (United States), gold, 100 m freestyle, 400 m freestyle & 200 m freestyle relay

1924 Paris

Paavo Nurmi (Finland, right), gold, cross-country

Ville Ritola (Finland, left), gold, 3,000 m steeplechase

Women's 100 m

1928
Amsterdam Netherlands

Games of the IX Olympiad

17 May – 12 August 1928

109 events ▪ 14 sports

46 competing nations ▪ 2,883 athletes

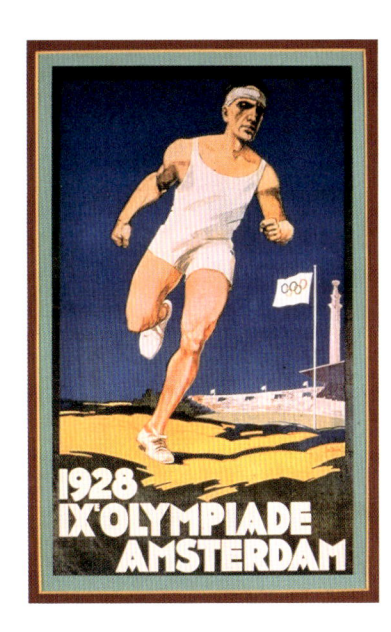

Herbert Hoover, president, United States

Portugal vs Chile, football

400 m, start

▲ Romeo Neri (Italy), silver, horizontal bars
▶ Alf Baxter (Great Britain), weightlifting

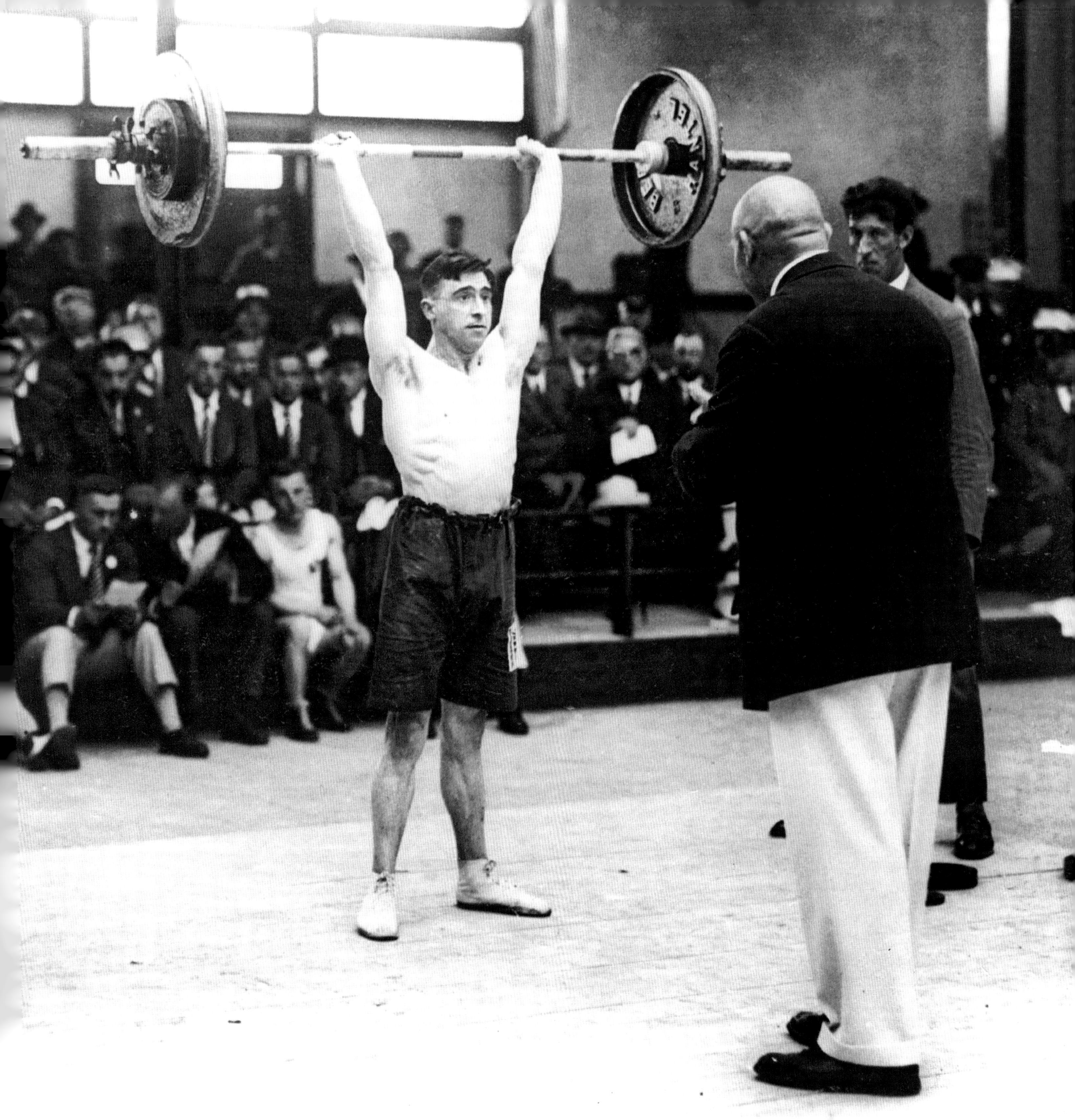

Percy Williams (Canada), gold, 100 m & 200 m

American athletes stretch on board ship

Horse racing (demonstration sport)

1928
St. Moritz Switzerland

II Olympic Winter Games

11-19 February 1928

14 events ▪ 4 sports

25 competing nations ▪ 464 athletes

Amelia Earhart flies the Atlantic

France vs Great Britain, 3–2, ice hockey

John O'Neill Farrell (United States), bronze, 500 m speed skating

▲ Bobsleigh
▶ Polish bobsleigh team

82   1928 St Moritz

1928 St Moritz

Skijoring

Women's figure skaters

1928 St Moritz

Birger Ruud (Norway), gold, ski jumping

1932

Lake Placid United States

III Olympic Winter Games

4-15 February 1932

14 events ▪ 4 sports

17 competing nations ▪ 252 athletes

Nazi Party, Germany

Dog sled racing

Brothers J. Herbert and Curtis Stevens (United States), gold, bobsleigh

Karl Schafer (Austria), gold, figure skating

Birger Ruud (Norway), gold, ski jumping

10,000 m speed skating, start

92 1932 Lake Placid

Ski jumping

Lauri A. Lethinen (Finland, left), gold, 400 m

1932

Los Angeles
United States

Games of the X Olympiad

30 July – 14 August 1932

117 events ▪ 14 sports

37 competing nations ▪ 1,332 athletes

Great Depression, New York City

'Babe' Didrickson (United States), gold, javelin & 80 m hurdles; silver, high jump

Pat O'Callaghan (Ireland), gold, hammer throw

Romeo Neri (Italy), gold, parallel bars

Bill Miller (United States), gold, pole vault

Tom Green (98, Great Britain), gold, 50 km walk

Smoky, official mascot

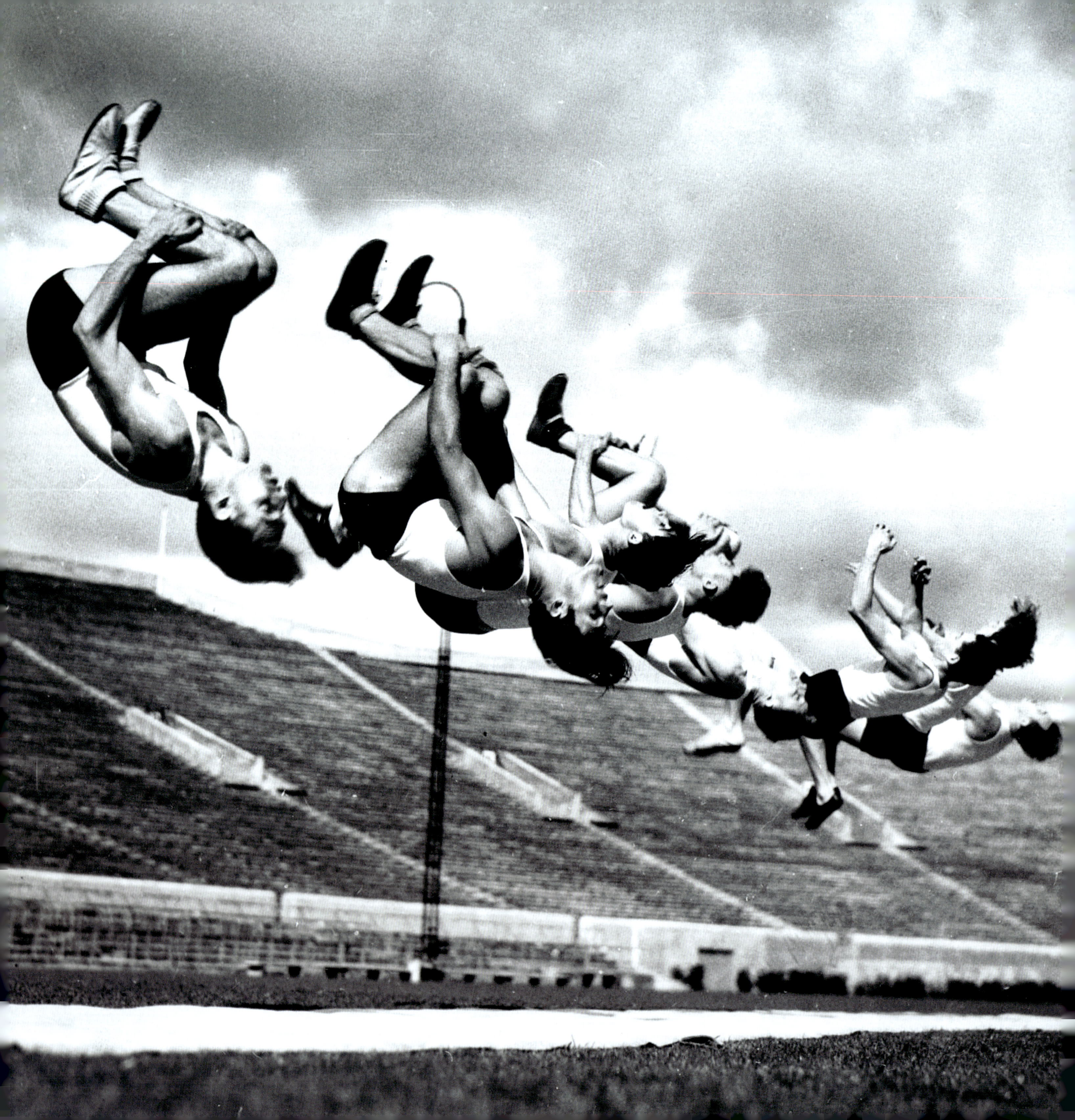

▲ Training dives
◀ Gymnasts training

1932 Los Angeles

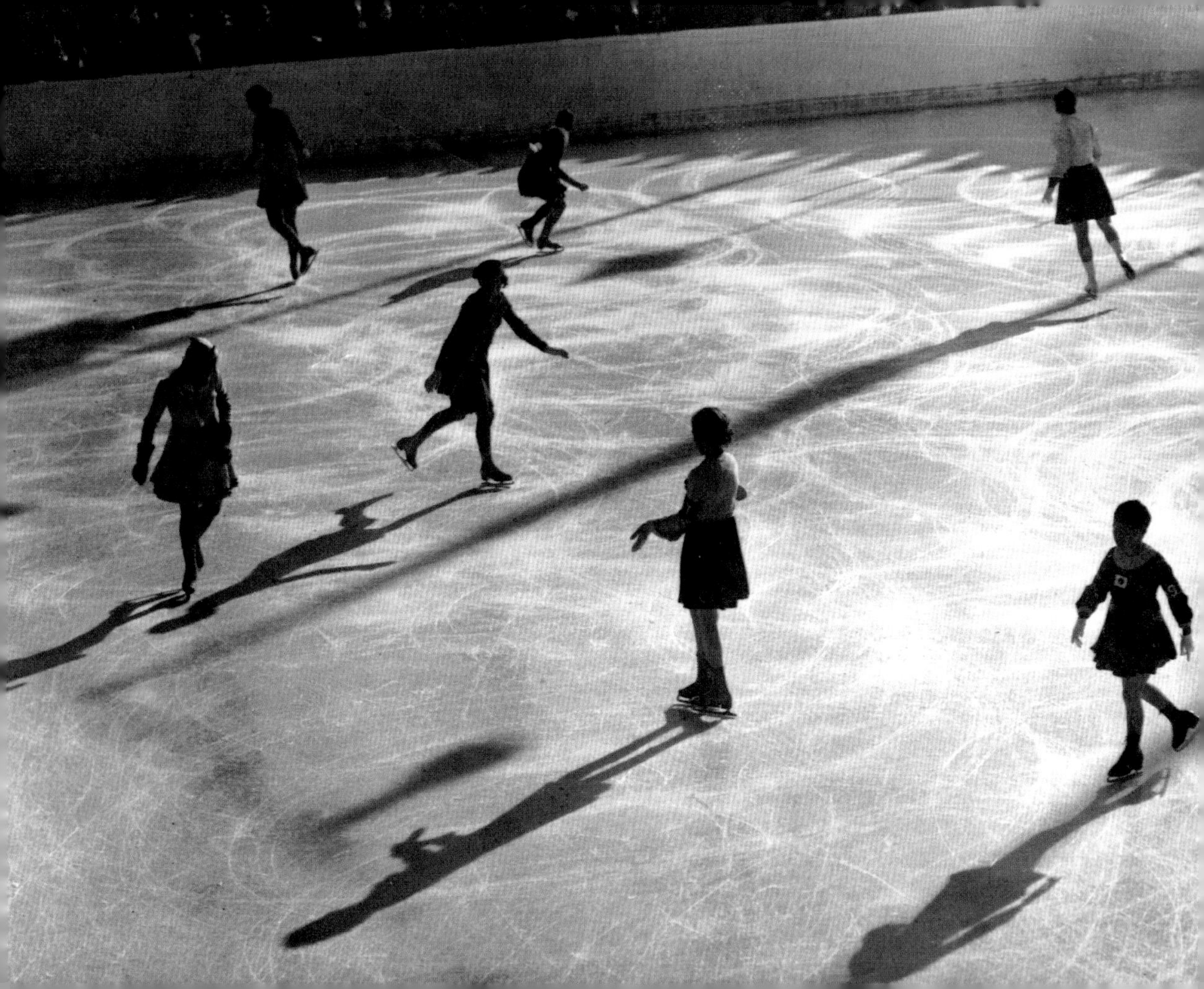

1936

Garmisch-Partenkirchen Germany

IV Olympic Winter Games

6 – 16 February 1936

17 events ▪ 4 sports

28 competing nations ▪ 646 athletes

Spanish Civil War

Cleaning the ice rink

Movie camera

▲ Cristl Cranz (Germany), gold, alpine skiing combined
▶ Closing ceremony

108 1936 Garmisch-Partenkirchen

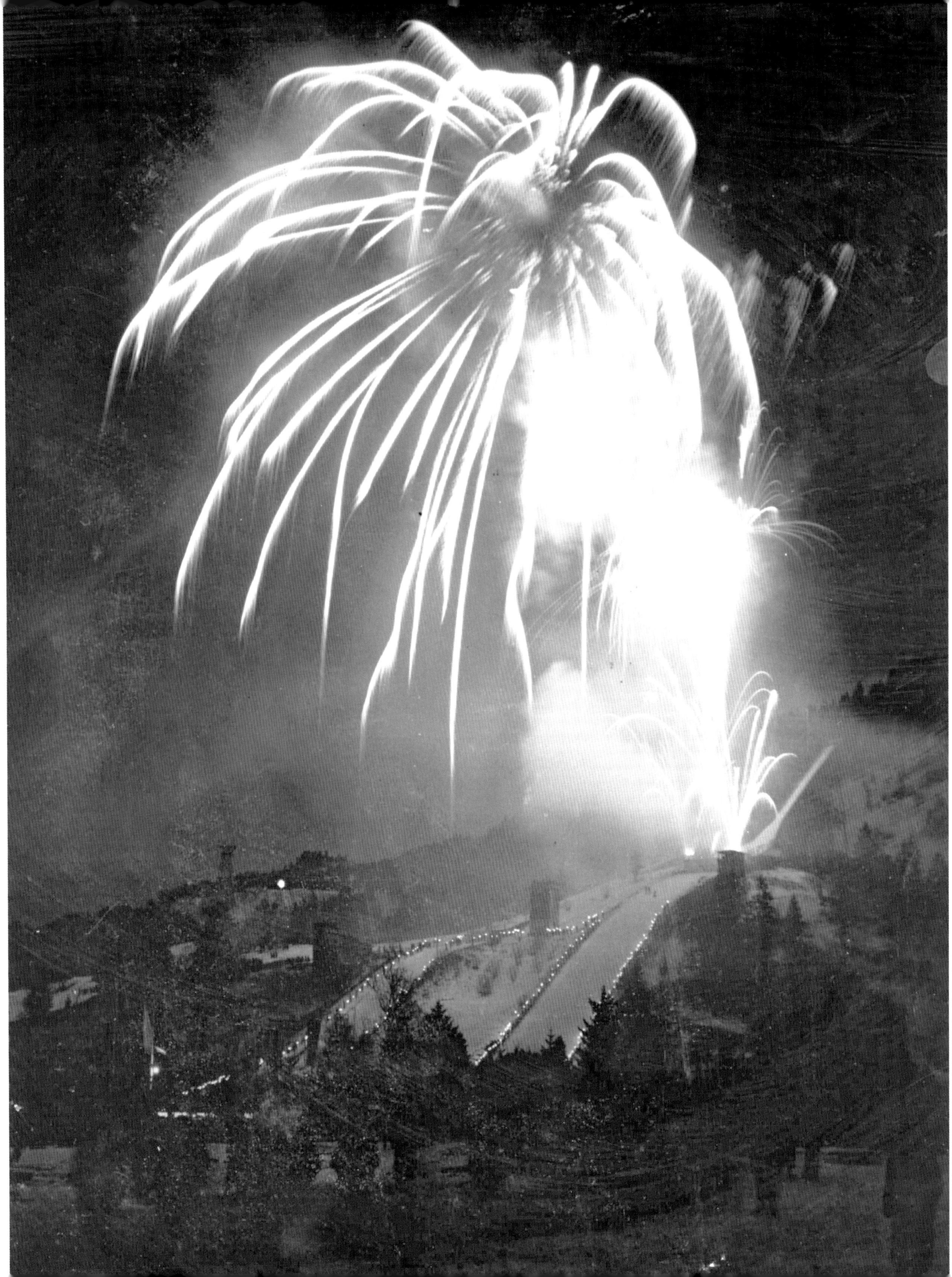

Birger Ruud (Norway), gold, ski jumping

Austrian athletes, opening ceremony

Jesse Owens (733, United States), gold, 100 m

1936

Berlin Germany

Games of the XI Olympiad

1 – 16 August 1936

129 events ▪ 19 sports

49 competing nations ▪ 3,963 athletes

Swastika flag, Olympic stadium

Jesse Owens (United States), gold, long jump, 100 m, 200 m & 4 x 100 m relay

Gisela Mauermayer (Germany), gold, discus

1936 Berlin

▲ Alfred Schwarzmann (Germany), bronze, horizontal bar
◄ The crowd give the Nazi salute at the closing ceremony

1936 Berlin

▲ Mexico (bronze) vs Philippines, basketball
▶ Austria (gold) vs Italy (silver), football

118 1936 Berlin

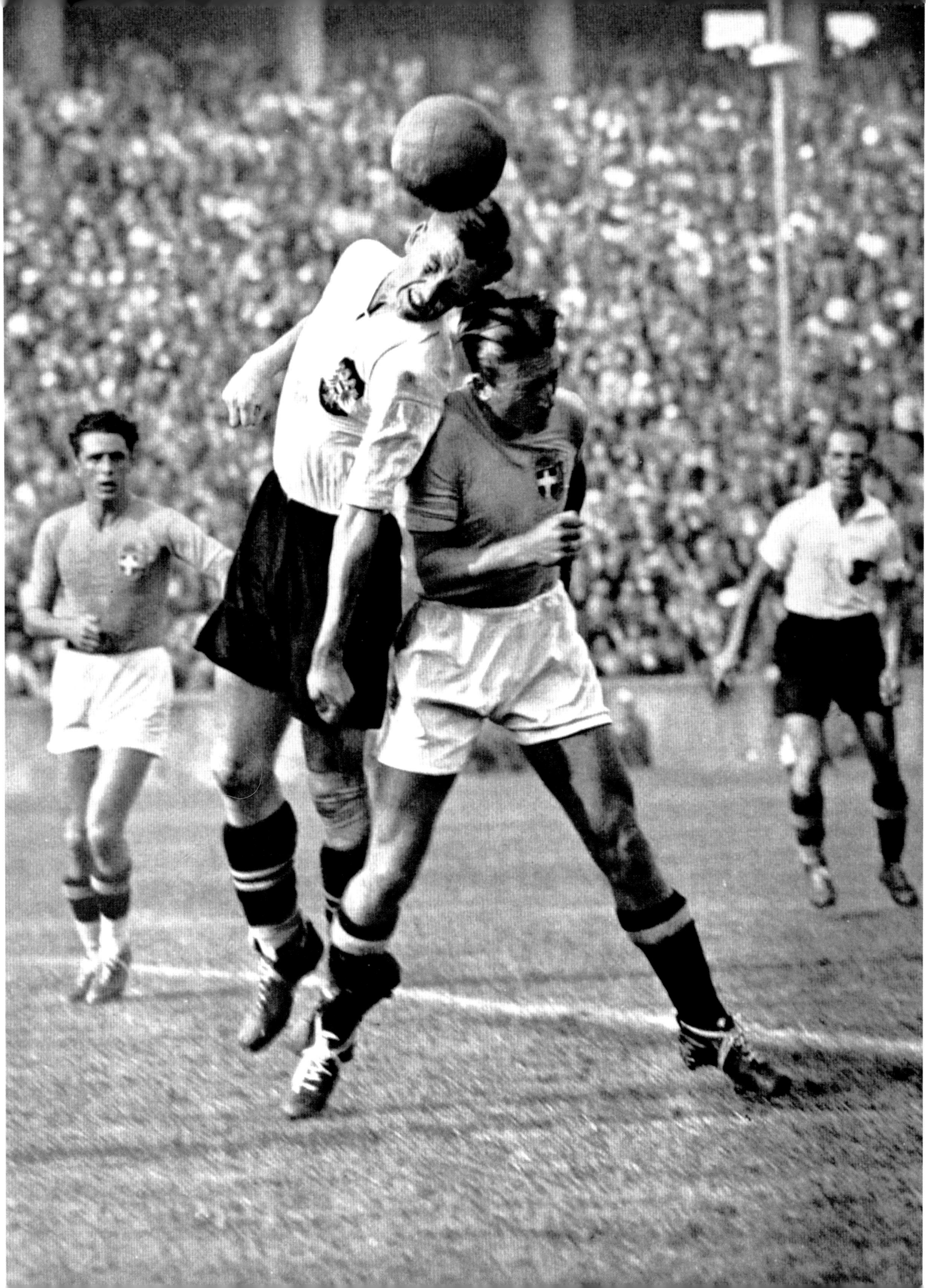

Mexican polo player

Judges, finish line

1936 Berlin

▲ ▶ Marjorie Gestring (United States), gold, 3 m springboard

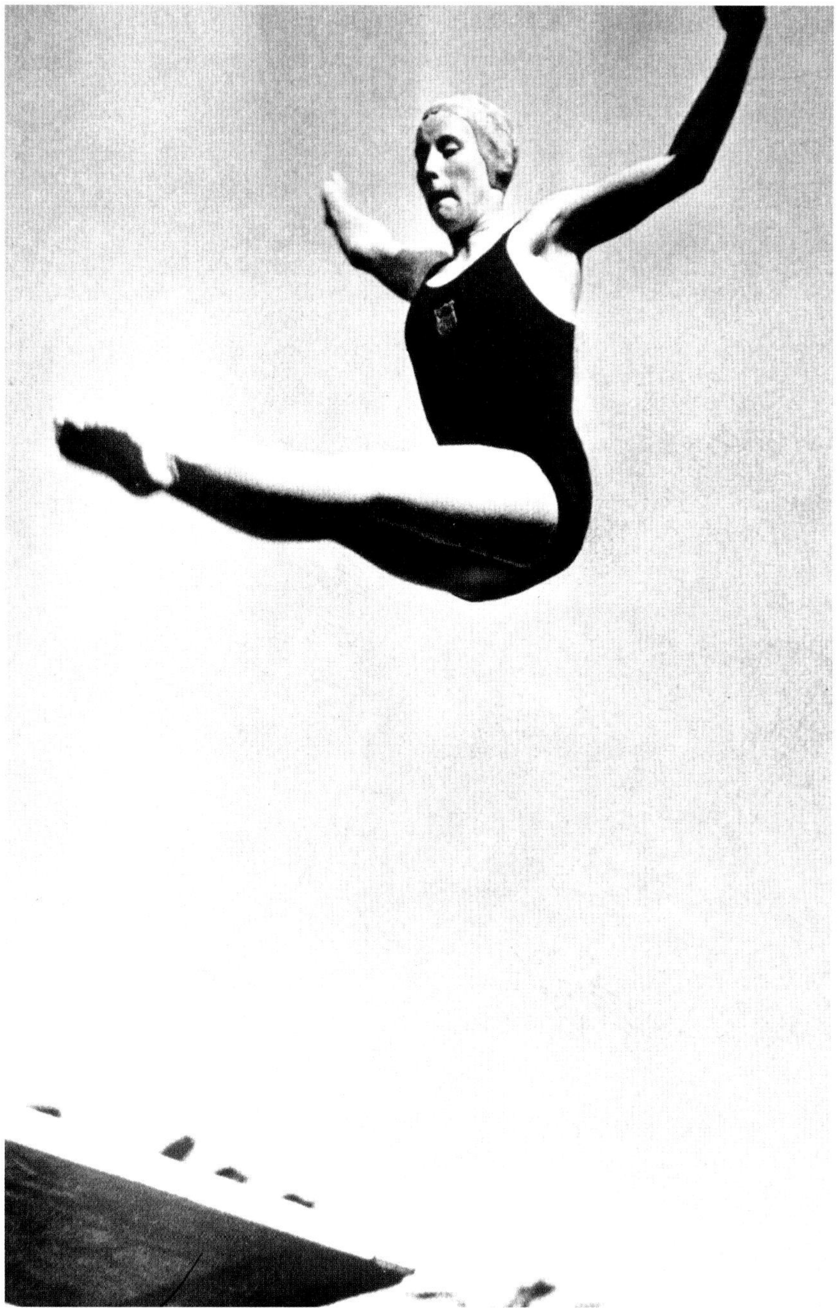

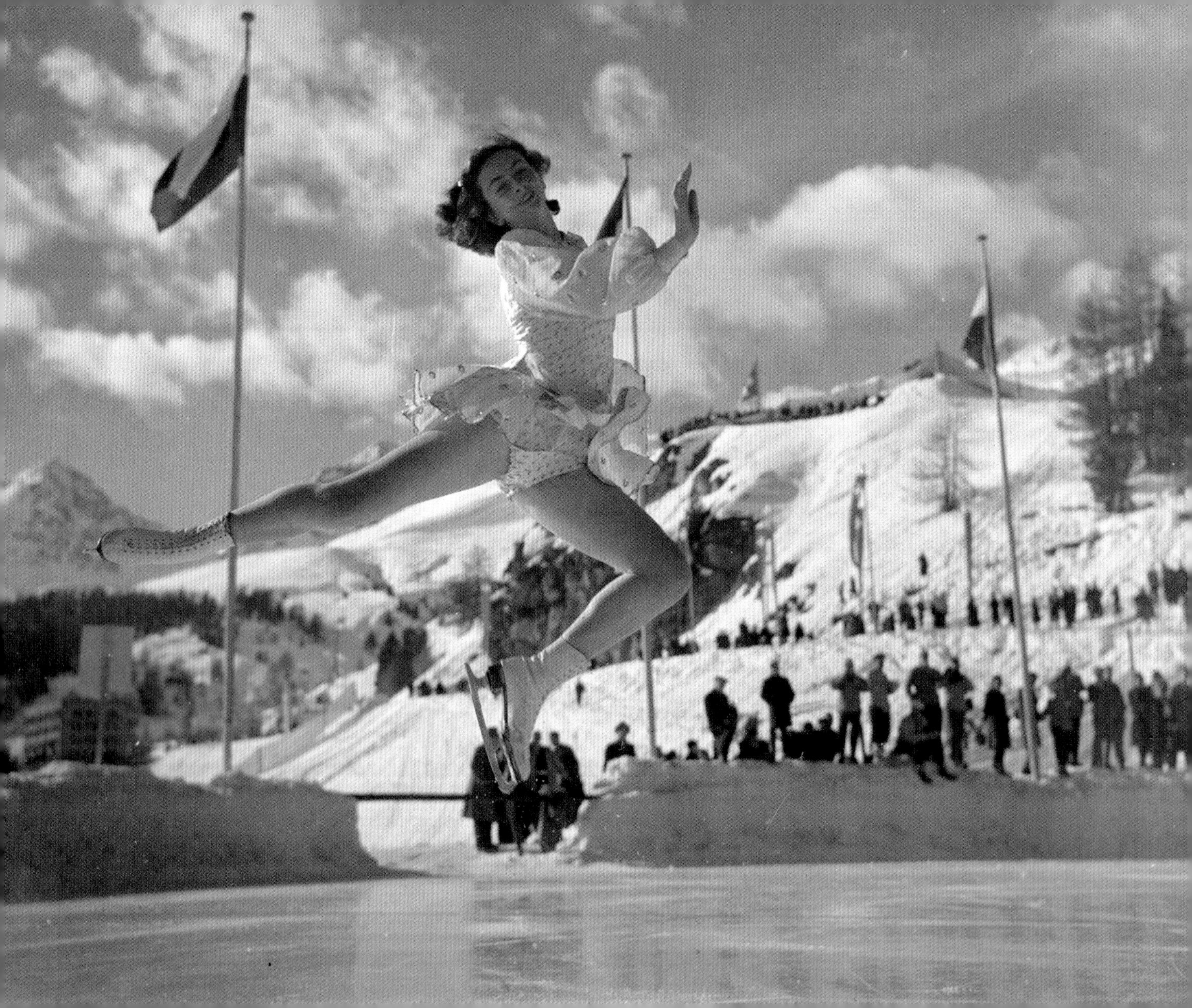

1948

St Moritz Switzerland

V Olympic Winter Games

30 January – 8 February 1948

22 events ▪ 4 sports

28 competing nations ▪ 669 athletes

Berlin air lift, West Germany

Great Britain, bobsleigh

Ken Bartholomew (United States), silver, 500 m speed skating

Richard Bott (Great Britain), skeleton bob

128 1948 St Moritz

Gretchen Fraser (United States), gold, women's slalom; silver, women's alpine combined skiing

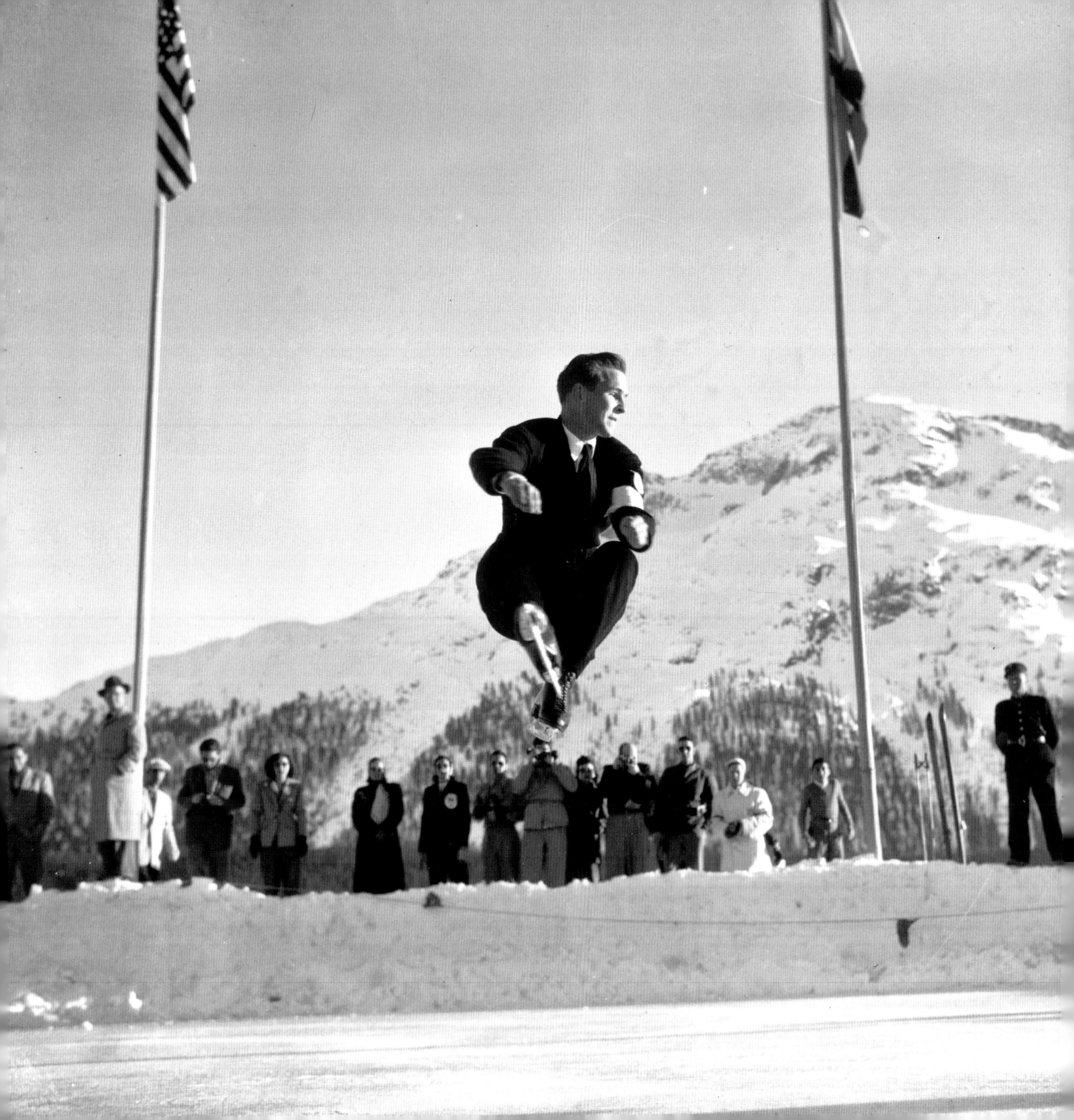

▲ Barbara Ann Scott (Canada), gold, figure skating
◀ Dick Button (United States), gold, figure skating

Fanny Blankers-Koen (Netherlands, right), gold, 80 m hurdles, 100 m, 200 m & 4 x 100 m relay

1948

London
Great Britain

Games of the XIV Olympiad

29 July – 14 August 1948

136 events ▪ 17 sports

59 competing nations ▪ 4,104 athletes

State of Israel

Tore Sjöstrand (357, Sweden), gold, 3,000 m steeplechase

Major N. Mikkelsen (Denmark), three-day eventing

▲ U.S. team, water polo
▶ U.S. divers

136   1948 London

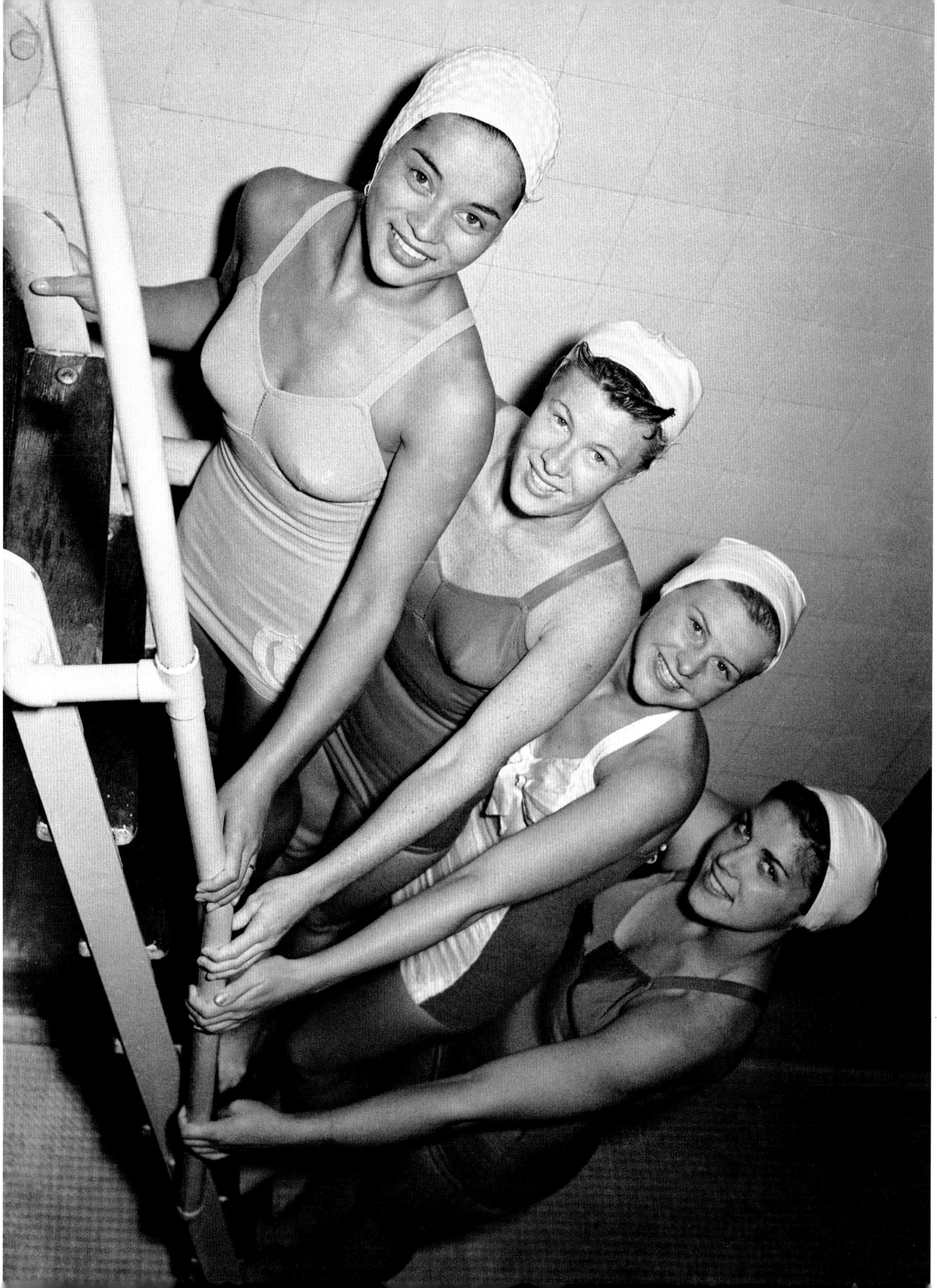

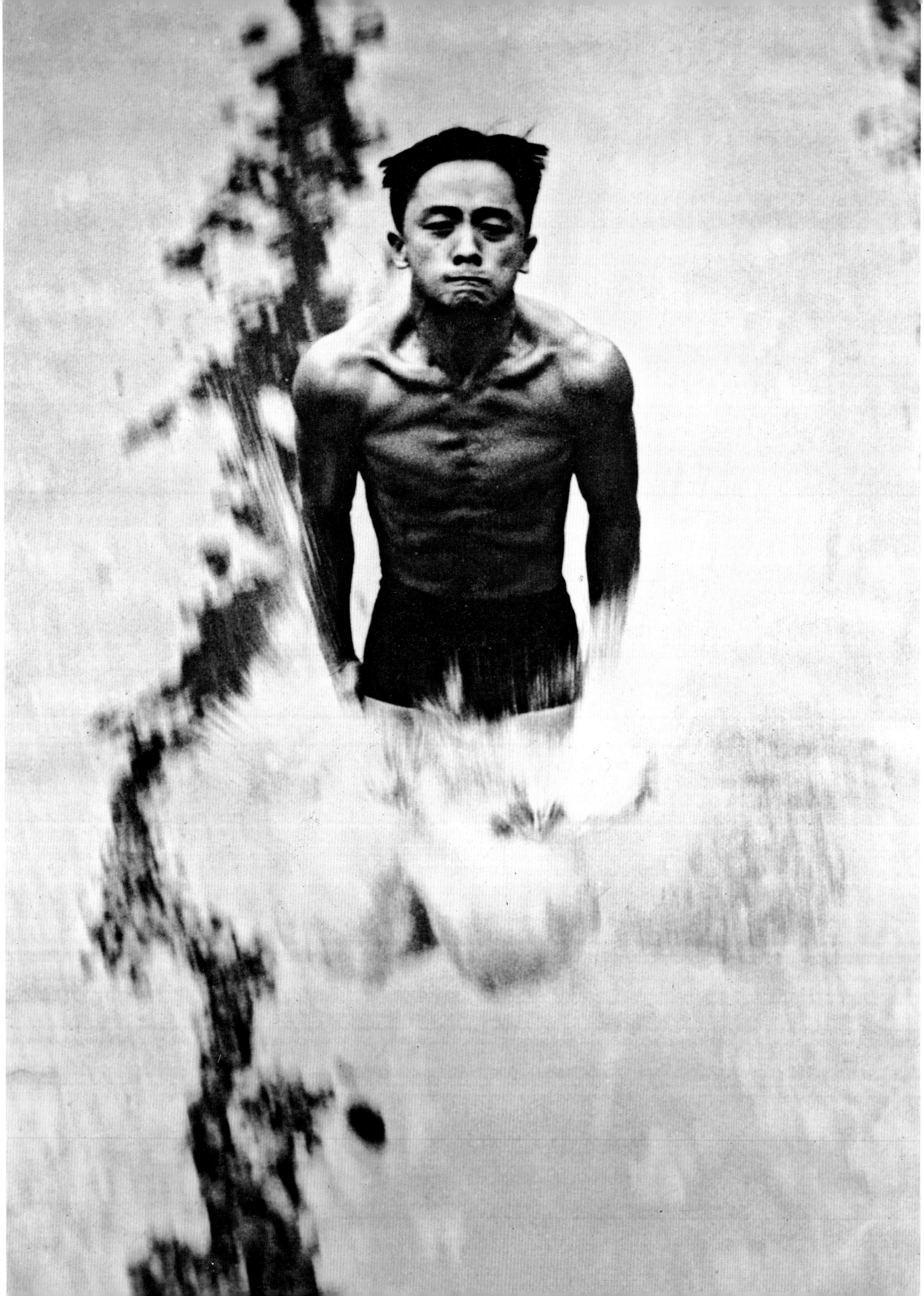

▲ Harrison Dillard (United States), gold, 100 m
◀ Sammy Lee (United States), gold, 10-m platform diving; bronze, 3-m springboard

1948 London

▲ Defeated wrestler
▶ Ahmet Kirecci (Turkey), gold, Greco-Roman wrestling

Javelin ▶

Shot put ▶▶

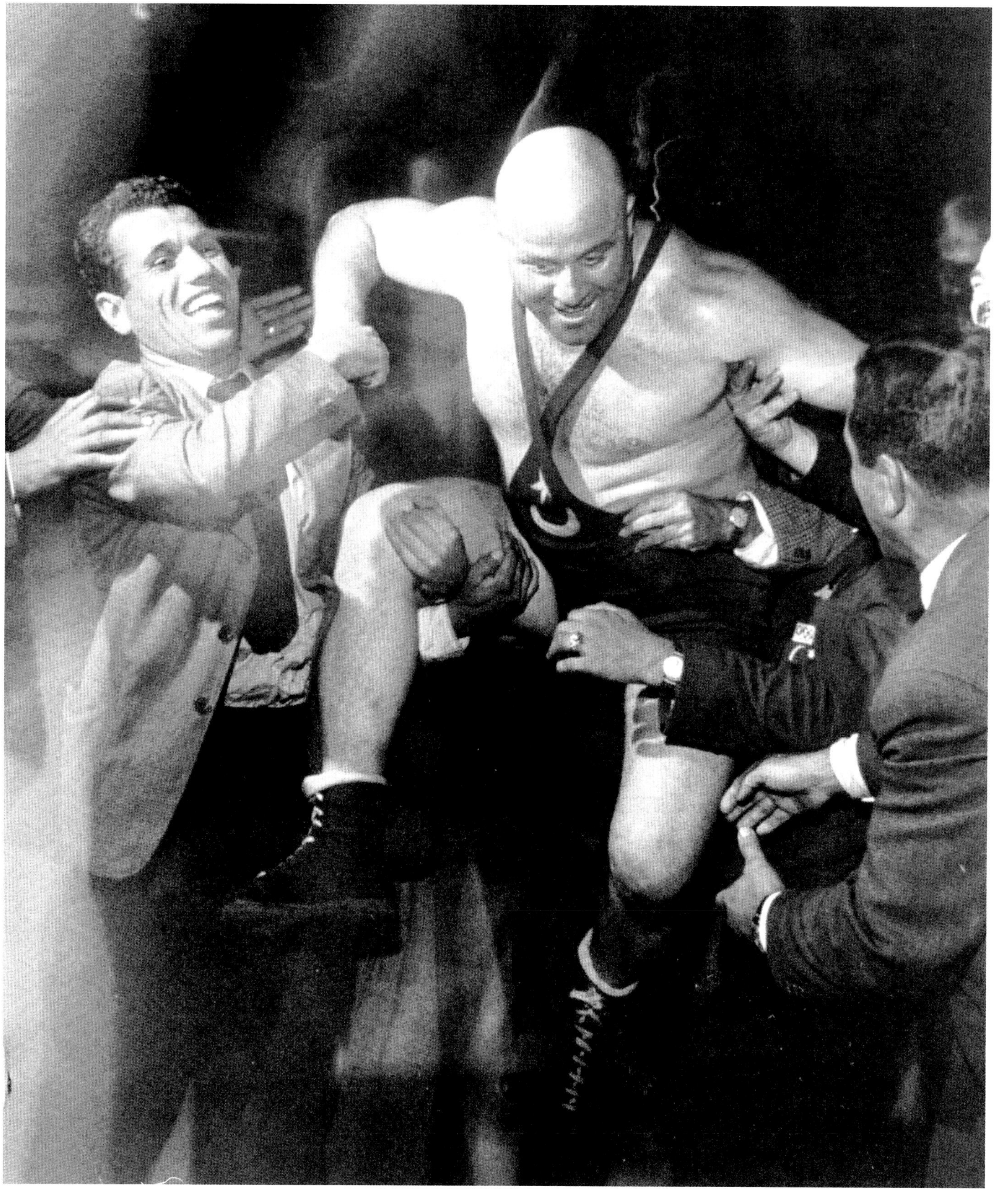

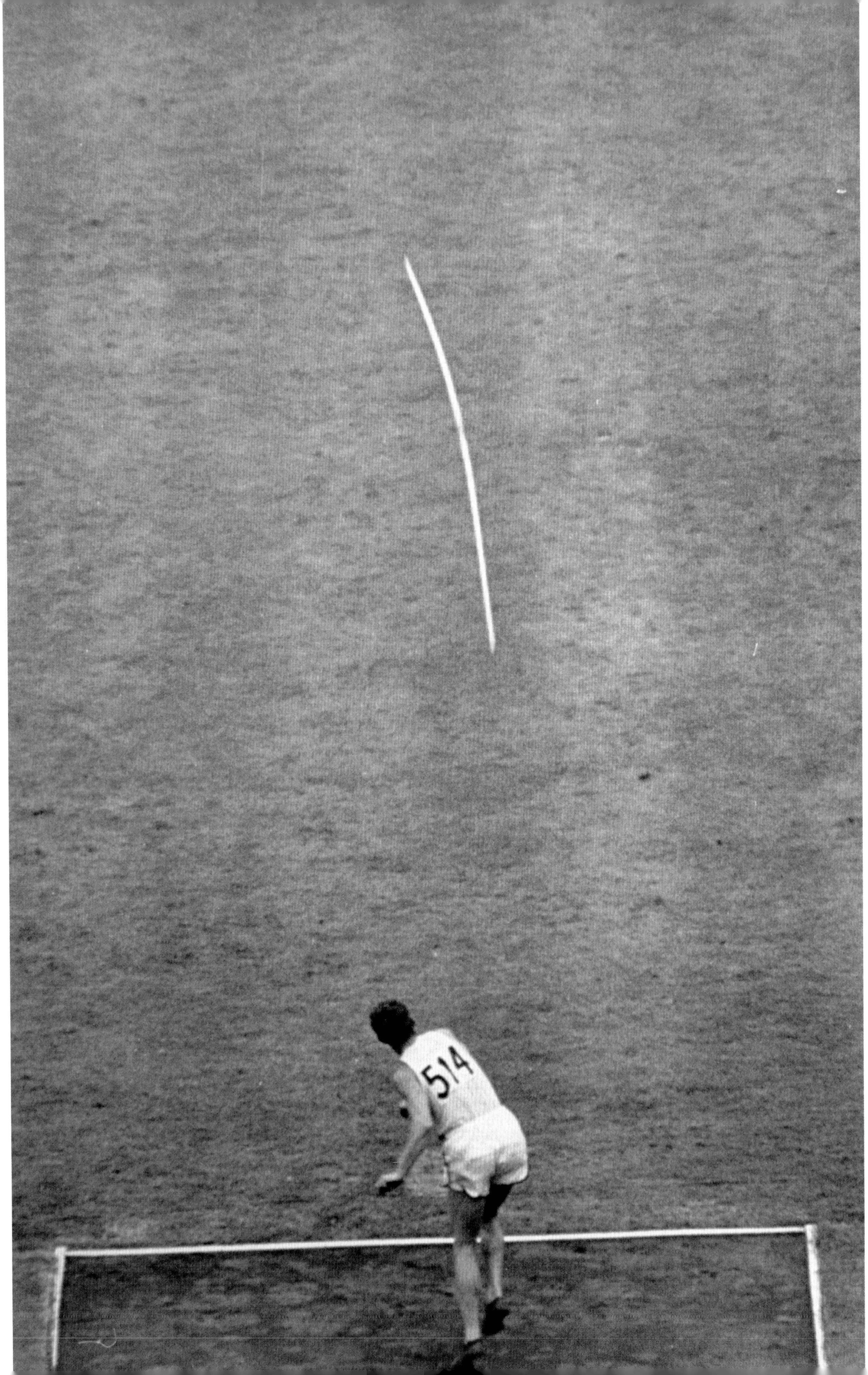
514

1948 London   143

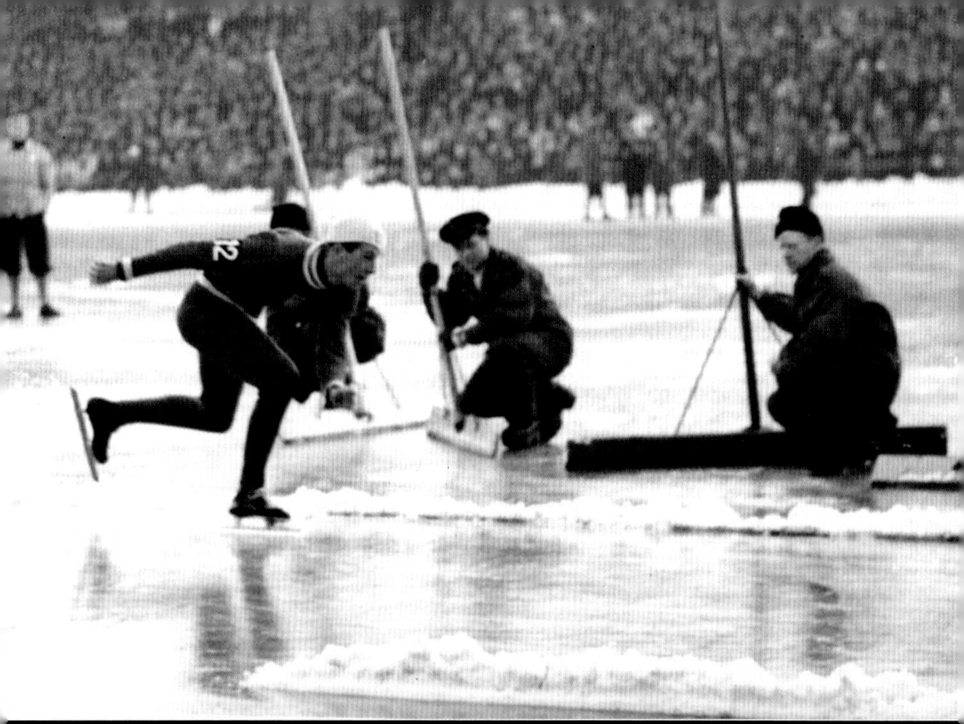

1952

Oslo
Norway

VI Olympic Winter Games

14 – 25 February 1952

22 events ▪ 4 sports

30 competing nations ▪ 694 athletes

Gary Cooper and Grace Kelly, *High Noon*

Alain Giletti (France), figure skating

Canada (gold) vs United States (silver), ice hockey

Veikko Hakulinen (Finland), gold, 50 km cross country

Hilary Laing (Great Britain), downhill skiing

1952 Oslo

▲ Skiers, women's slalom
◀ Vlastimil Melich (Czechoslovakia), Nordic combined

Greco-Roman wrestling

1952

Helsinki Finland

Games of the XV Olympiad

19 July – 3 August 1952

149 events ▪ 17 sports

69 competing nations ▪ 4,955 athletes

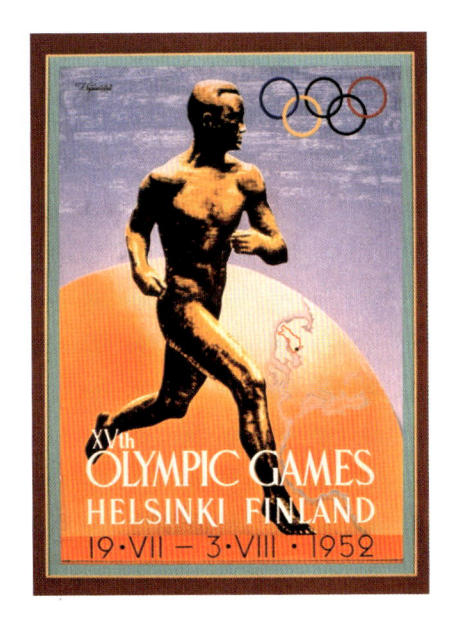

Christian Dior salon, Paris

▲ Chris Chataway (Great Britain, left), Alain Mimoun (France, centre) & Emil Zatopek (Czechoslovakia, right), gold, 5,000 m, 10,000 m & marathon
▶ Pat McCormick (United States), gold, springboard diving & platform diving

1952 Helsinki

Women's 100 m hurdles

Bob Mathias (United States), gold, decathlon

Soviet Union, gold, women's team gymnastics

Soviet gymnast, balance beam

Bob Mathias (United States), gold, decathlon

4,000 m team pursuit, men's cycling

India, gold, hockey

Jean Boiteaux (France), gold, 200 m freestyle, and his father

Sixten Jernberg (Sweden), gold, 50 km cross-country; silver, 15 km & 30 km; bronze, 4 x 10 km relay

1956

Cortina d'Ampezzo
Italy

VII Olympic Winter Games

26 January – 5 February 1956

24 events ▪ 4 sports

32 competing nations ▪ 821 athletes

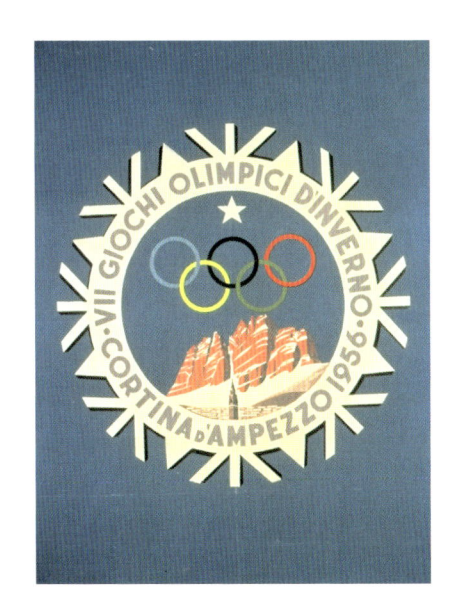

Elvis Presley

Denis Brodeur (Canada), bronze, ice hockey

Men's slalom

Canada vs Italy, 3–1, ice hockey

Speed skaters

1956 Cortina d'Ampezzo

Toni Sailer (Austria), gold, men's downhill, slalom & giant slalom

Radia Yeroshina (Soviet Union, right), silver, & Lyubov Kozyreva (Soviet Union), gold, respectively, women's 10 km cross-country

Ski jump tower

1956 Cortina d'Ampezzo

Spain, bobsleigh

Men's fencing

1956

Melbourne Australia

Games of the XVI Olympiad

22 November – 8 December 1956

145 events ▪ 17 sports

72 competing nations ▪ 3,314 athletes

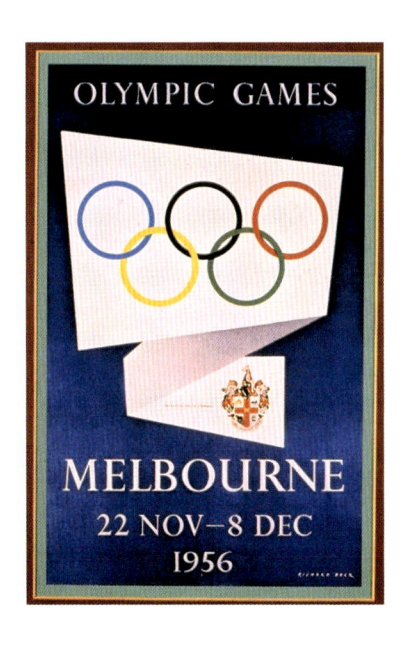

Grace Kelly & Prince Rainier, Monaco

Larisa Latynina (Soviet Union), 4 gold, 1 silver, 1 bronze, gymnastics

Arkadi Vorobyev (Soviet Union, gold), David Sheppard (United States, silver) and Jean Debuf (France, bronze), weightlifting

Women's 100 m, start

Dawn Fraser (Australia, left), gold, 100 m freestyle & 4 x 100 m freestyle relay; silver, 400 m freestyle

1956 Melbourne

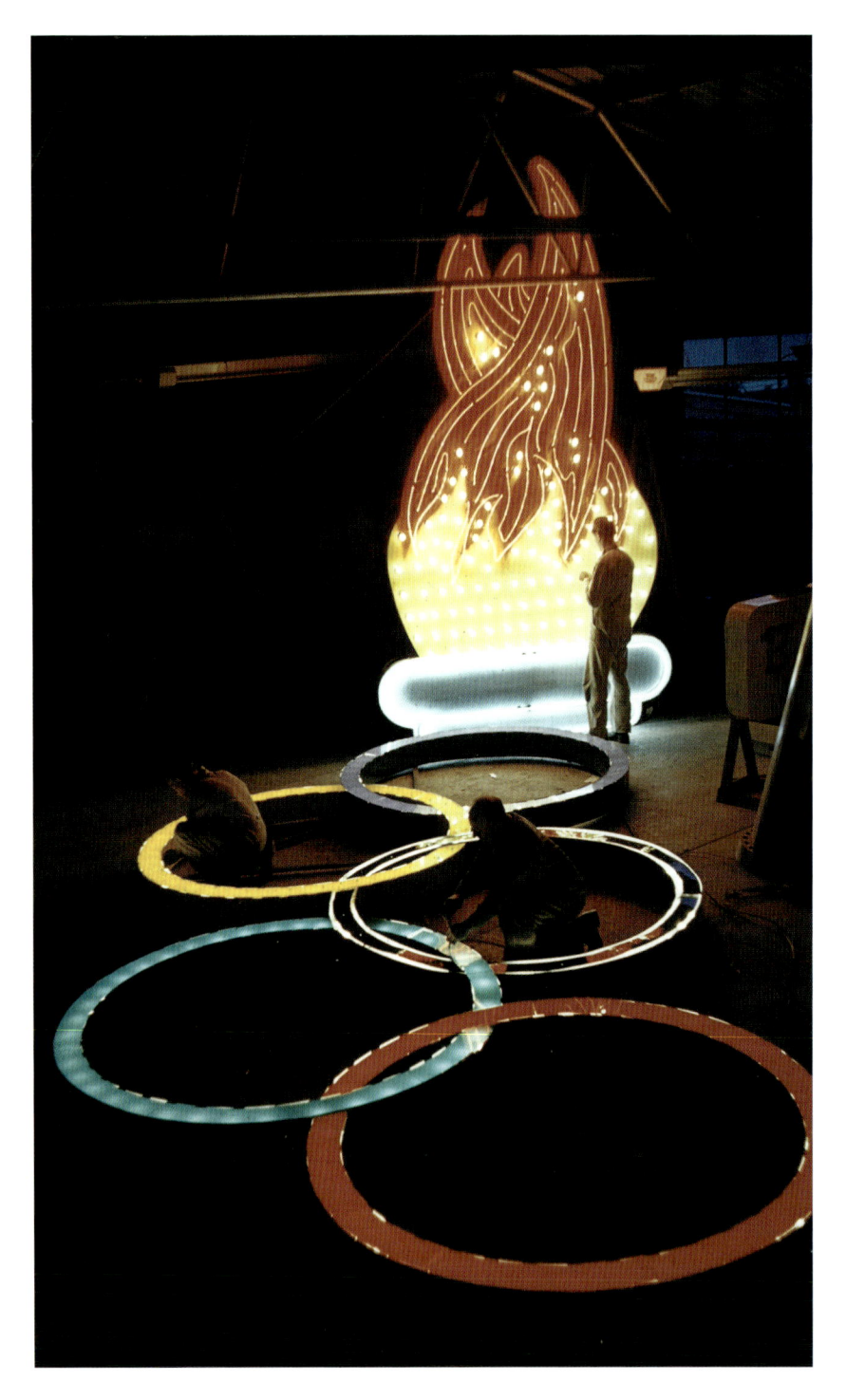

▲ Neon rings
▶ Practice, diving

1956 Melbourne

Glenn Davis (278, United States), gold, 400 m hurdles

Gunhild Larking (Sweden), high jump

1956 Melbourne

Oleg Fedoseyev (Soviet Union), long jump

Jose Telles Da Conceicau (Brazil), high jump

Canadian and U.S. gymnasts

Finish-line judges

Men's slalom

1960

Squaw Valley United States

VIII Olympic Winter Games

18 – 28 February 1960

27 events ▪ 4 sports

30 competing nations ▪ 665 athletes

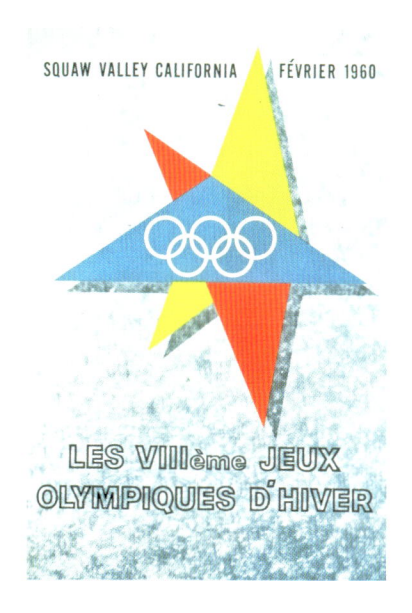

John F. Kennedy, president, United States

Ski jumping

Yevgeny Grishin (Soviet Union), gold, 500 m & 1,500 m speed skating

Figure skating ▶

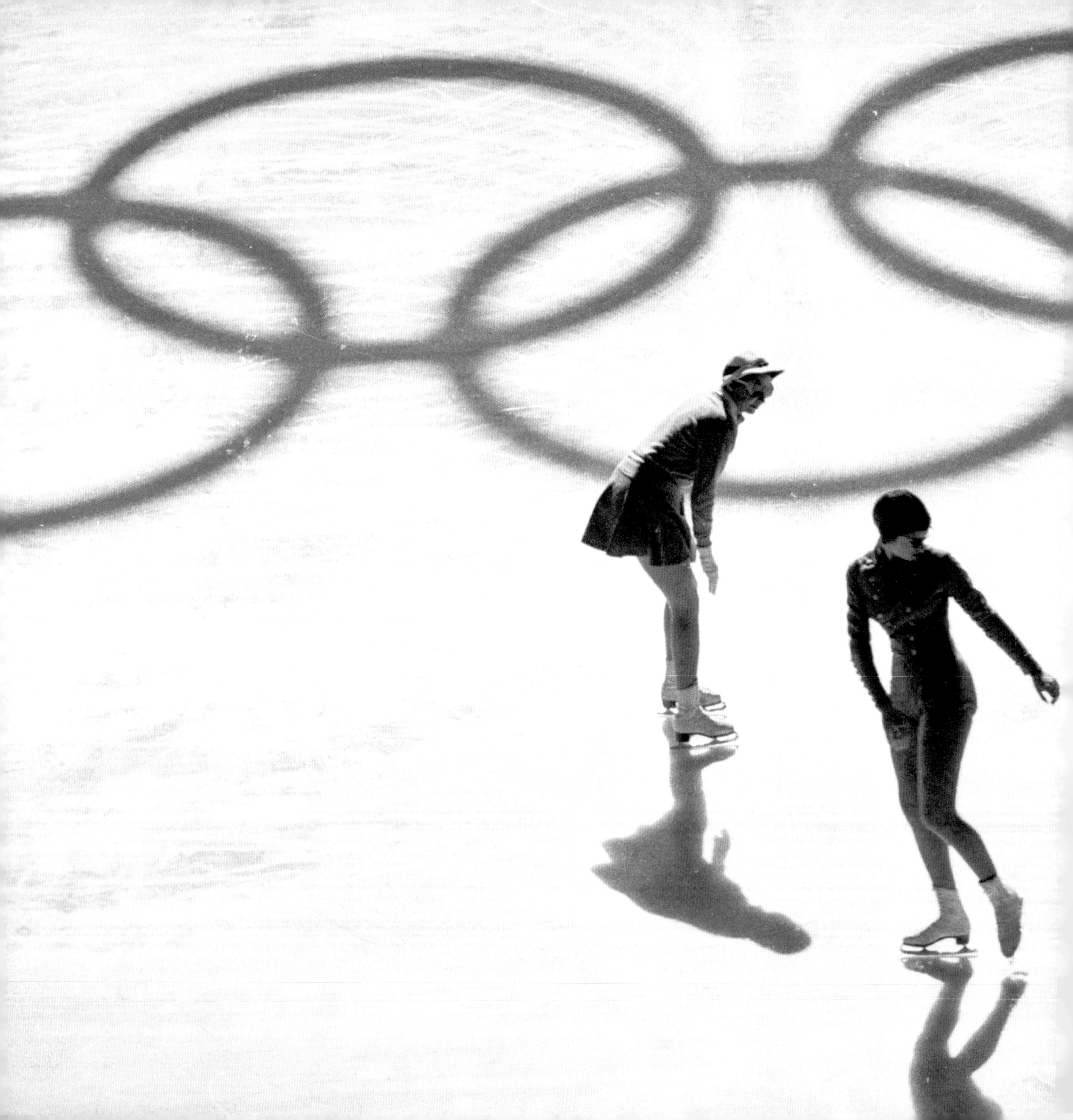

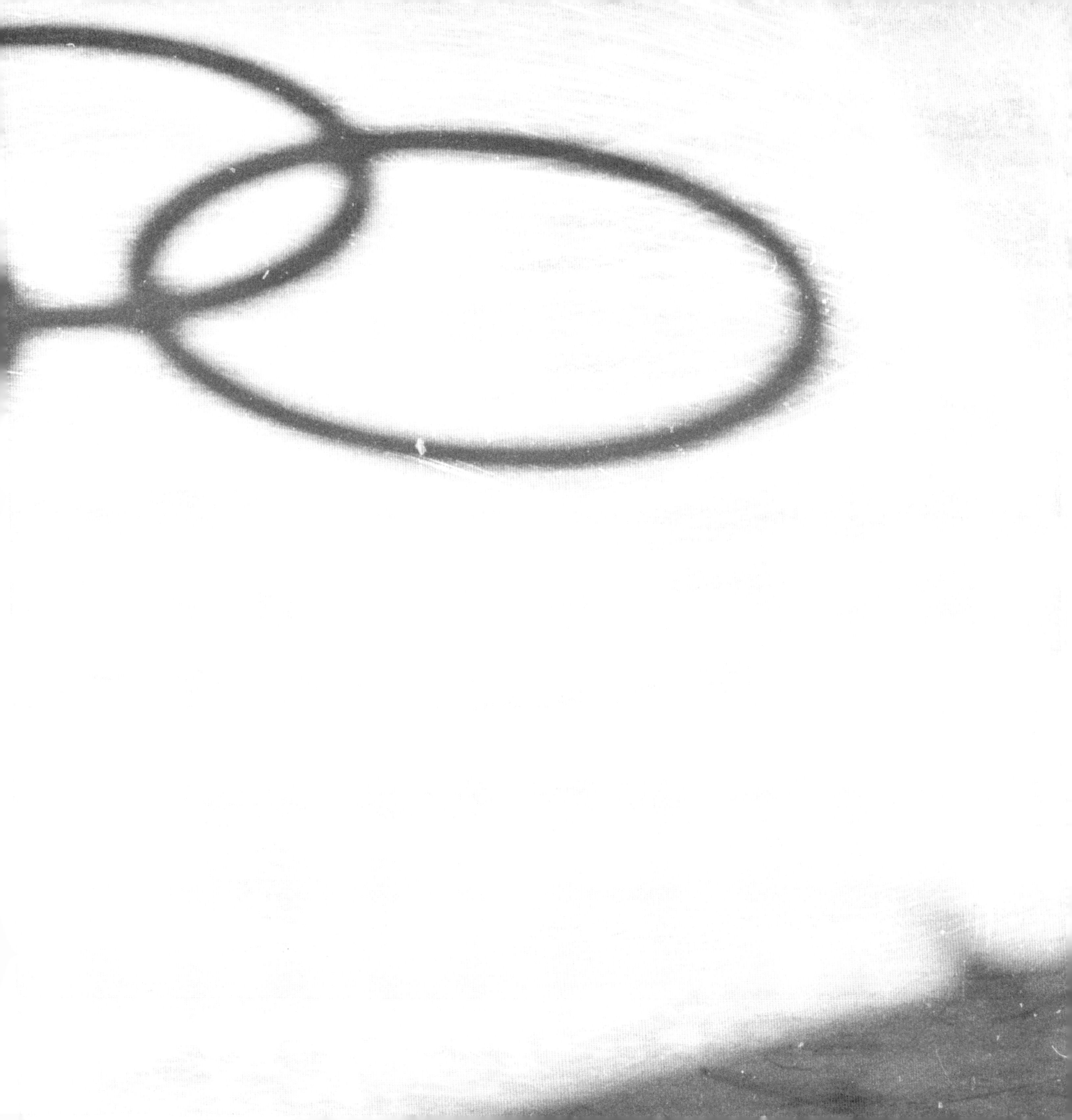

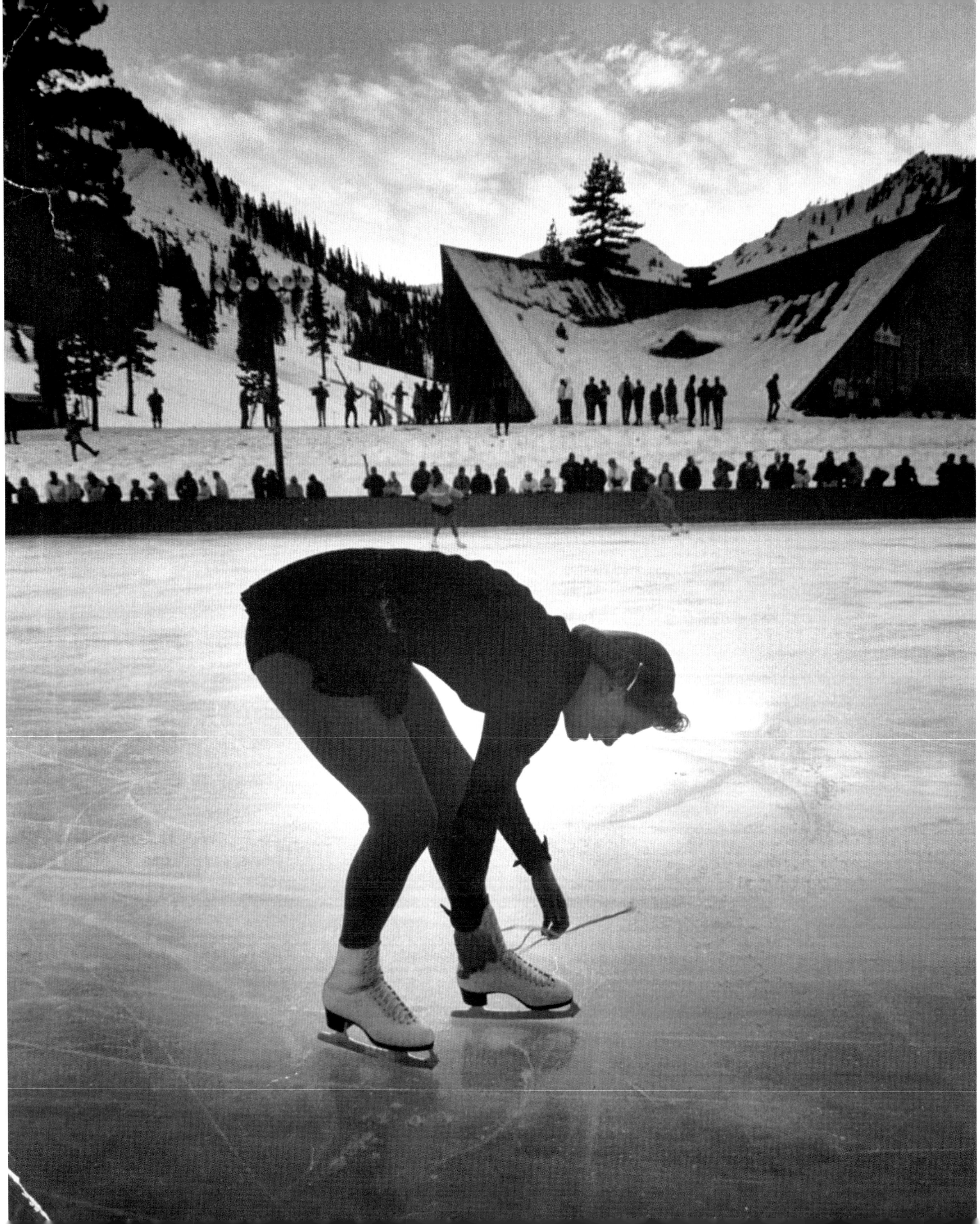

▲ Cross-country skier
◀ Carol Heiss (United States), gold, figure skating

1960 Squaw Valley

▲ Competitors, women's skiing
▶ Slalom course

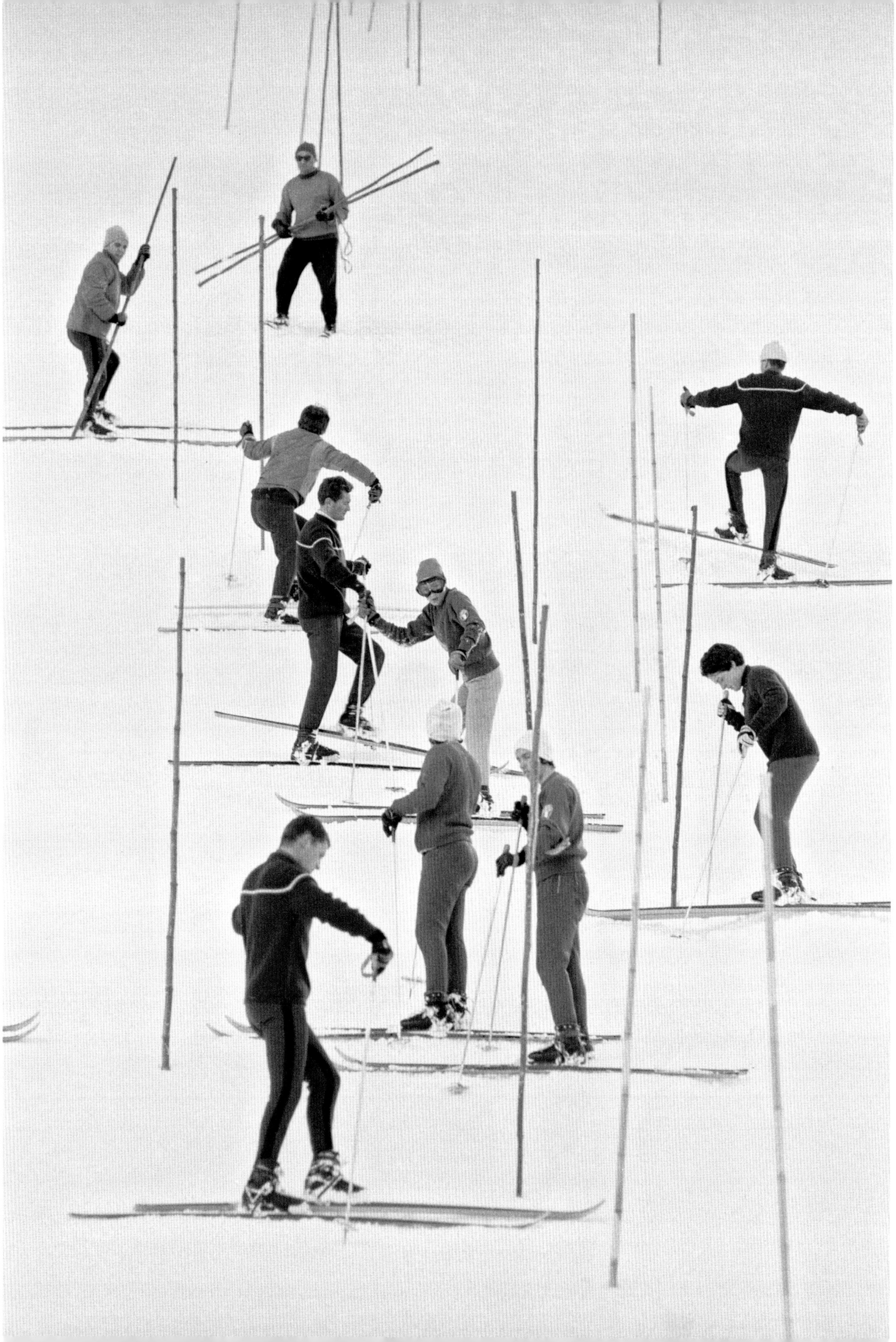

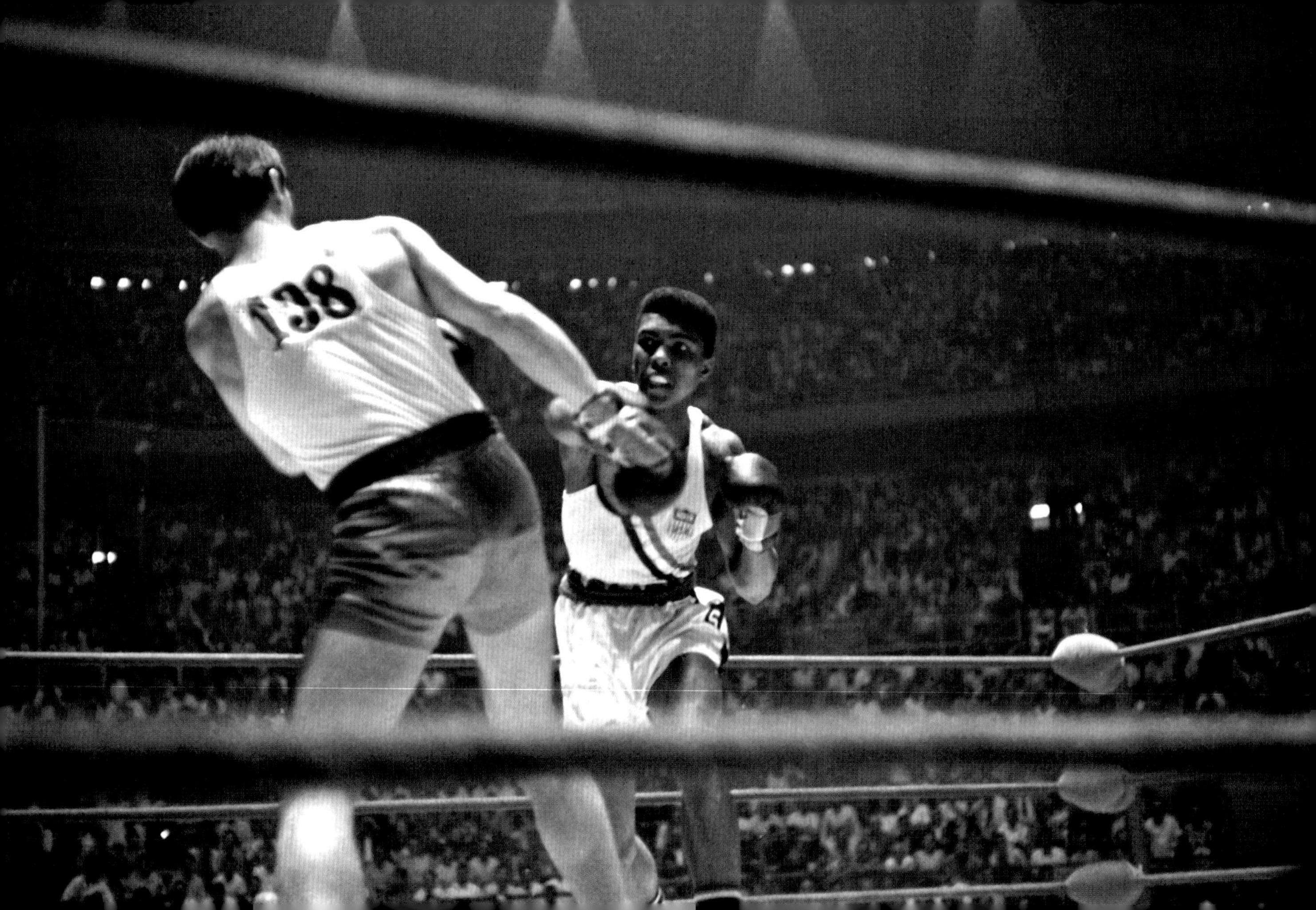
138

1960

Rome
Italy

Games of the XVII Olympiad

25 August – 11 September 1960

150 events ▪ 17 sports

83 competing nations ▪ 5,338 athletes

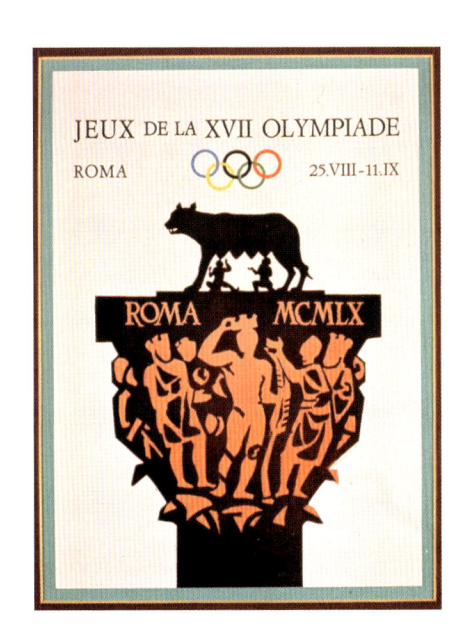

Janet Leigh, *Psycho*

100 m, start

Wilma Rudolph (United States, left), gold, women's 100 m, 200 m & 4 x 100 m relay

▲ Team mates help Knud Enemark (Denmark), 100 km team time trial; Enemark collapsed & later died
▶ Losing sprinters, 100 m final

1960 Rome 203

Marathon runner, Constantine's Arch

Abebe Bikila (Ethiopia), gold, marathon

Doris Fuchs (left) and Sharon Richardson, U.S. gymnasts

Greco-Roman wrestling, Basilica of Maxentius

Men's 1,000 m kayak

Al Oerter (United States), gold, discus

Cassius Clay (United States), gold, boxing

Louis Martin (Great Britain), bronze, weightlifting

Ski jumping

1964
Innsbruck Austria

IX Olympic Winter Games

29 January – 9 February 1964

34 events ▪ 6 sports

36 competing nations ▪ 1,091 athletes

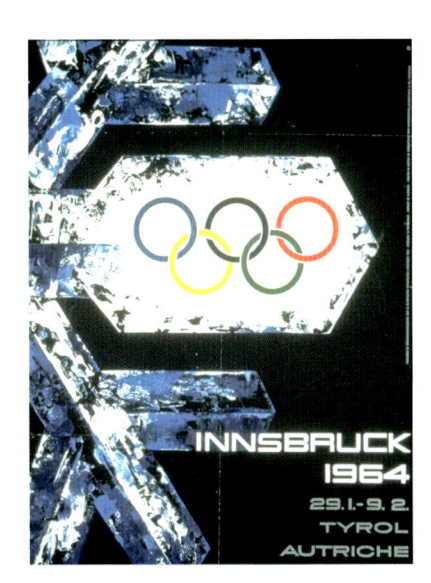

Martin Luther King, Nobel peace prize

Jonny Nilsson (Sweden), gold, 10,000 m speed skating

Christine Goitschel (France), gold, women's slalom; silver, giant slalom

Lidya Skoblikova (Soviet Union), gold, 500 m, 1,000 m, 1,500 m & 3,000 m speed skating

Deutschland II (Germany), bobsleigh

Canada (white) vs Soviet Union, gold, ice hockey

Spectators

Takashi Ono (Japan), gold, men's team gymnastics

1964

Tokyo
Japan

Games of the XVIII Olympiad

10 – 24 October 1964

163 events ▪ 19 sports

93 competing nations ▪ 5,151 athletes

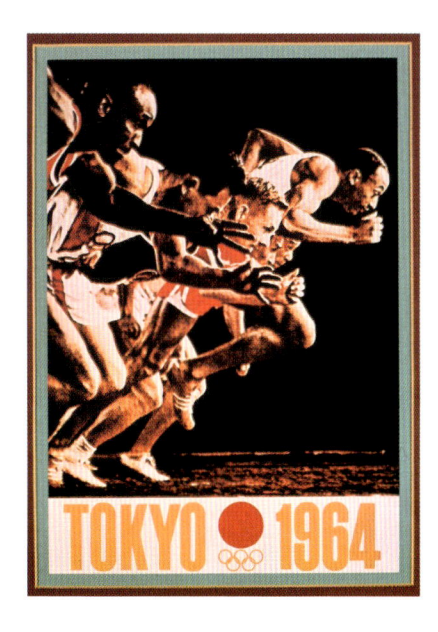

Cassius Clay, world champion

Women's swimming start

Female diver

Japan (white, gold) vs Soviet Union (silver), women's volleyball

Tamara Press (Soviet Union), gold, women's shot put & discus throw

Osamu Watanabe (Japan, right), gold, freestyle wrestling

Betty Cuthbert (Australia, centre), gold, women's 400 m, with Ann Packer (Great Britain, left, silver) & Judy Amoore (Australia, bronze)

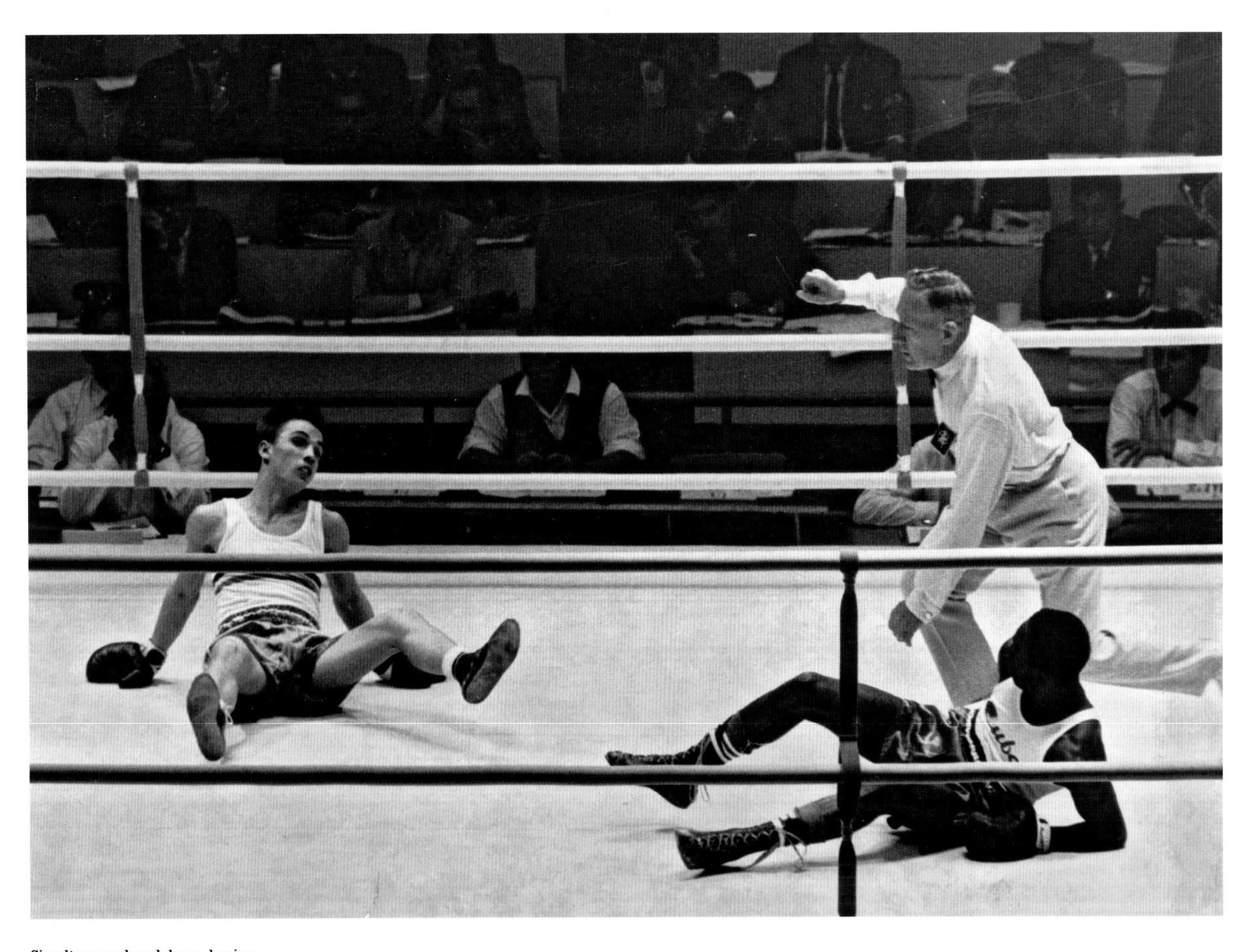

Simultaneous knockdown, boxing

Judo, demonstration sport

Daniel Revenu (France) vs Roland Losert (Australia), foil

Walt Hazzard (United States), gold, basketball

Gösta Pettersson (Sweden), bronze, team time trial

Philip K. Shinnick (United States), long jump

1964 Tokyo 233

Olga Pall (Austria), gold, women's downhill

1968

Grenoble France

X Olympic Winter Games

6 – 18 February 1968

35 events ▪ 6 sports

37 competing nations ▪ 1,158 athletes

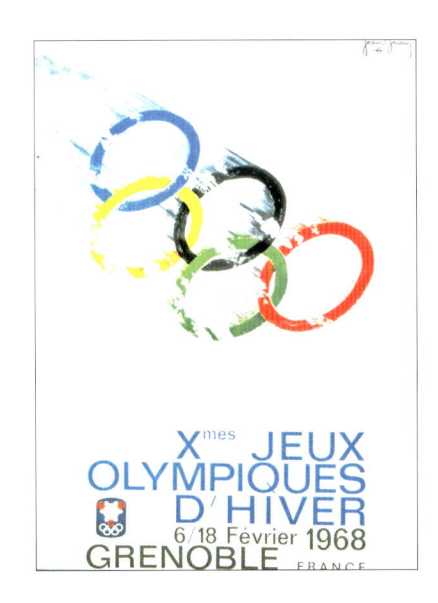

Martin Luther King, assassination

▲ Ski jumpers polish their skis
▶ Bobsleigh run

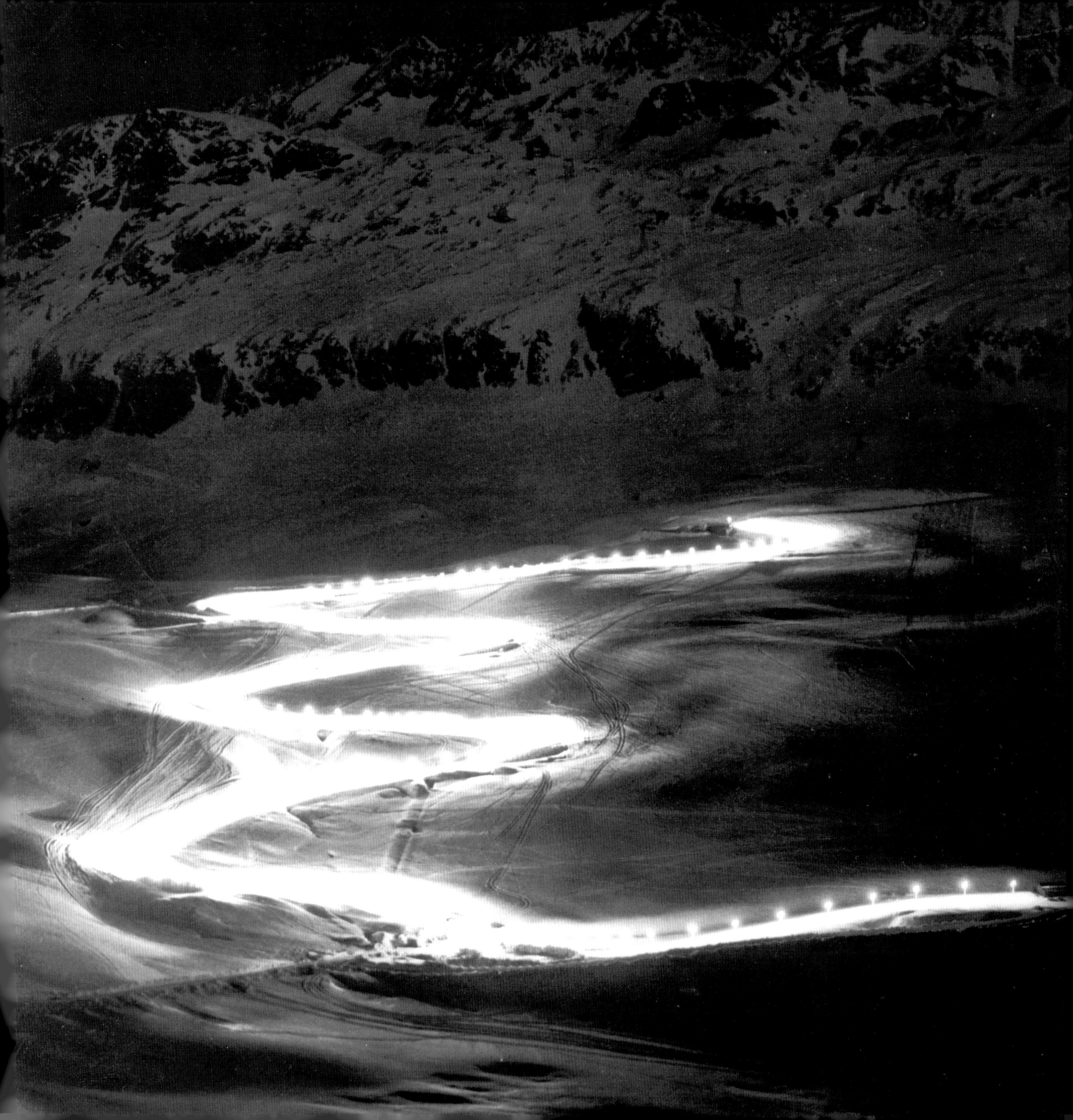

Jean-Claude Killy (France), gold, giant slalom, slalom & downhill

Speed skating practice

1968 Grenoble

Peggy Fleming (United States), gold, figure skating

Soviet Union (gold) vs Czechoslovakia (silver), ice hockey

Jean-Claude Killy (France), gold, giant slalom, slalom & downhill

Audrey Hepburn (left) with Jean-Claude Killy (France)

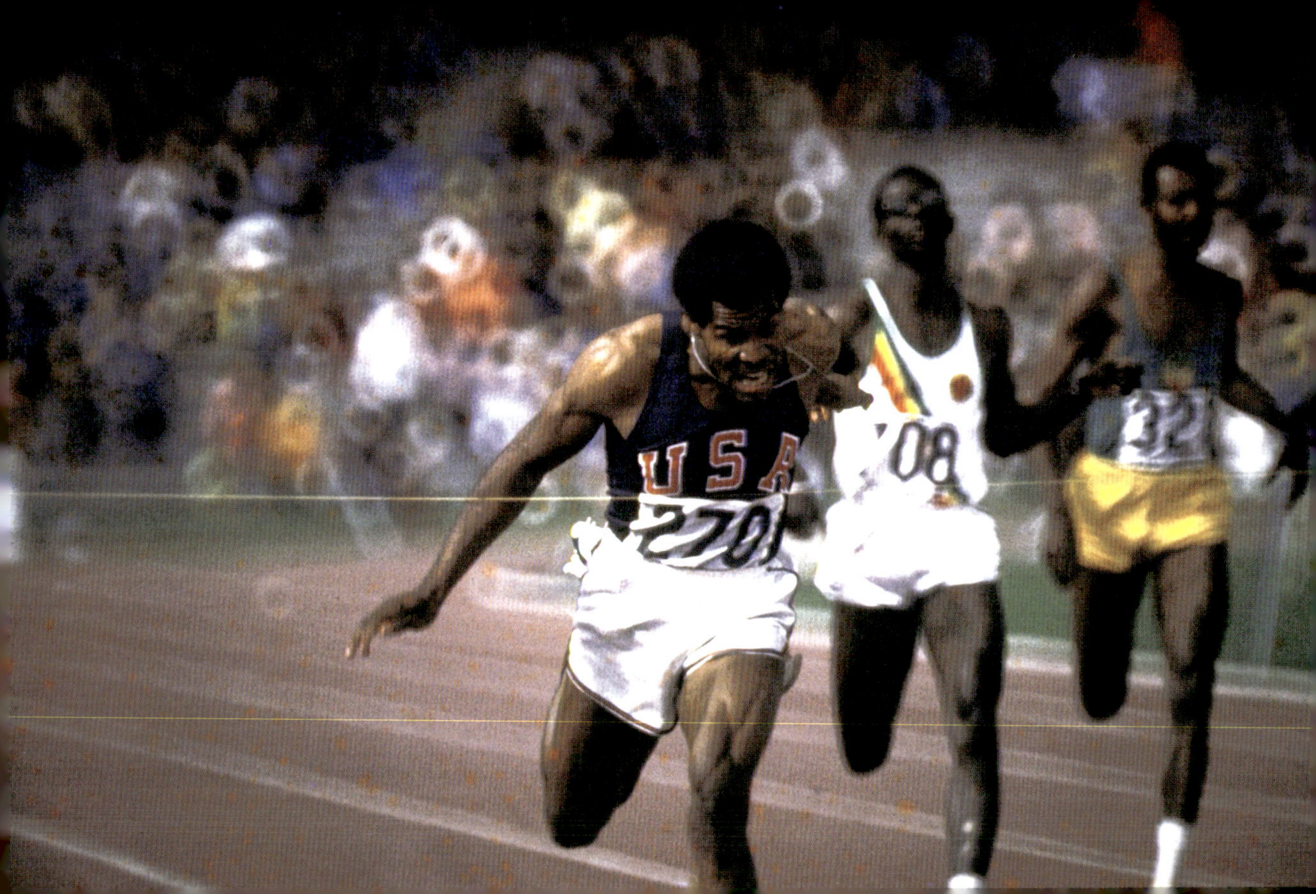
USA
270
08
32

1968

Mexico City
Mexico

Games of the XIX Olympiad

12 – 22 October 1968

172 events ▪ 20 sports

112 competing nations ▪ 5,516 athletes

Spectators

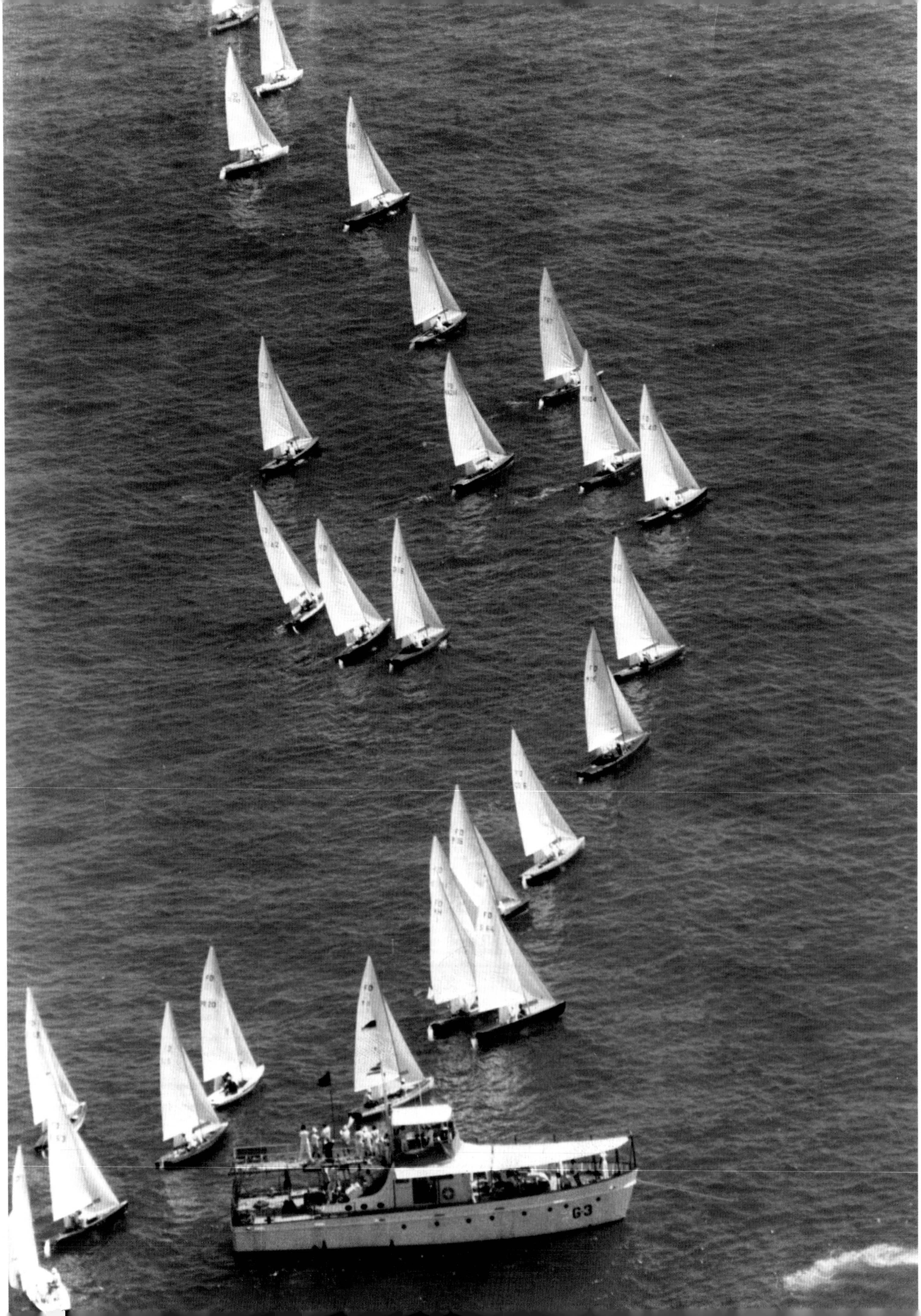

▲ Road race
◀ Flying Dutchman class, start

1968 Mexico City 247

Charlie Green (United States), gold, 4 x 100 m relay; bronze, 100 m

Soviet Union (red), gold, men's tandem sprint

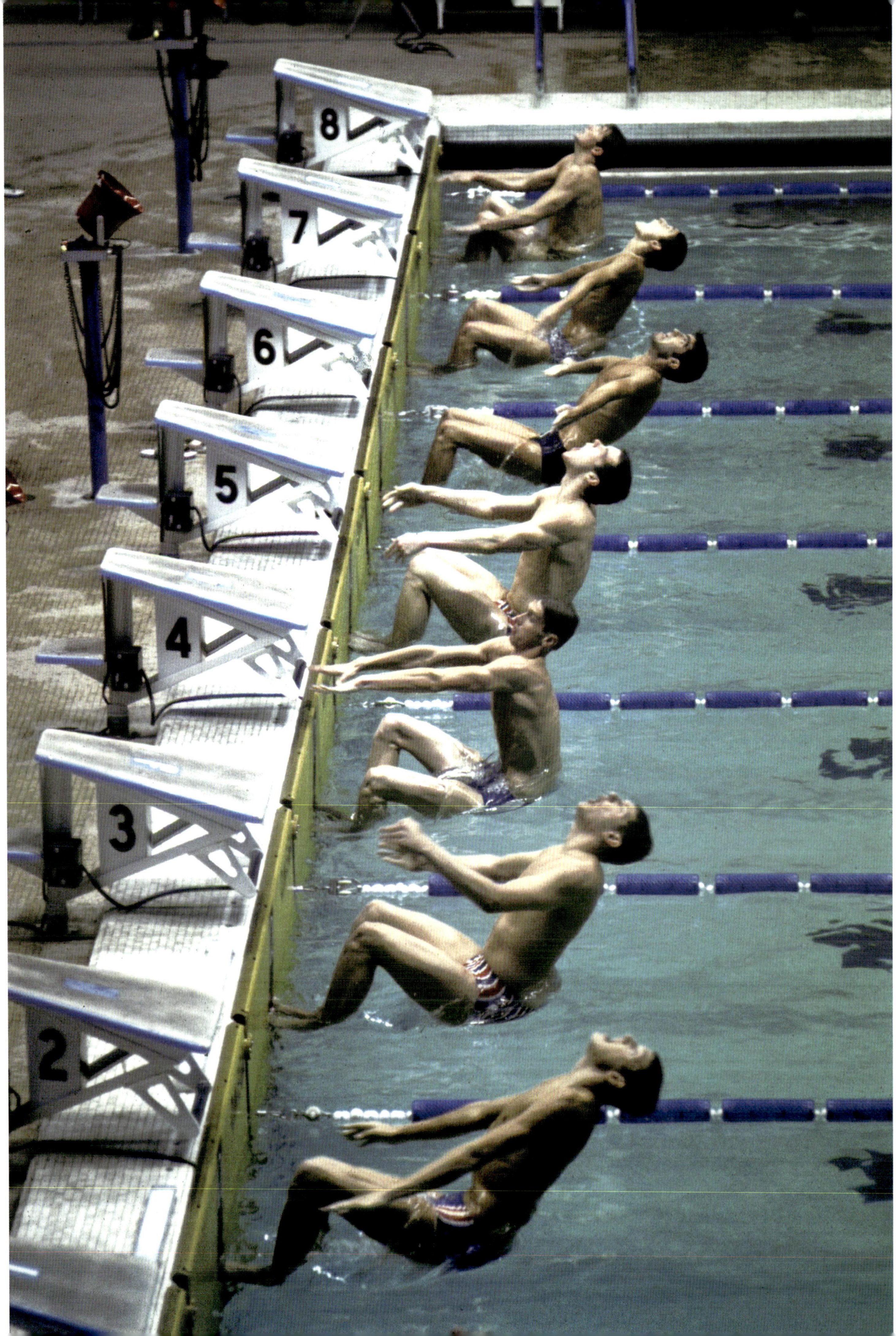

▲ Debbie Meyer (United States), gold, women's 200 m, 400 m & 800 m freestyle

◀ Men's 200 m backstroke, start

1968 Mexico City

Black Power salute, men's 200 m medal ceremony: Peter Norman (Australia, silver, left); Tommie Smith (United States, gold, centre); John Carlos (United States, bronze, right)

Bob Beamon (United States), gold, men's long jump

William Steinkraus & Snowbound (United States), gold, show jumping

Dick Fosbury (United States), gold, high jump

Mamo Wolde (Ethiopia), gold, marathon

Vera Caslavska (Czechoslovakia), 4 gold, 2 silver, gymnastics

1968 Mexico City 257

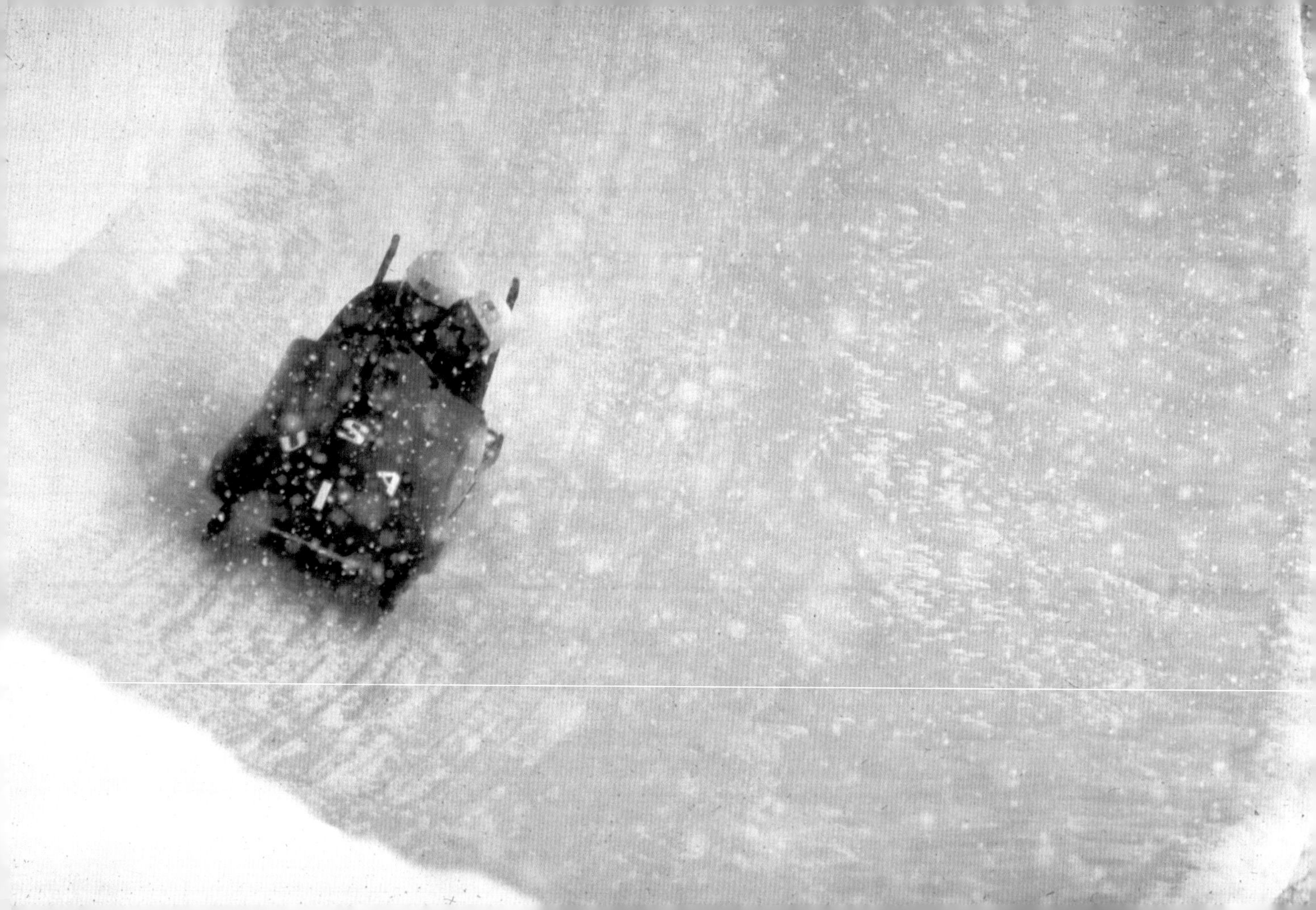
USA I

1972

Sapporo
Japan

XI Olympic Winter Games

3 – 13 February 1972

35 events ▪ 6 sports

35 competing nations ▪ 1,006 athletes

Moon buggy, Apollo 16

Marie-Theres Nadig (Switzerland), gold, downhill & giant slalom

Magnar Solberg (Norway), gold, 20 km biathlon

Francisco Fernandez Ochoa (Spain), gold, men's slalom

Yukio Kasaya (Japan, centre top), gold; Seiji Aochi (Japan, left, bronze); Akitsugu Konno (Japan, right, silver), 70 m ski jumping

Ard Schenk (Netherlands), gold, 1,500 m, 5,000 m & 10,000 m speed skating

Irina Rodnina & Alexei Ulanov (Soviet Union), gold, pairs figure skating

Bobsleigh run ▶
Olympic flame ▶▶

266   1972 Sapporo

1972 Sapporo 267

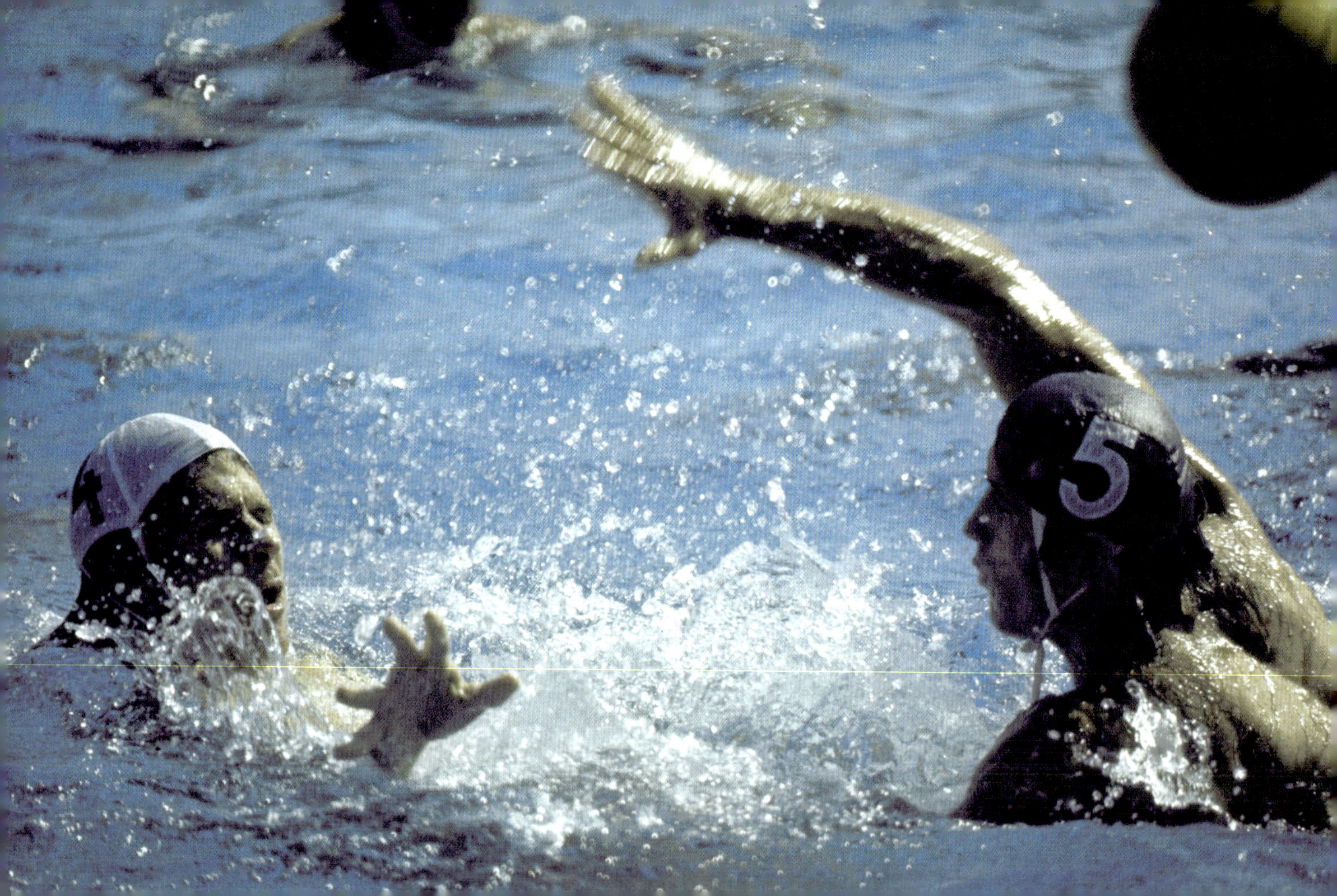

1972

Munich
West Germany

Games of the XX Olympiad

26 August – 11 September 1972

195 events ▪ 23 sports

121 competing nations ▪ 7,134 athletes

Terrorist siege, Olympic Village

Soviet Union (red) vs United States, 51–50, men's basketball final

Kip Keino (Kenya), gold, 3,000 m steeplechase

▲ Olga Korbut (Soviet Union), gold, floor, beam & team; silver, uneven bars
▶ Vasiliy Alekseyev (Soviet Union), gold, weightlifting

1972 Munich

Mark Spitz (United States), gold, 100 m & 200 m butterfly, 100 m & 200 m freestyle, 4 x 100 m & 4 x 200 m freestyle, & 4 x 100 m medley

Mark Spitz (United States, top) 200 m butterfly

Valeri Borzov (Soviet Union), gold, 100 m & 200 m; silver, 4 x 100 m relay

Lasse Viren (Finland), gold, 5,000 m & 10,000 m

Duane Bobick (United States), boxing

Wayne Wells (United States, top), gold, freestyle wrestling

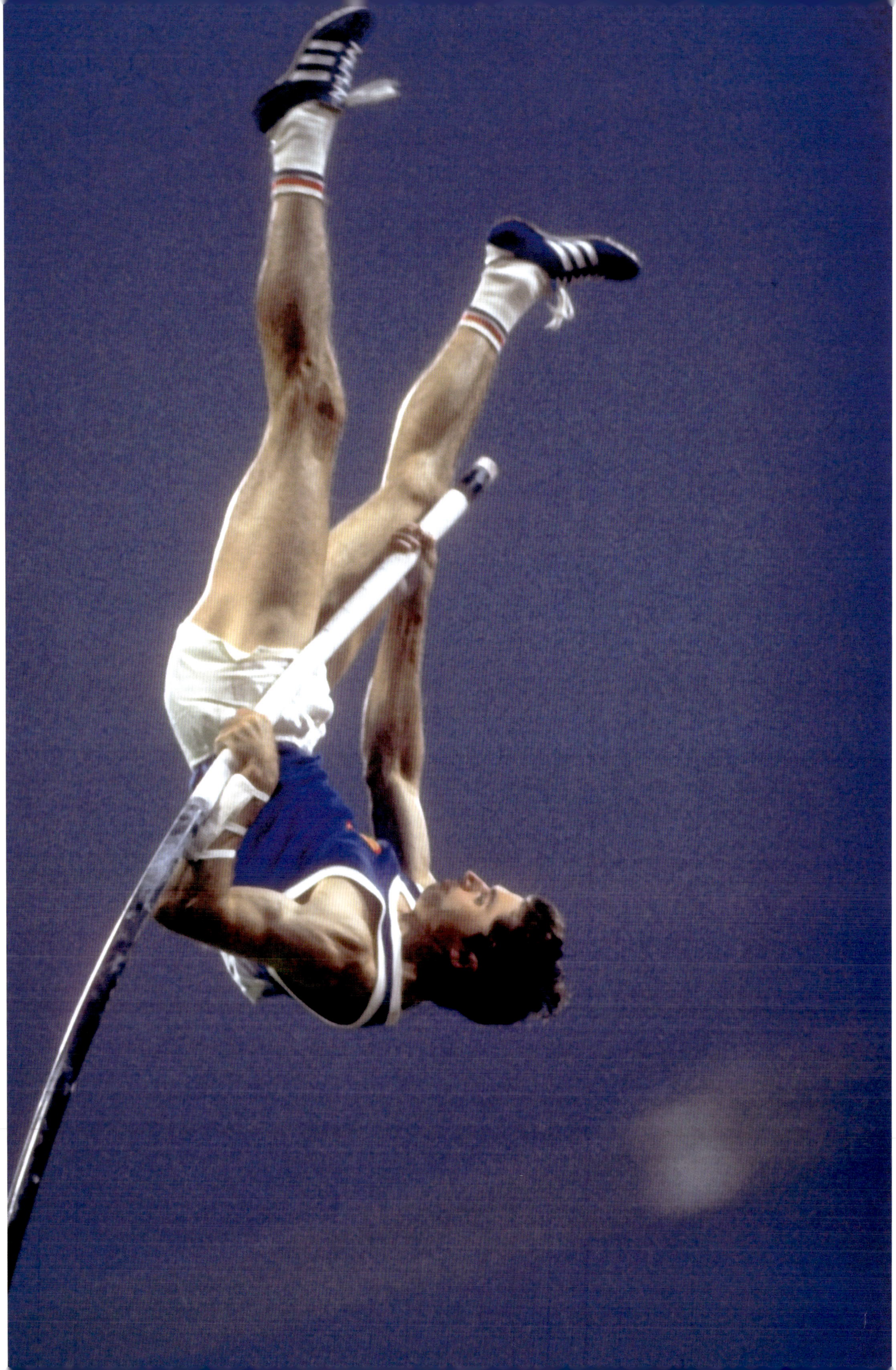

▲ Gail Neall (Australia), gold, 400 m individual medley
◀ Wolfgang Nordwig (East Germany), gold, pole vault

1972 Munich

Men's archery

Chess, Olympic Village

1972 Munich

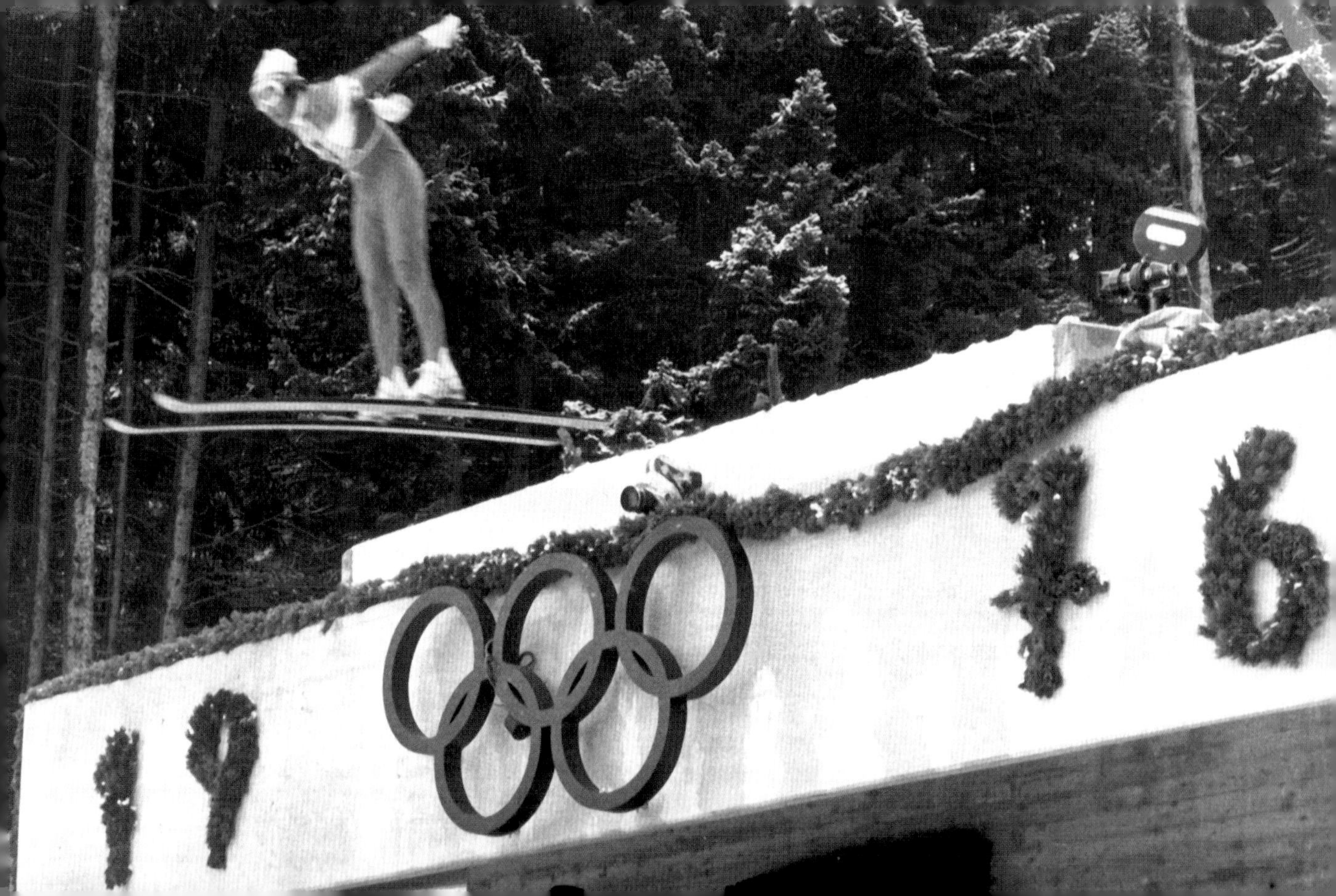
19
76

1976

Innsbruck Austria

XII Olympic Winter Games

4 – 15 February 1976

37 events ▪ 6 sports

37 competing nations ▪ 1,123 athletes

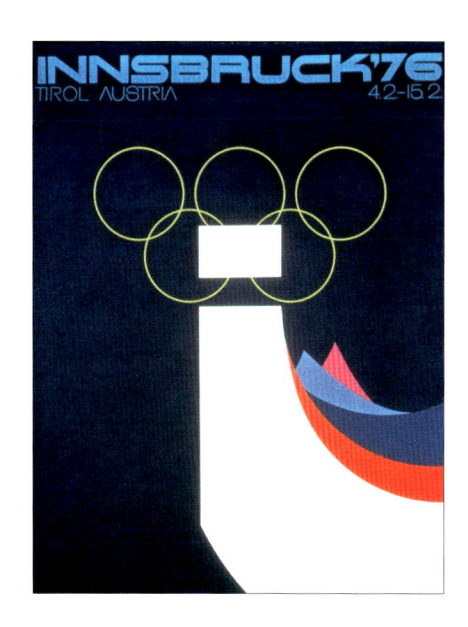

Concorde, first commercial flight

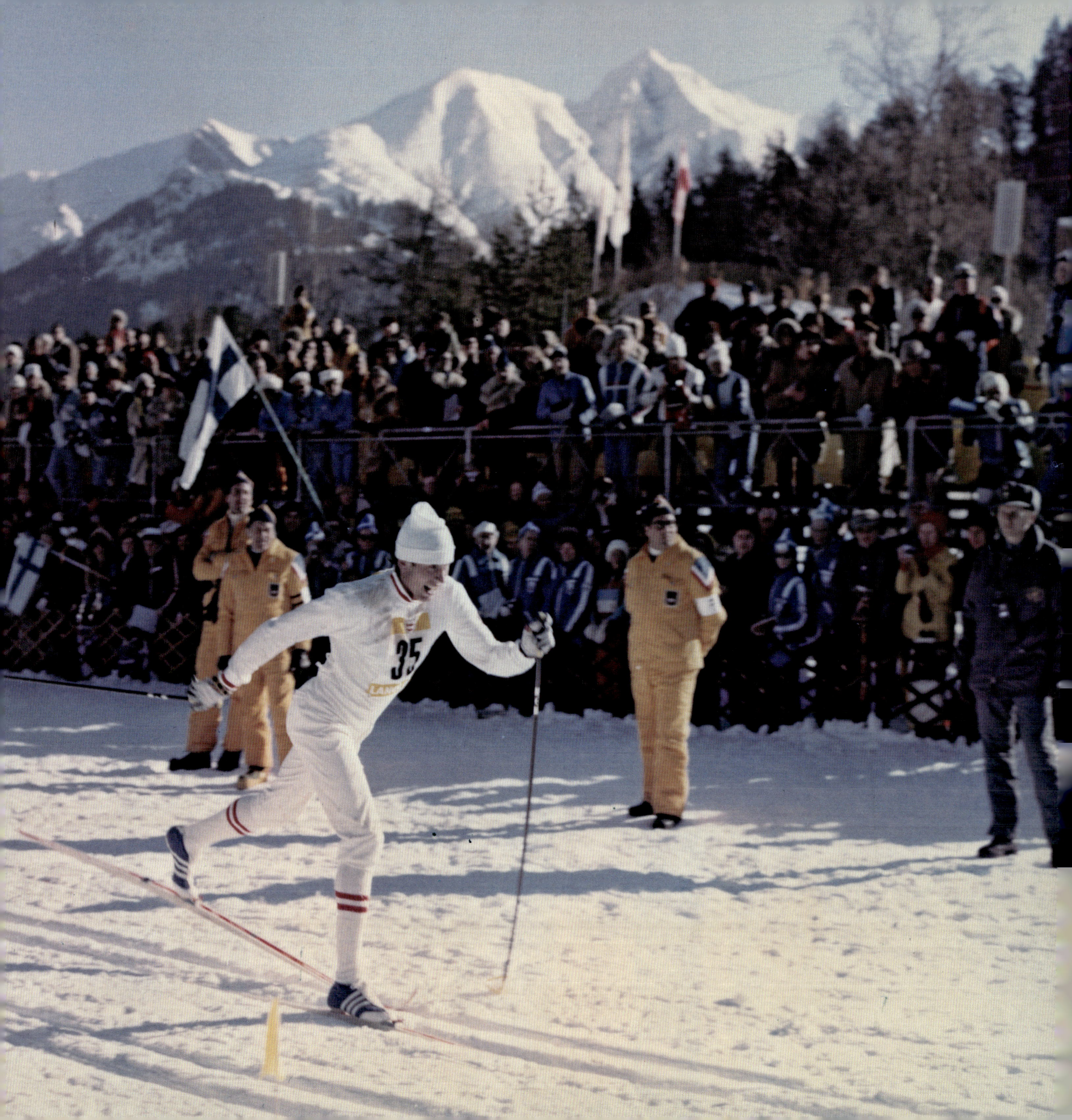
35

▲ Rosi Mittermaier (West Germany), gold, downhill & slalom; bronze, giant slalom

◄ Sergei Saweljew (Soviet Union) gold, 15 km cross-country

1976 Innsbruck

Sheila Young (United States), gold, 500 m speed skating; silver, 1,500 m; bronze, 1,000 m

Elisabeth Demleitner (West Germany), bronze, luge, with Formula 1 champion Jackie Stewart

1976 Innsbruck 289

Opening ceremony

Dorothy Hamill (United States, centre), gold, figure skating, with Dianne de Leeuw (Netherlands, silver, right) & Christine Errath (East Germany, bronze)

1976 Innsbruck

Galina Kulakova (Soviet Union), gold, women's 4 x 5 km cross-country relay

Irina Moiseyeva & Andrei Minenko (Soviet Union), silver, pairs figure skating

Ingemar Stenmark (Sweden), men's slalom

John Curry (Great Britain), gold, figure skating

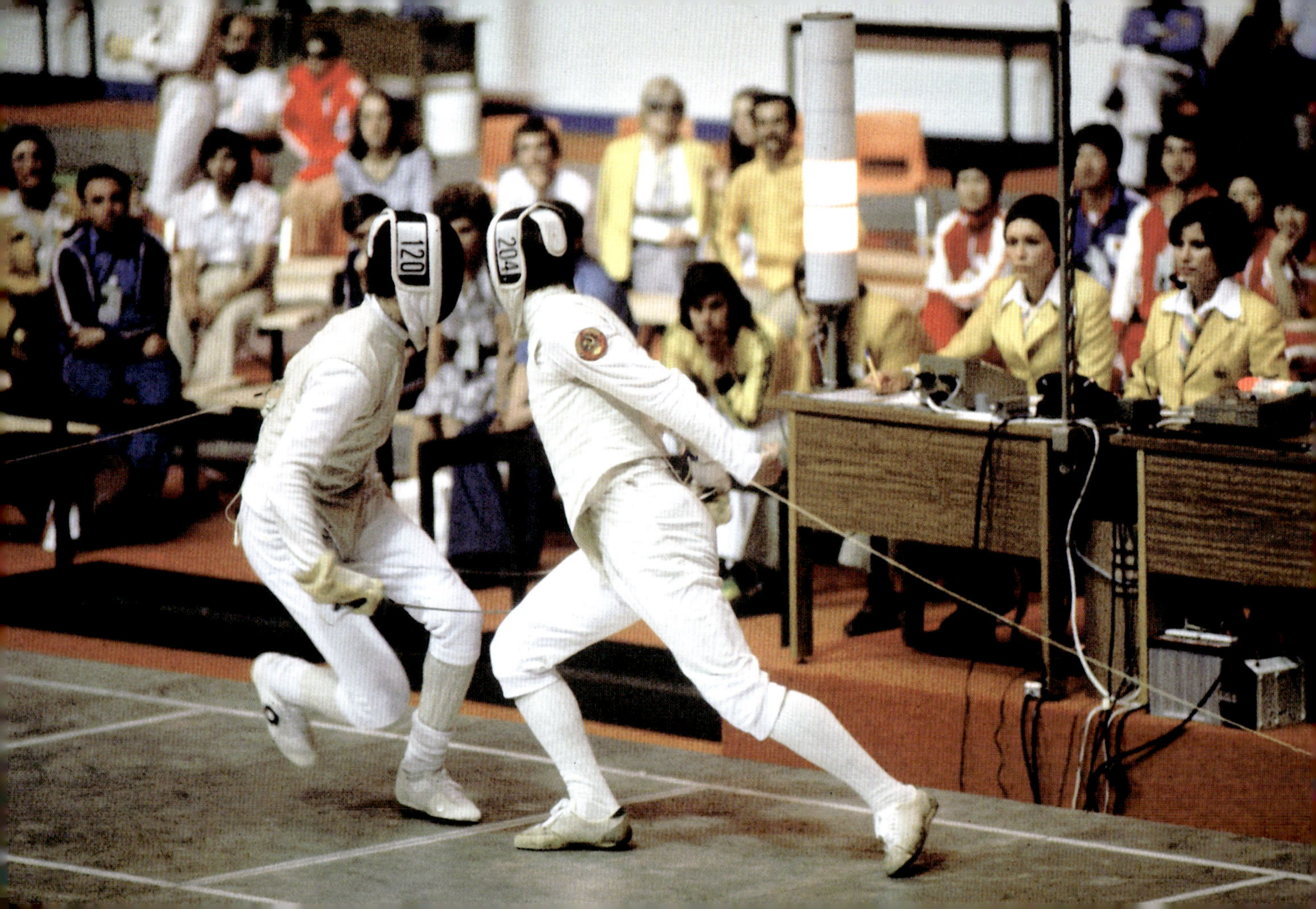
120
204

1976

Montreal Canada

Games of the XXI Olympiad

17 July – 1 August 1976

198 events ▪ 21 sports

92 competing nations ▪ 6,084 athletes

Death of Chairman Mao Zedong, China

Hasely Crawford (Trinidad and Tobago, gold) Don Quarrie (Jamaica, silver), Valeri Borzov (Soviet Union, bronze), men's 100 m

Adrian Dantley (United States) vs Canada, basketball

East Germany (gold) vs Poland (silver), football

Arnie Robinson (United States), gold, long jump

John Walker (New Zealand, right), gold, 1,500 m

Alberto Juantorena (Cuba), gold, 400 m & 800 m

Men's team pursuit

David Roberts (United States), bronze, pole vault

1976 Montreal

1976 Montreal

▲ Olga Korbut (Soviet Union), gold, team; silver, beam
◀ Klaus Dibiasi (Italy), gold, men's 10-m platform diving

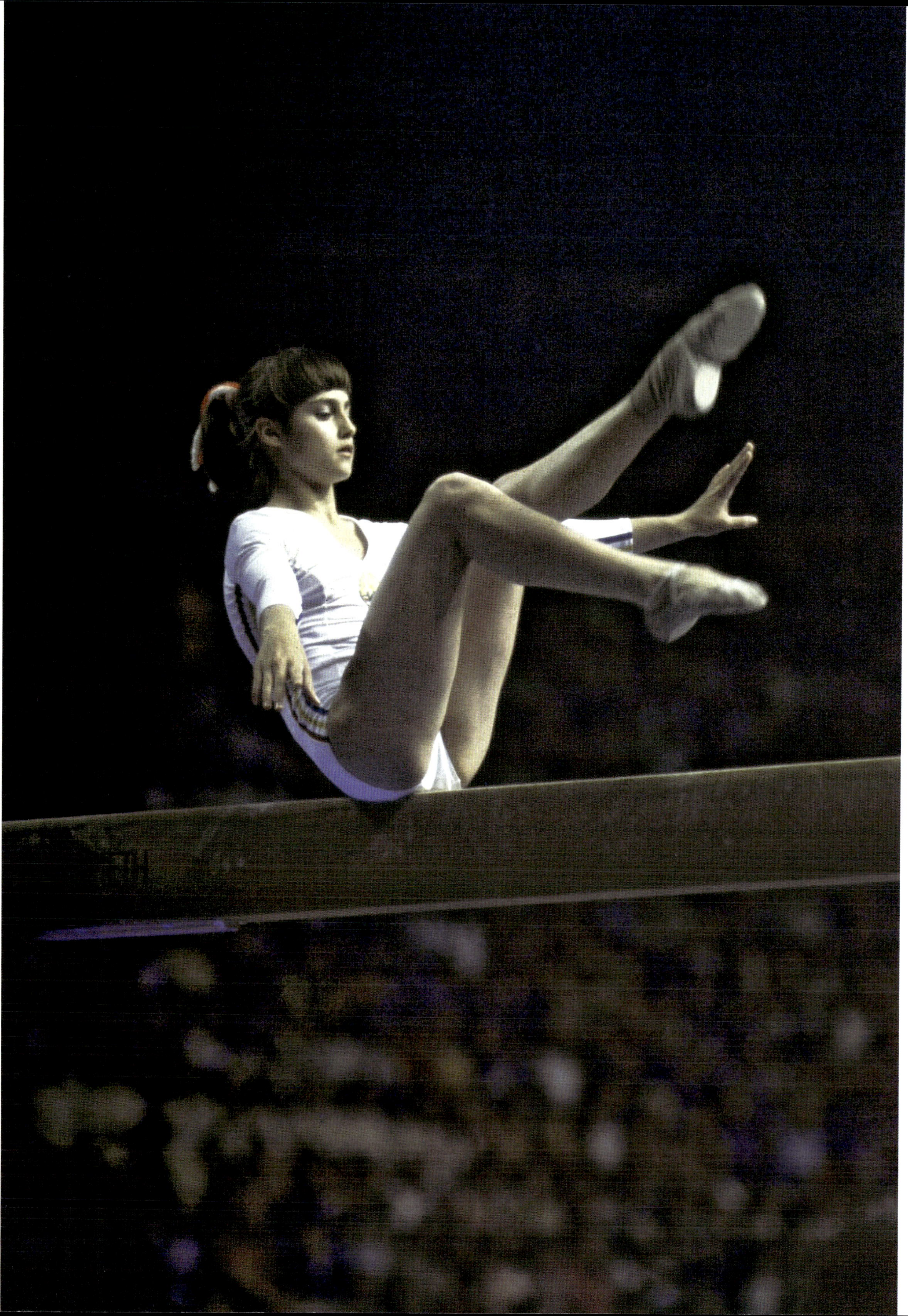

▲ Soviet Union, gold, handball
◀ Nadia Comaneci (Romania), 3 gold, 1 silver, 1 bronze, gymnastics

1976 Montreal   309

Leon Spinks (United States), gold, boxing

Sugar Ray Leonard (United States), gold, boxing

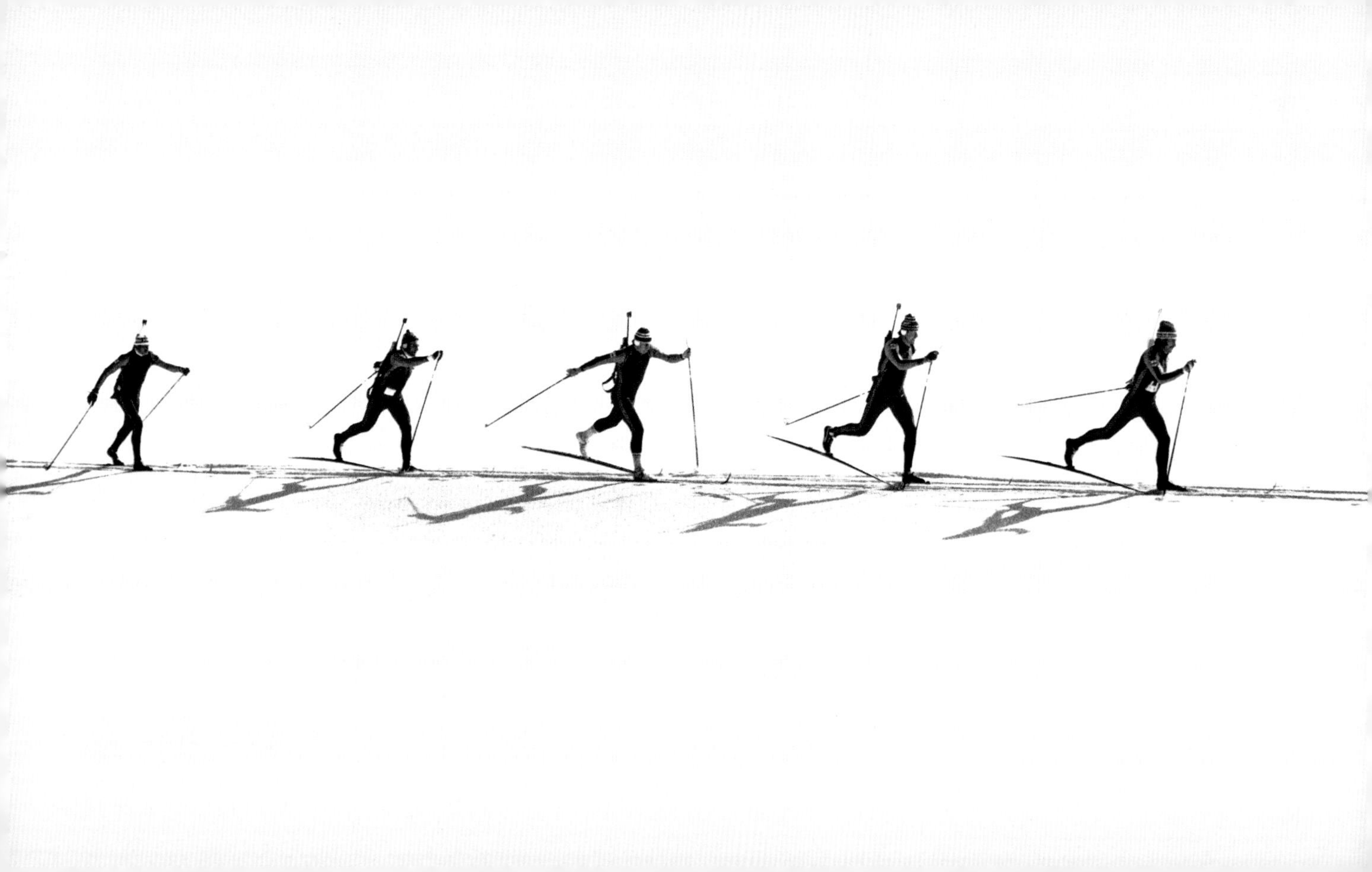

1980

Lake Placid
United States

XIII Olympic Winter Games

13 – 24 February 1980

38 events ▪ 6 sports

37 competing nations ▪ 1,072 athletes

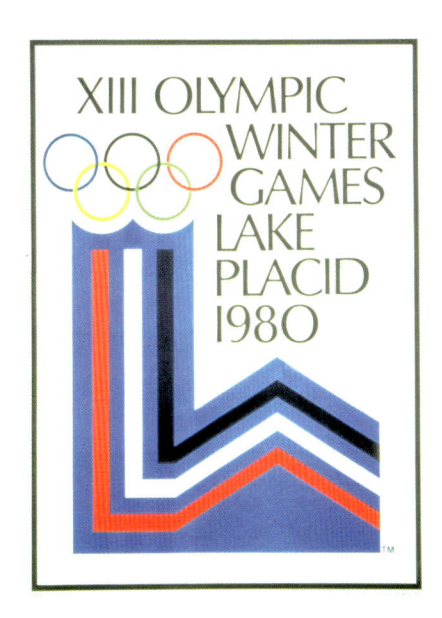

Solidarity trade union, Poland

▲ Alpine skiing course
▶ James Denney (United States), ski jumping

1980 Lake Placid 315

Hanni Wenzel (Lichtenstein), gold, women's giant slalom & slalom; silver, downhill

Nikolay Zimyatov (Soviet Union), gold, men's 30 km, 50 km & 4 x 10 km cross-country relay

▲ ▶ United States defeat the Soviet Union 4–3 in the 'Miracle on Ice' semi-final, before taking gold, men's ice hockey

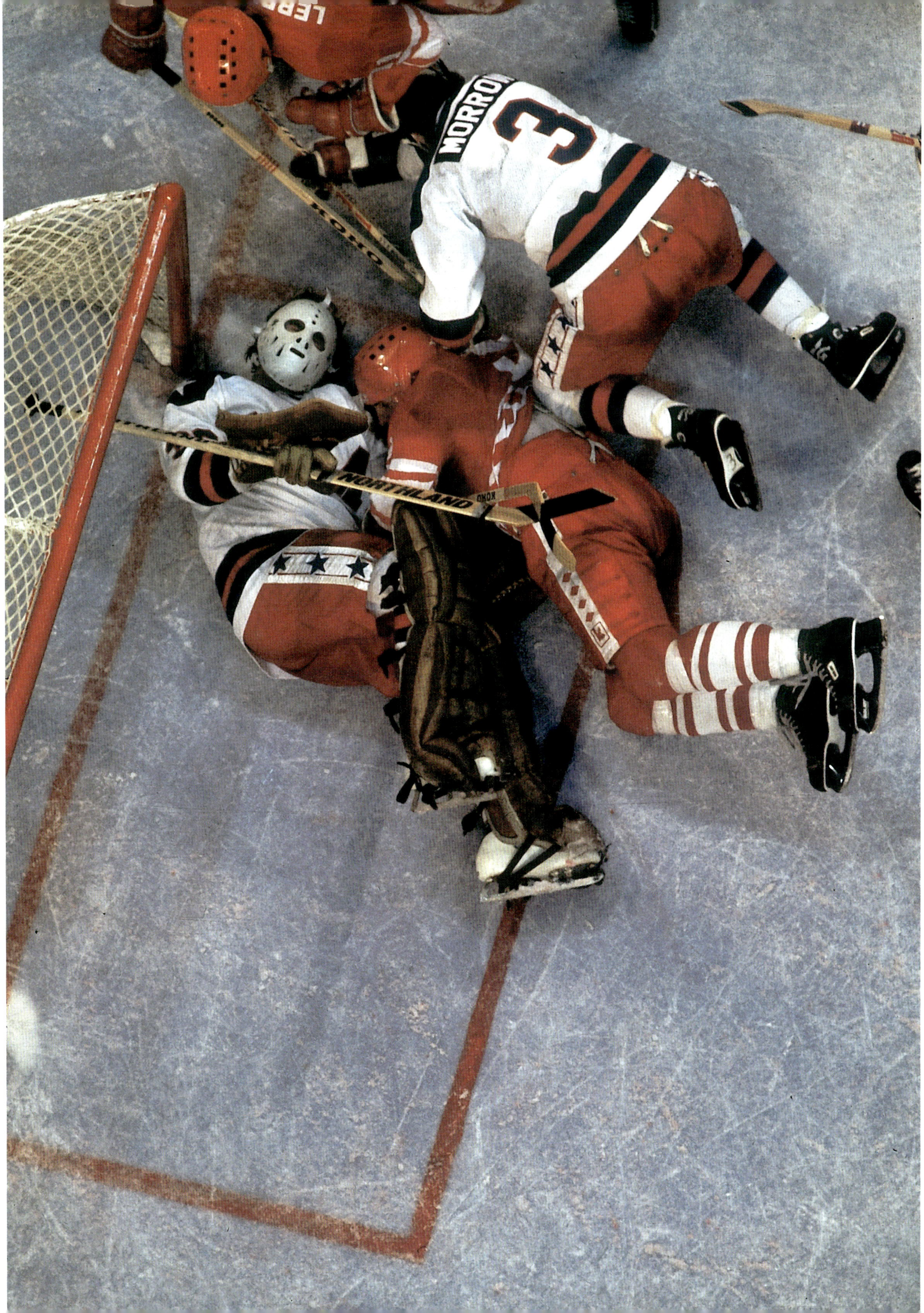
3
NORTHLAND

▲ Robin Cousins (Great Britain), gold, men's figure skating
▶ Eric Heiden (United States), gold, 500 m, 1,000 m, 1,500 m, 5,000 m & 10,000 m speed skating

321

Alexander Tikhonov (Soviet Union), gold, 4 x 7.5 km biathlon relay

Hans Rinn (front) and Norbert Hahn (East Germany), gold, pairs luge

Sebastian Coe (254, Great Britain), gold, 1,500 m; silver, 800 m

1980

Moscow
Soviet Union

Games of the XXII Olympiad

19 July – 3 August 1980

203 events ▪ 21 sports

80 competing nations ▪ 5,179 athletes

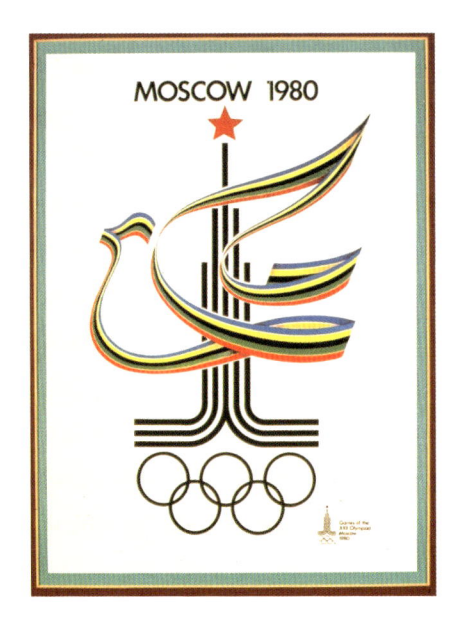

Iranian Embassy siege, London

▲ Opening ceremony

▶ Frank Paschek (East Germany), silver, long jump

1980 Moscow

Marita Koch (East Germany), gold, 400 m; silver, 4 x 400 m relay

Sultan Rakhmanov (Soviet Union), gold, weightlifting

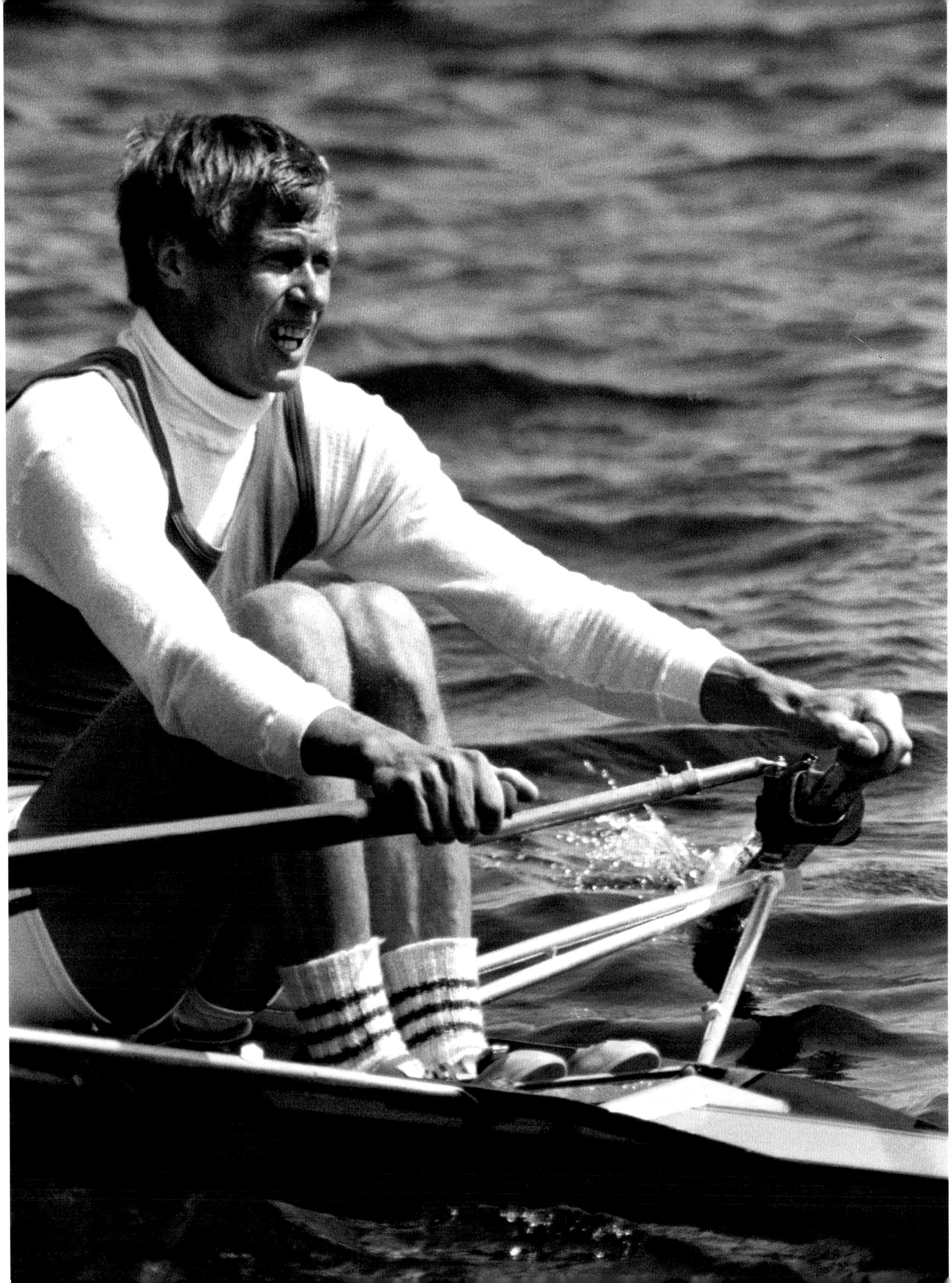

▲ Soviet Union (red, gold) vs Bulgaria (silver), women's basketball
◀ Pertti Karppinen (Finland), gold, sculls

1980 Moscow 331

3,000 m steeplechase

Duncan Goodhew (Great Britain), gold, 100 m breaststroke; bronze, 4 x 100 m medley

Allan Wells (Great Britain, left), gold, 100 m; silver, 200 m

1980 Moscow

Daley Thompson (Great Britain), gold, decathlon

Nelly Kisi (Soviet Union), beam

Teofilo Stevenson (Cuba, left), gold, vs Pyotr Zaev (Soviet Union), boxing

Alexander Dityatin (Soviet Union), 3 gold, 4 silver, 1 bronze, gymnastics

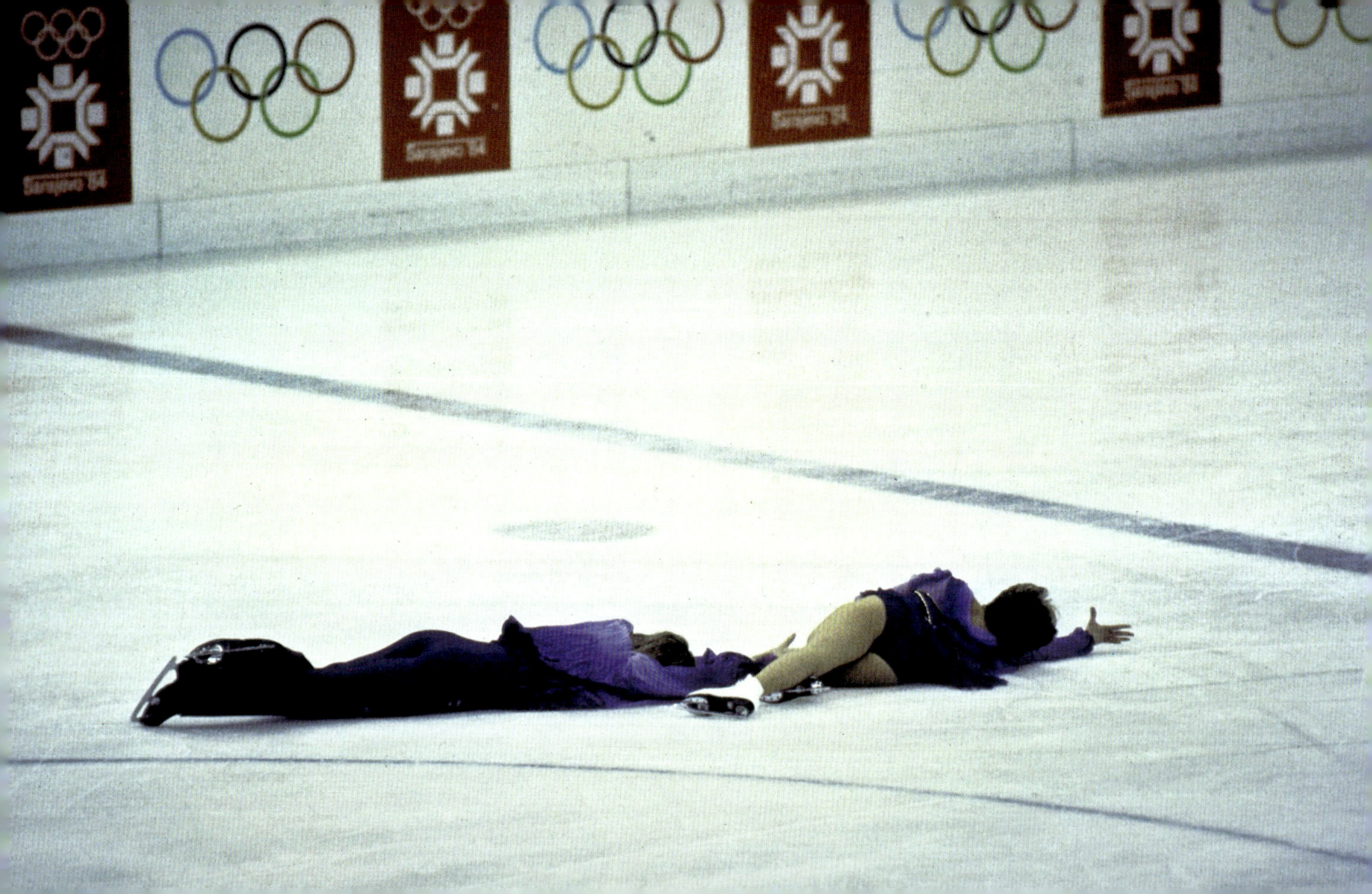
Sarajevo '84

1984
Sarajevo Yugoslavia

XIV Olympic Winter Games

8 – 19 February 1984

39 events ▪ 6 sports

49 competing nations ▪ 1,272 athletes

Indira Ghandi assassination, India

Katarina Witt (East Germany), gold, figure skating

Men's luge

Karin Enke (East Germany), gold, women's 1,000 & 1,500 m speed skating; silver 500 m & 3,000 m

Soviet Union, bobsleigh

Bill Johnson (United States), gold, men's downhill

346   1984 Sarajevo

Bill Johnson (United States), gold, men's downhill

1984 Sarajevo

Jens Weissflog (East Germany), gold, 70-m ski jump; silver, 90-m ski jump

Marja-Liisa Hämäläinen (Finland), gold, women's 5 km, 10 km & 20 km cross-country; bronze, 4 x 5 km relay

1984 Sarajevo

Cross-country

U.S. twins Phil (right) & Steve Mahre, gold & silver, giant slalom

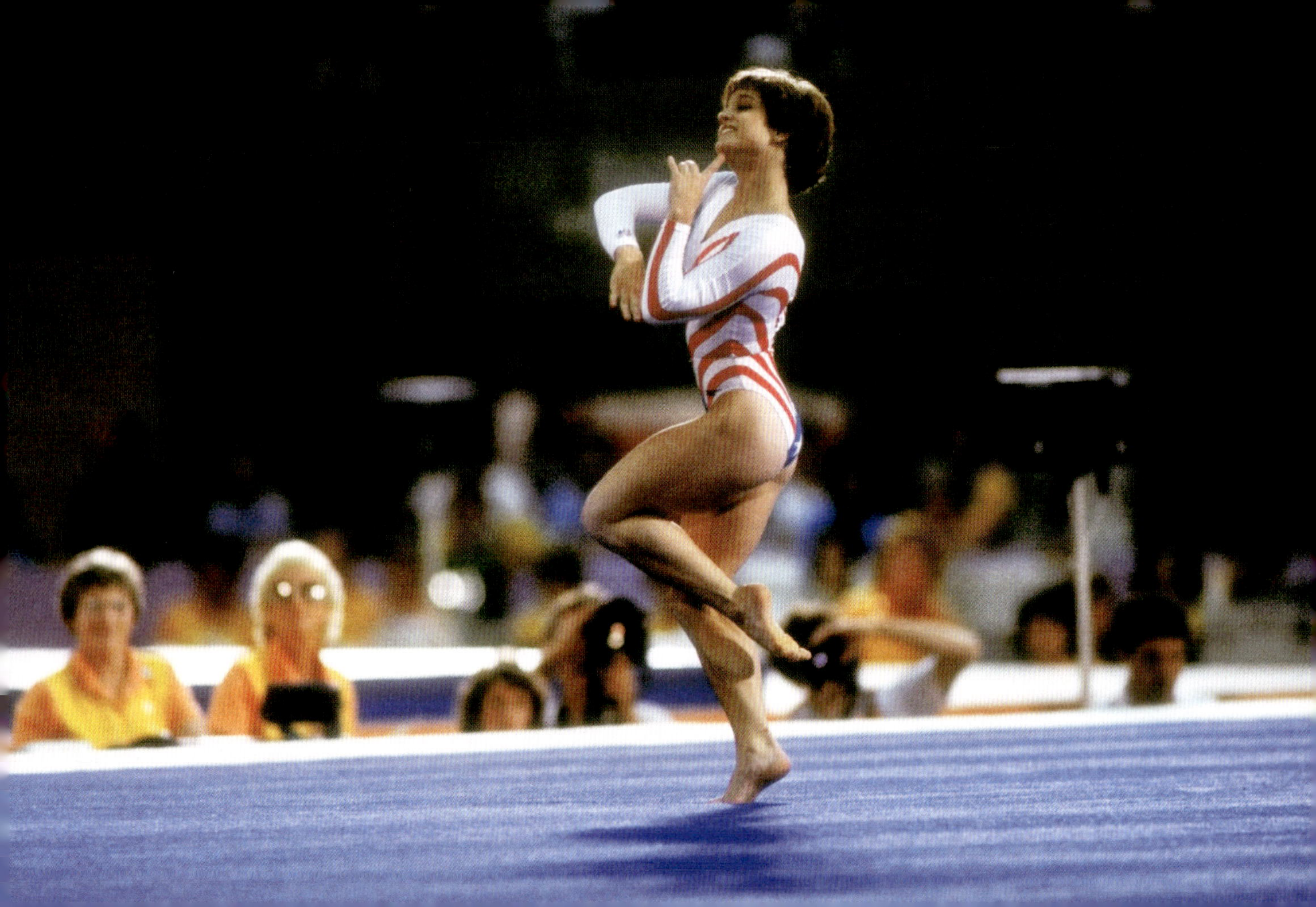

1984
Los Angeles
United States

Games of the XXIII Olympiad

28 July – 12 August 1984

221 events ▪ 23 sports

140 competing nations ▪ 6,829 athletes

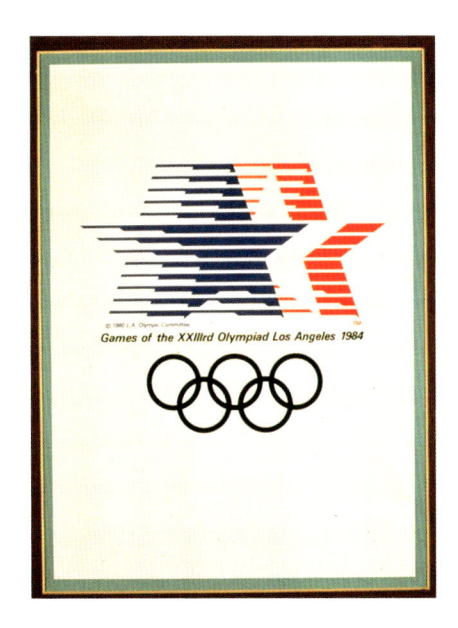

Contras vs Sandanistas, Nicaragua

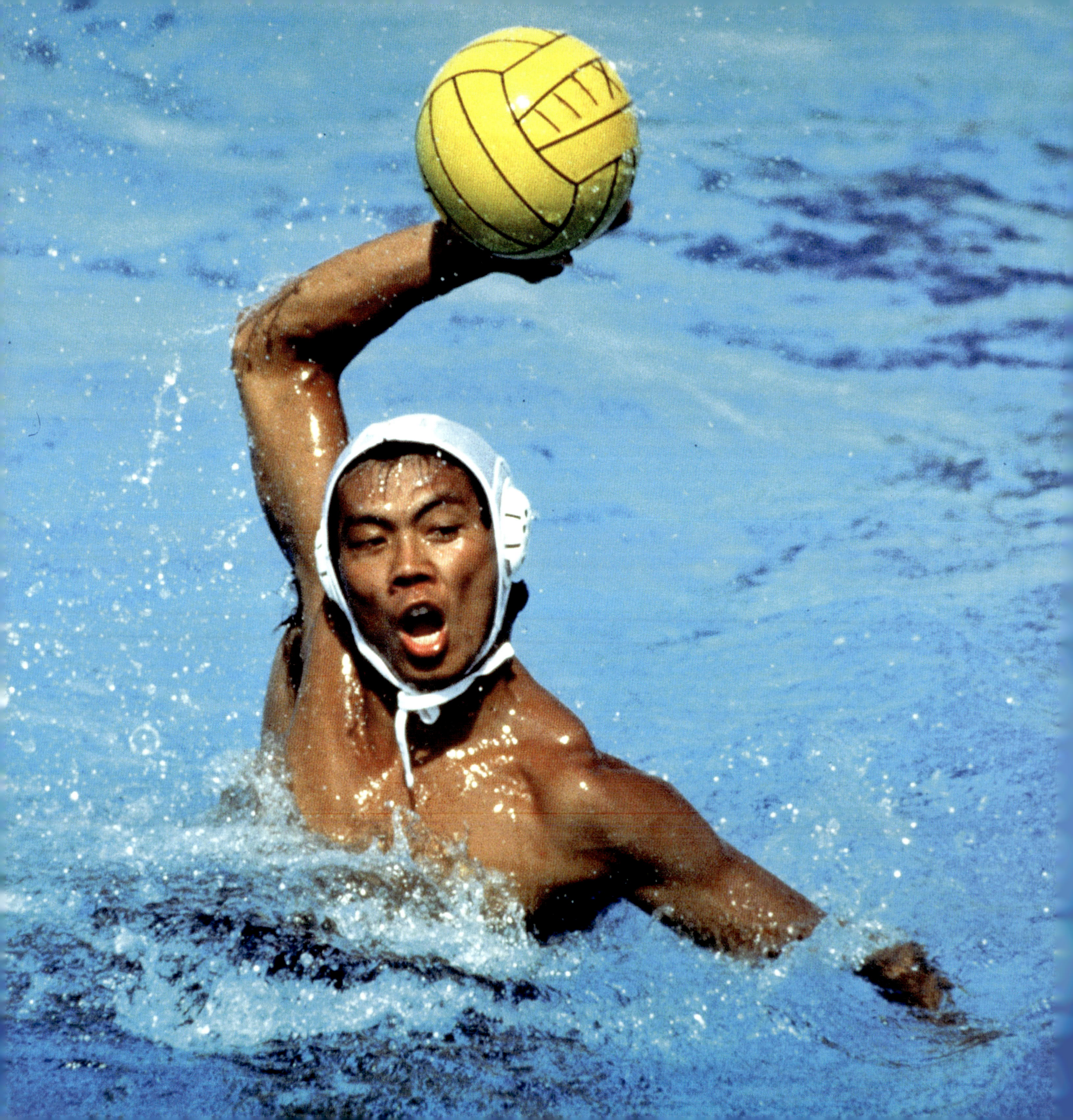

▲ Candie Costie & Tracie Ruiz (United States), gold, synchronized swimming

◂ Hisaharu Saito (Japan), water polo

China (red), gold, vs United States, women's volleyball final

Steve Hegg (United States), gold, individual pursuit; silver, team pursuit

Three-day eventing

Peter Evans (New Zealand), 470 sailing class

1984 Los Angeles

Greg Louganis (United States), gold, 3-m springboard and 10-m platform diving

Mary Decker (United States), 3,000 m

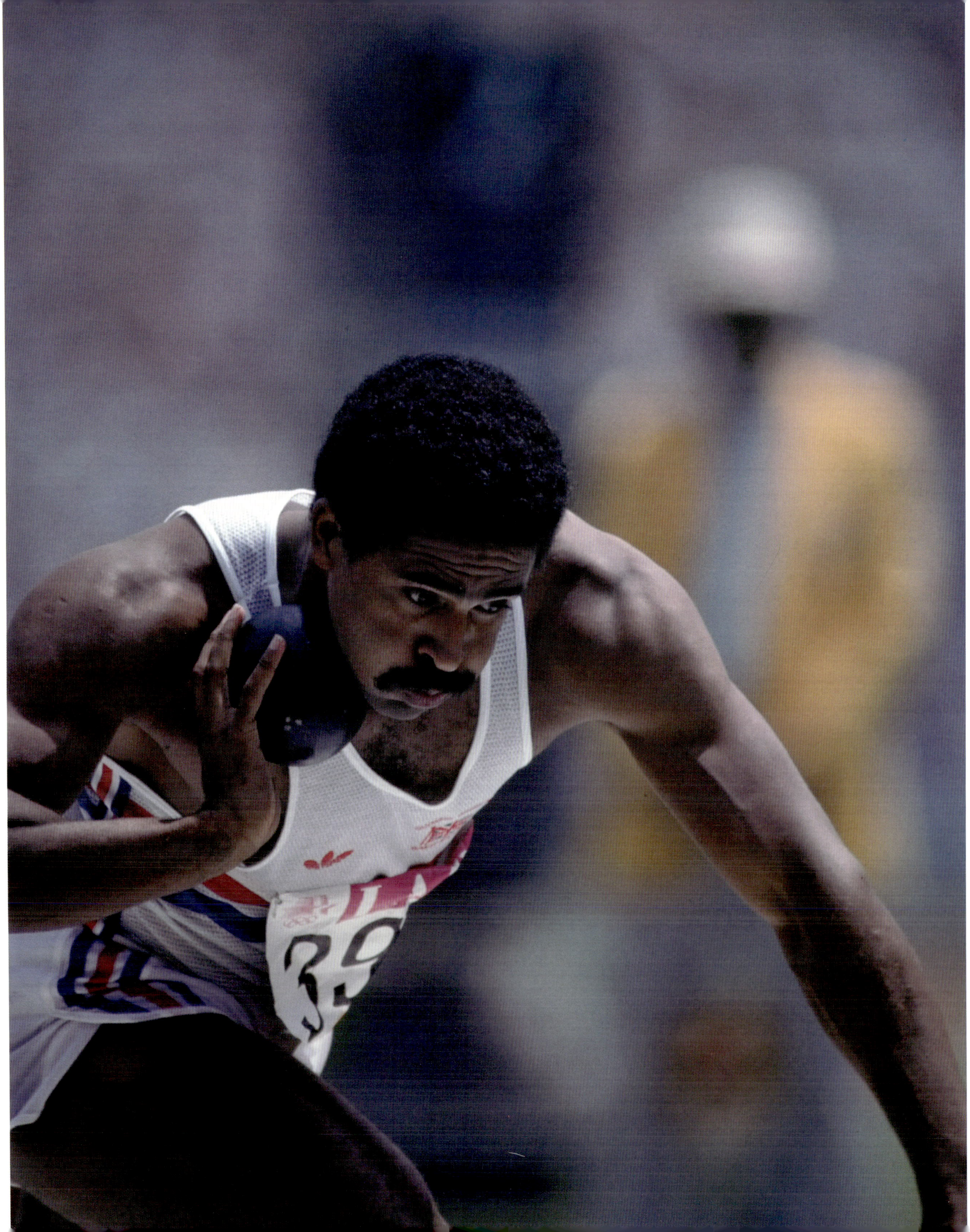

▲ Tim Daggett (United States), gold, team; bronze, pommel horse
◀ Daley Thompson (Great Britain), gold, decathlon

Edwin Moses (United States), gold, 400 m hurdles

Carl Lewis (United States), gold, long jump, 100 m, 200 m & 4 x 100 m relay

Men's 4 x 100 m freestyle relay ▶
Women's marathon ▶▶

1984 Los Angeles 365

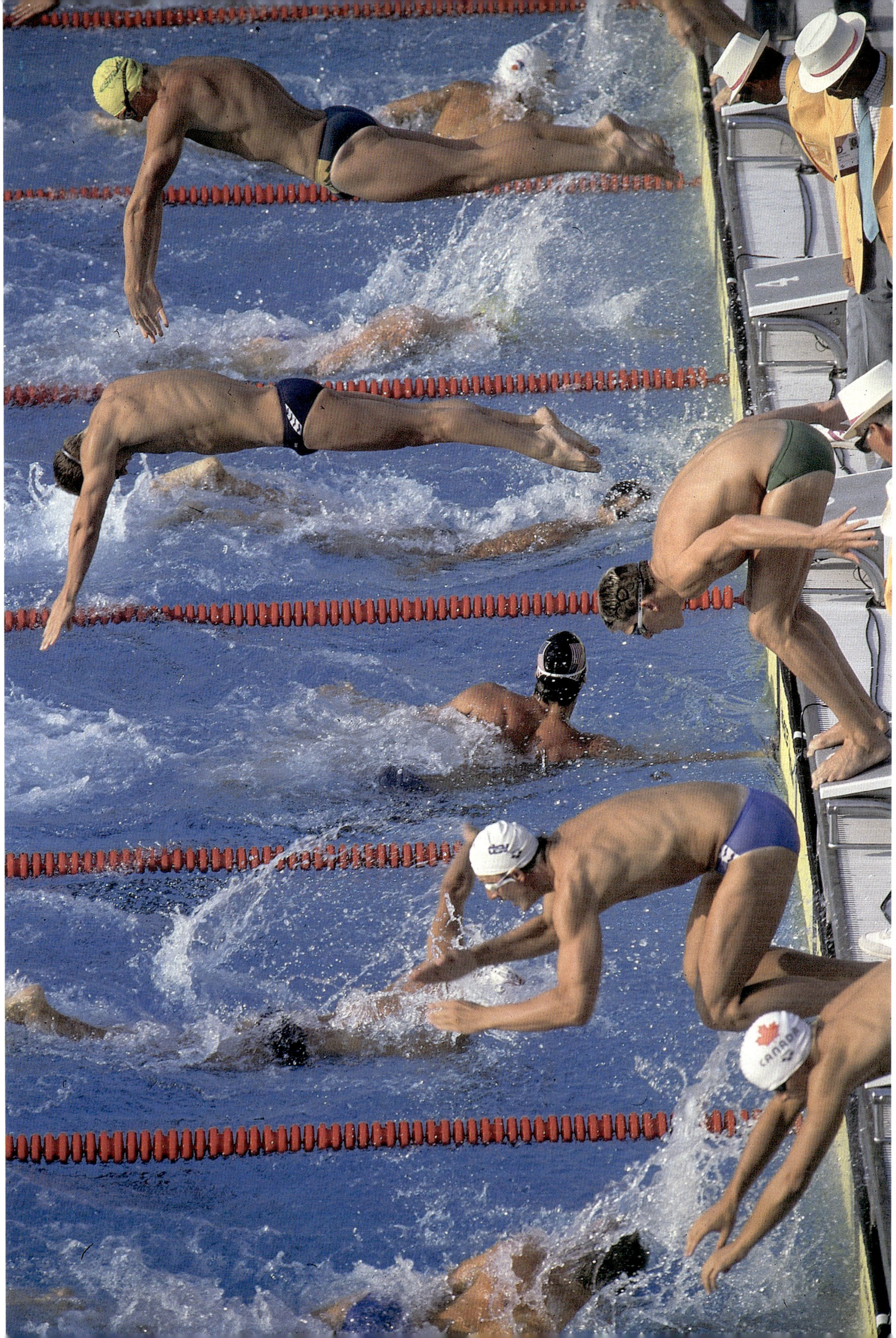
CANADA

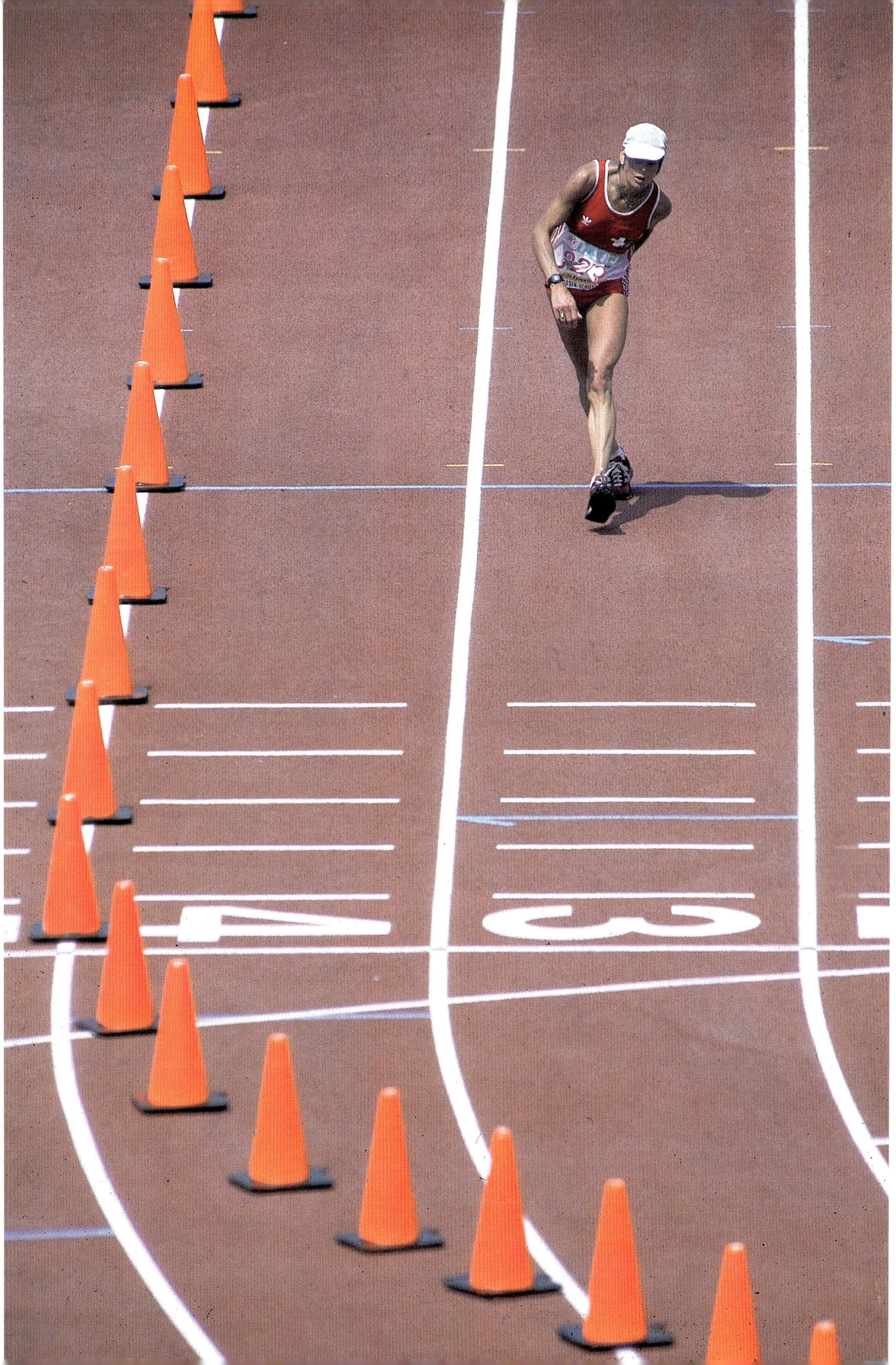
4
3

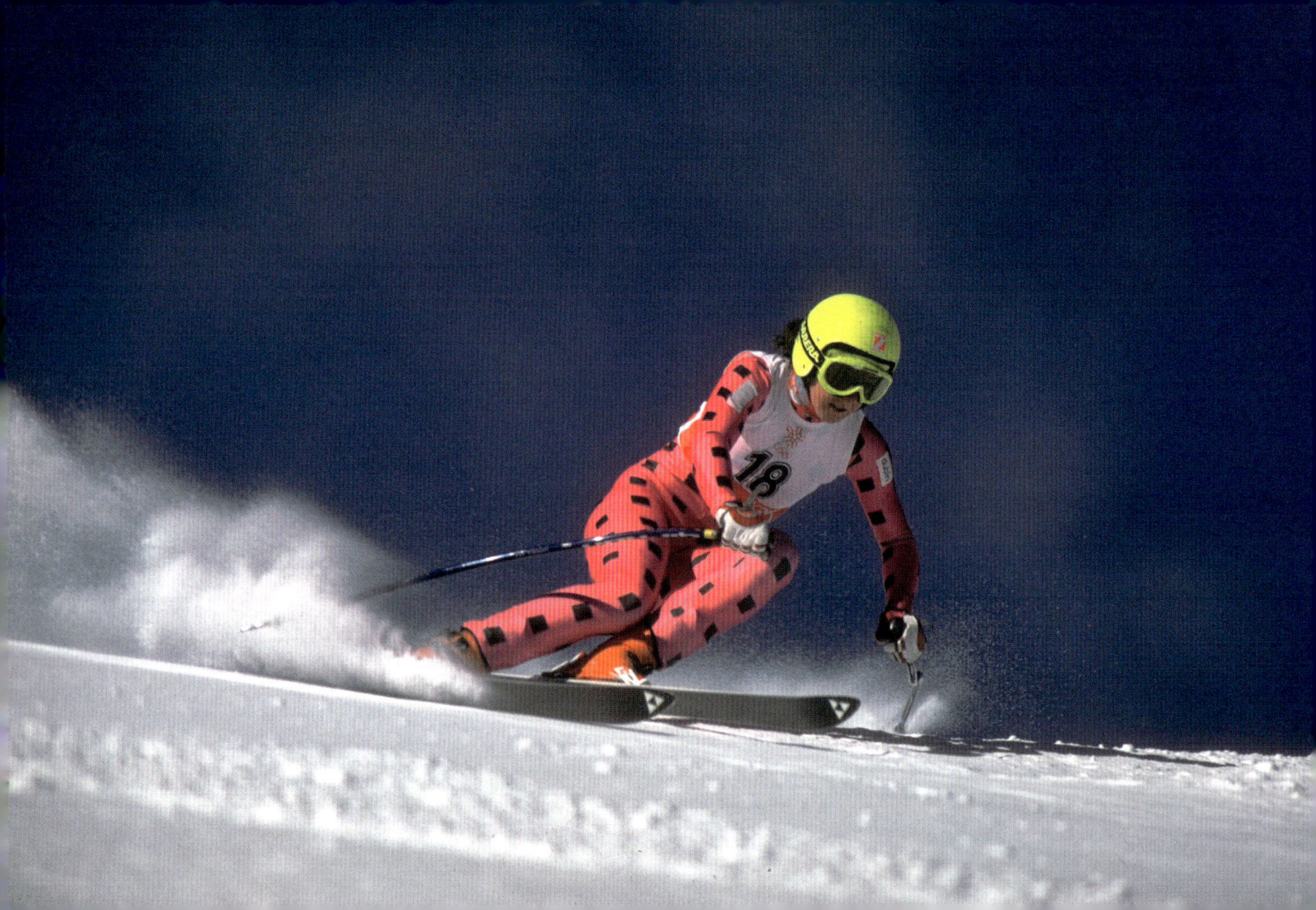
18

1988
Calgary Canada

XV Olympic Winter Games

13 – 28 February 1988

46 events ▪ 6 sports

57 competing nations ▪ 1,423 athletes

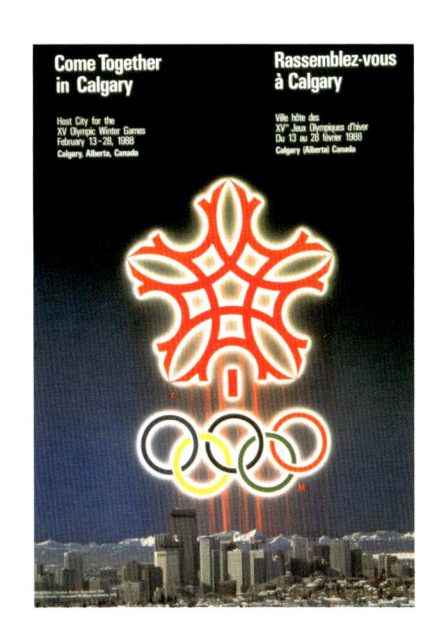

Pan Am Flight 103, Lockerbie, Scotland

Start, women's short track speed skating

Jamaica bobsleigh

Dan Jansen (United States), 500 m speed skating

Katarina Witt (East Germany), gold, figure skating

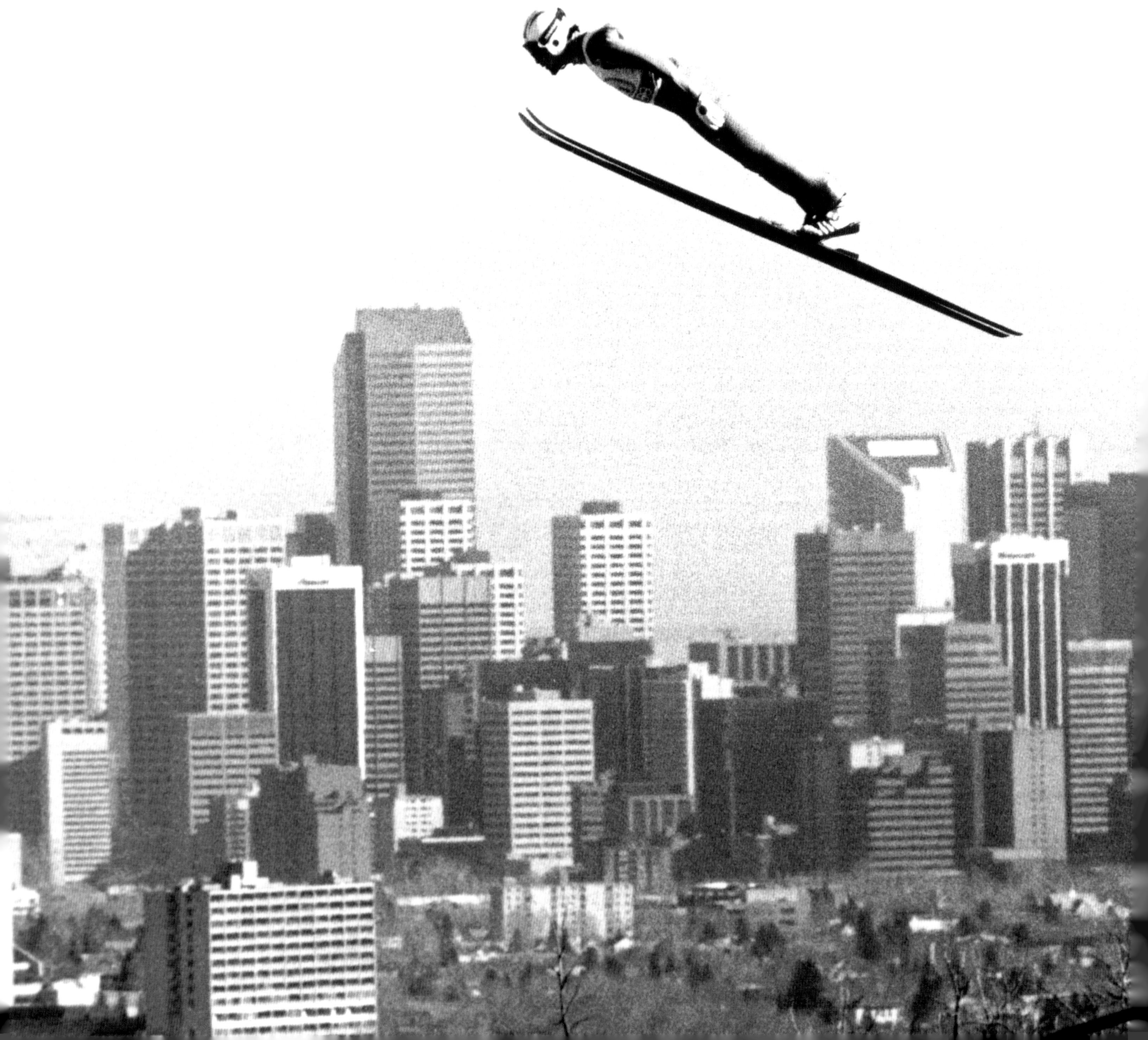

Ski jumping

1988 Calgary 375

Czechoslovakia vs Finland, men's ice hockey

Men's figure skating

Judd Bankert (Guam), biathlon

Men's 4 x 10 km cross-country relay, start

Ben Johnson (Canada, right), 100 m; disqualified for drug abuse

1988

Seoul
South Korea

Games of the XXIV Olympiad

17 September – 2 October 1988

237 events ▪ 25 sports

159 competing nations ▪ 8,391 athletes

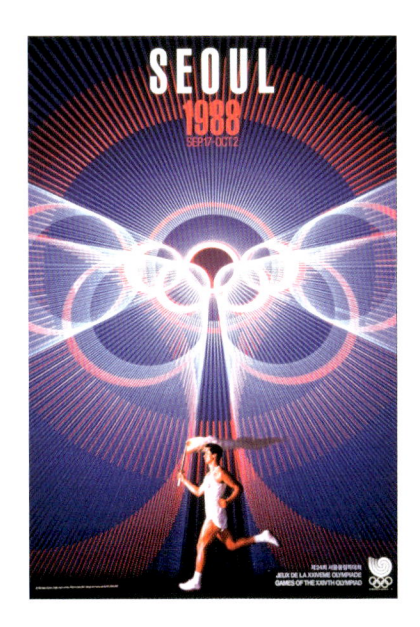

Benazir Bhutto, prime minister, Pakistan

Pamagiota Sitsela (Soviet Union), rhythmic gymnastics

Hiroaki Izumikawa (Japan), modern pentathlon

Men's team pursuit, cycling ▶
Jackie Joyner-Kersee (United States), gold, long jump & heptathlon ▶▶

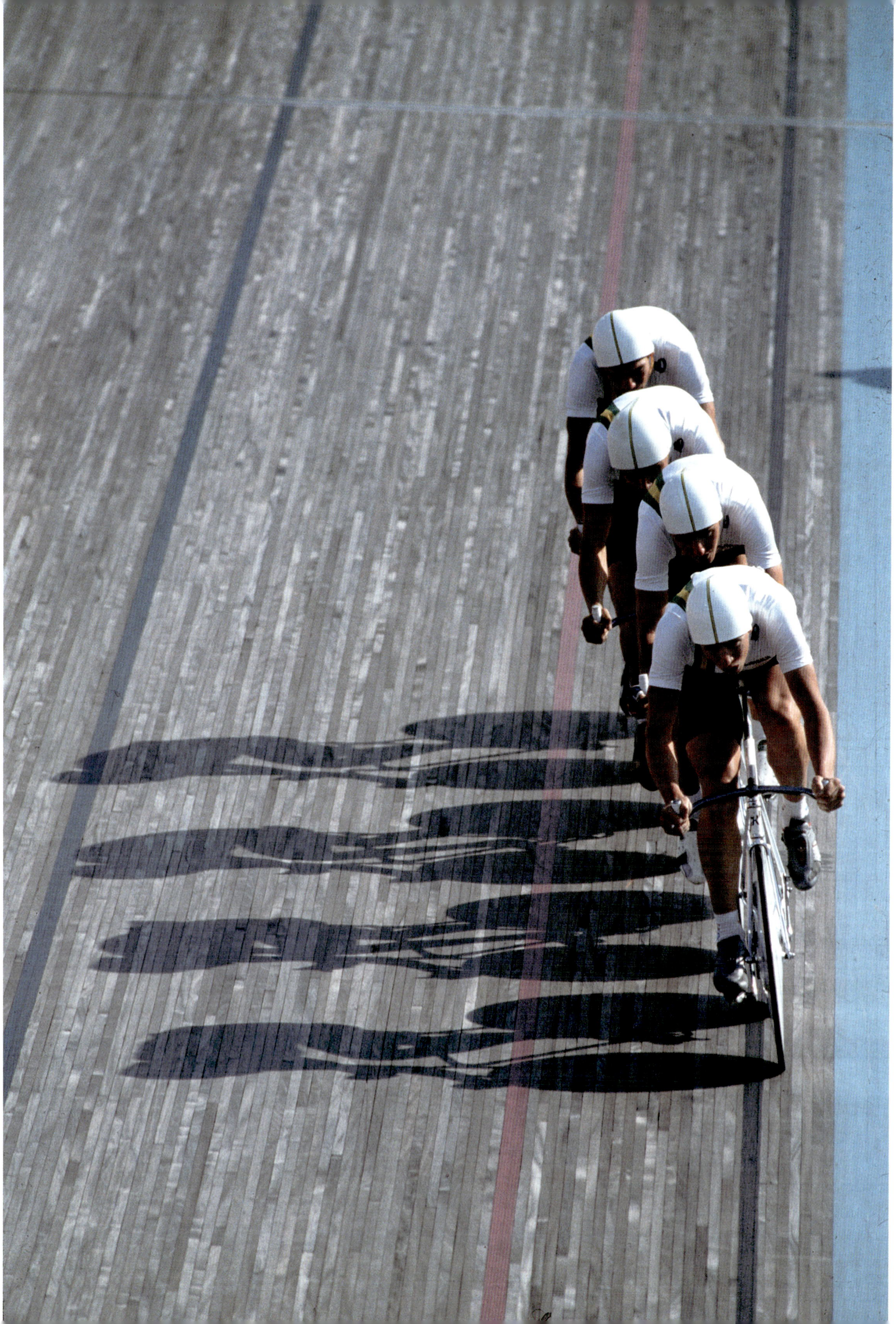

1988 Seoul

Matt Biondi (United States), 5 gold, 2 silver, 1 bronze, swimming

Jim Abbott (United States), gold, vs Japan, silver, men's baseball

Malcolm Cooper (Great Britain), gold, small-bore, three position rifle shooting

Women's K4 500 m

Byun Jong Il (South Korea), protest after losing boxing match

Anja Fichtel-Mauritz (West Germany), gold, women's individual foil & team foil

Florence 'Flo-Jo' Joyner Griffith (United States), gold, 100 m, 200 m & 4 x 100 m relay; silver, 4 x 400 m relay

Gymnast, balance beam

Alexandra Timochenko (Soviet Union), bronze, rhythmic gymnastics

Soviet Union synchronized swimming duet

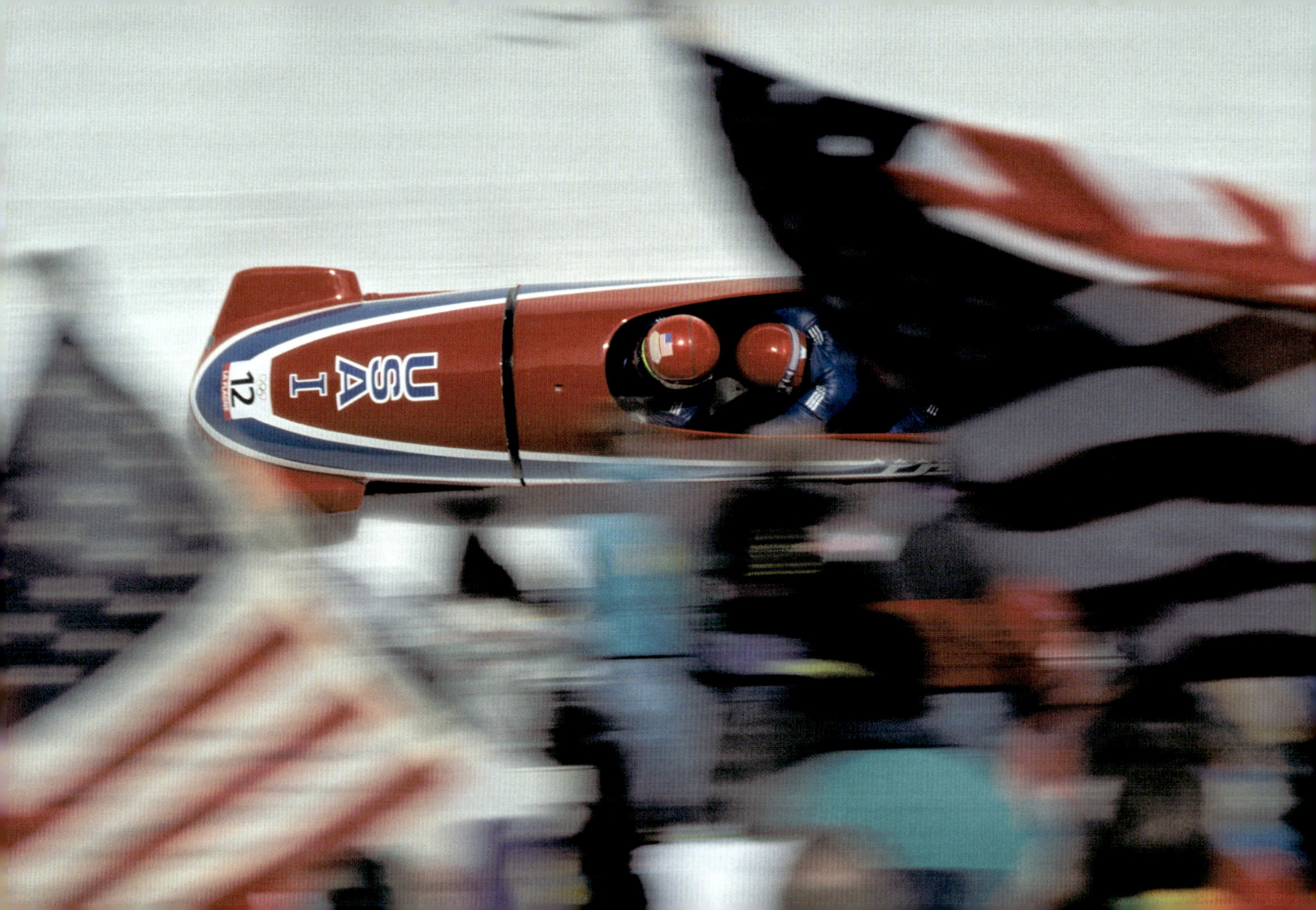
USA I
12

1992
Albertville
France

XVI Olympic Winter Games

8 – 23 February 1992

57 events ▪ 7 sports

64 competing nations ▪ 1,801 athletes

World's largest shopping mall, United States

Dordi Nordby (Norway), silver, curling

Women's cross-country

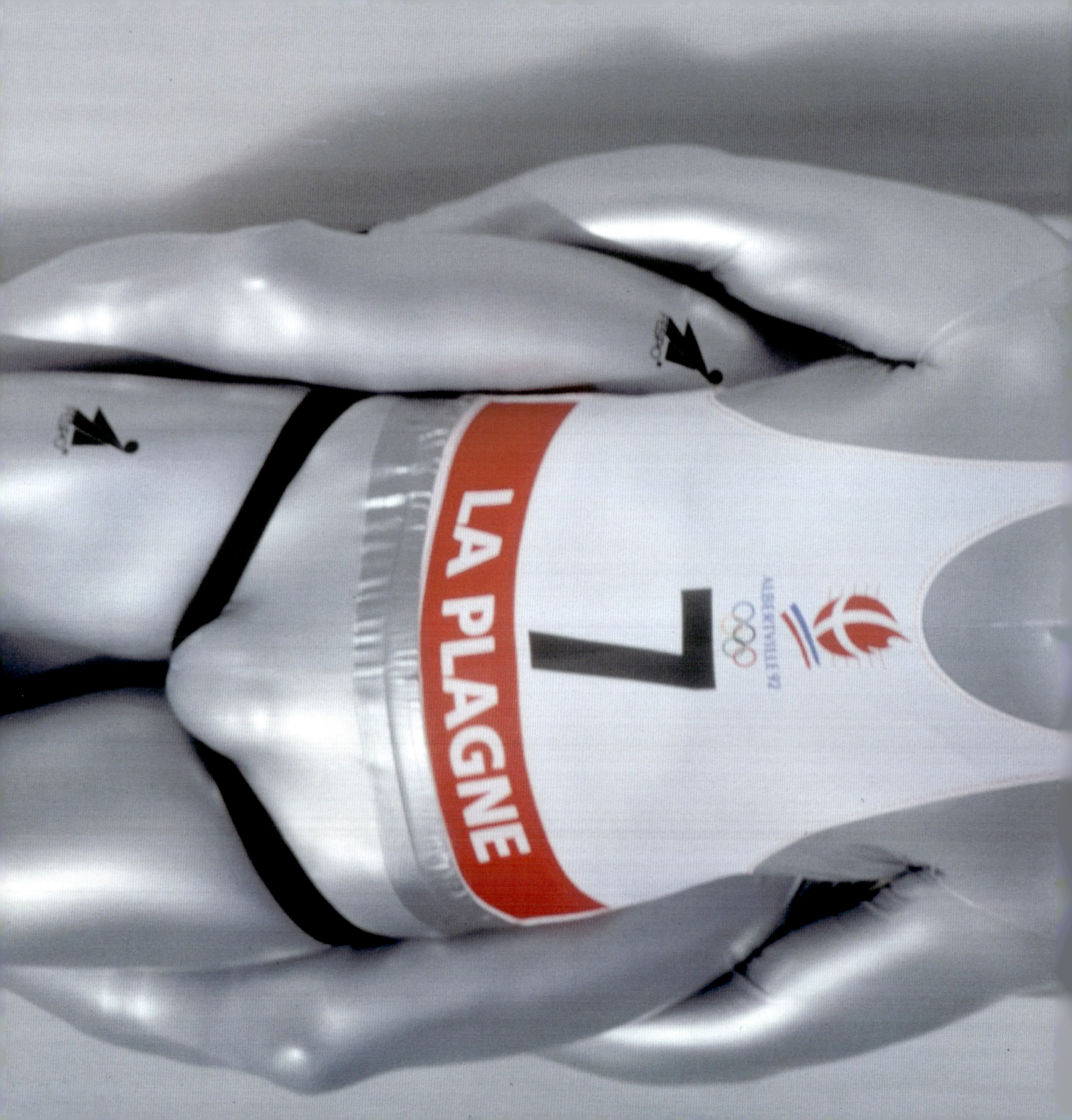
LA PLAGNE
7

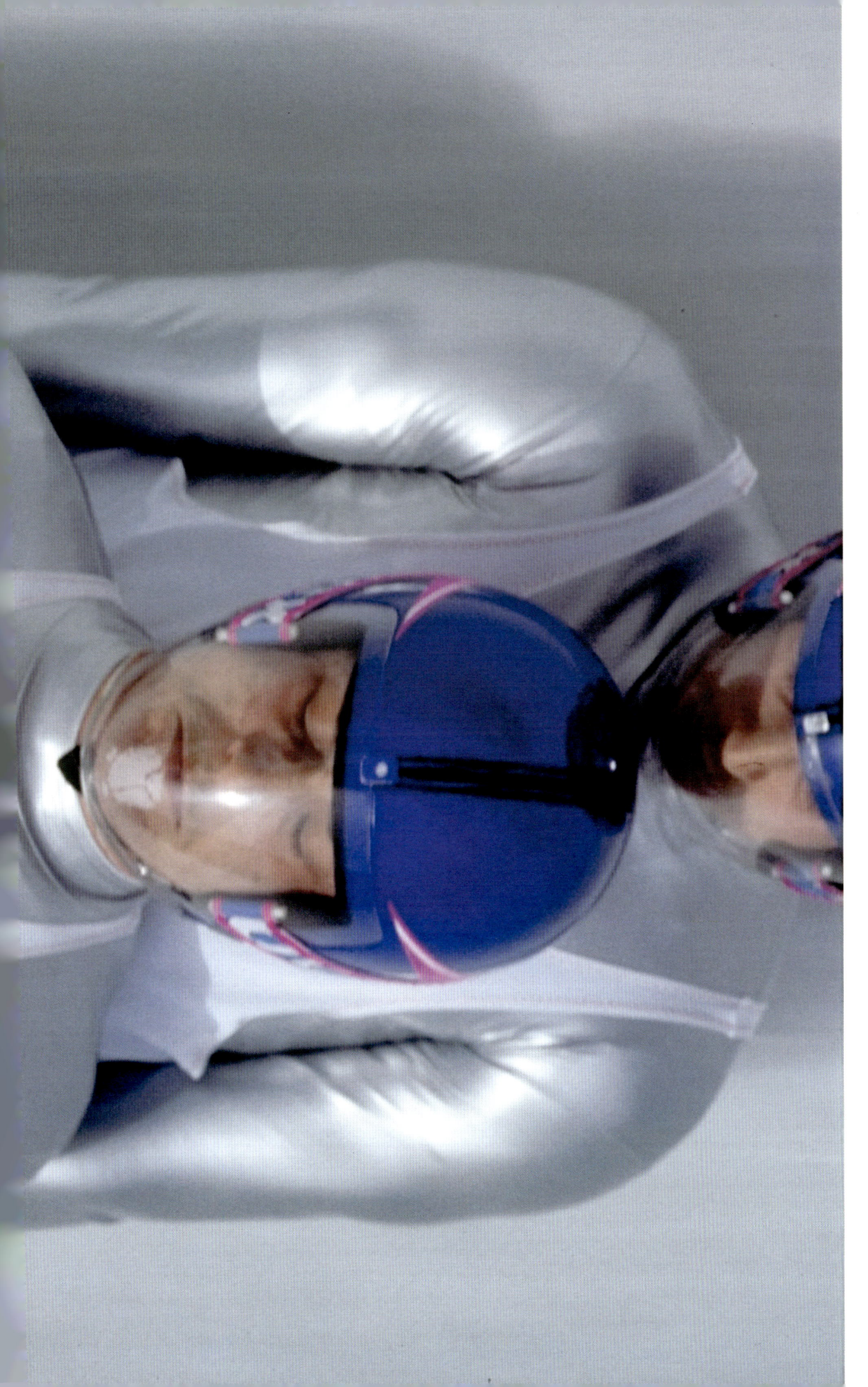

Men's doubles luge

Men's 120 m ski jump

Women's 4 x 5 km cross-country relay

1992 Albertville

▲ Men's 10,000 m speed skating

▶ Marina Klimova & Sergei Ponomarenko (Unified Team), gold, ice dancing

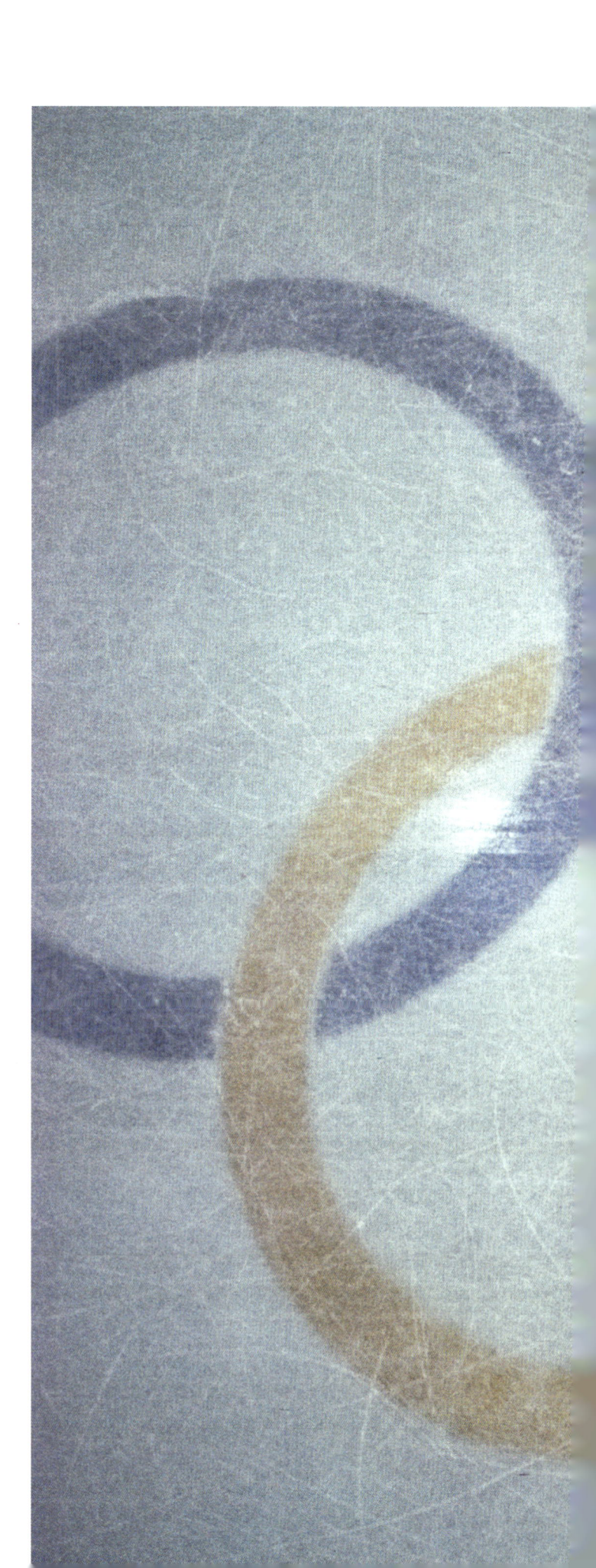

1992 Albertville

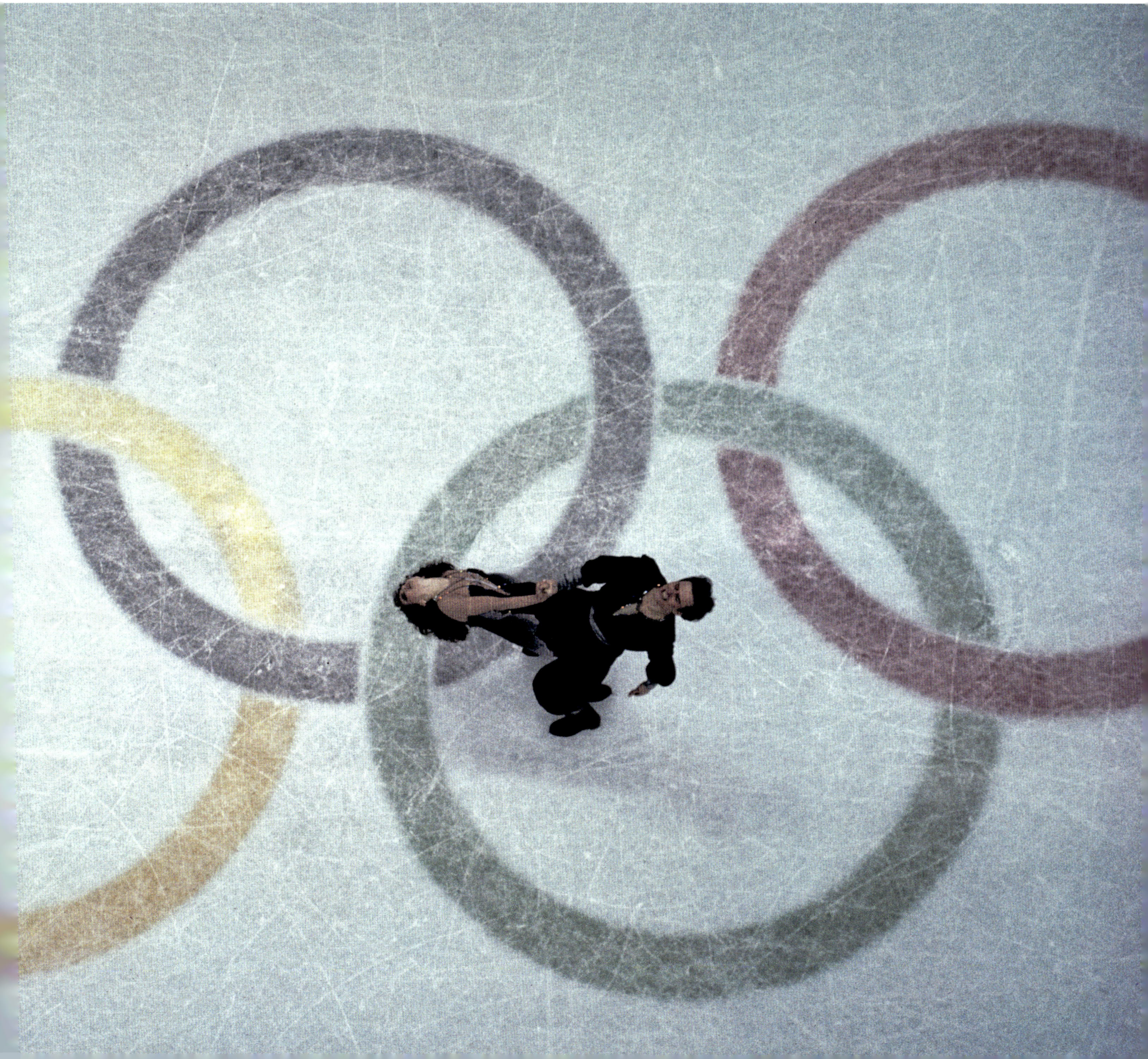

▲ Kristin Krone (United States), women's downhill combined
▶ Kurt Browning (Canada), men's ice dancing

1992 Albertville

Women's platform diving

1992

Barcelona Spain

Games of the XXV Olympiad

25 July – 9 August 1992

257 events ▪ 28 sports

169 competing nations ▪ 9,356 athletes

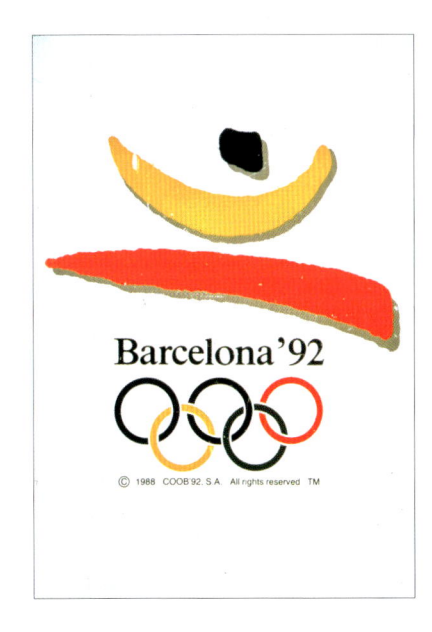

Rodney King trial riots, Los Angeles

Gail Devers (United States) falls, 100 m hurdles final

United States, gold, women's 4 x 100 m freestyle

1992 Barcelona

Arlindo Gouveia Colina (Venezuela), gold, taekwondo

Dressage

Michael Jordan (United States), 'Dream Team', gold, basketball

Jennifer Capriati (United States), gold, singles tennnis

Mel Stewart (United States), gold, 200 m butterfly & 4 x 100 m medley relay; bronze, 4 x 200 m freestyle

Canadian pairs canoeing

1992 Barcelona

Rhythmic gymnastics

Masanori Sugiura (Japan), bronze, baseball

Linford Christie (Great Britain), gold, 100 m

Derek Redmond (Great Britain), 400 m

▲ Women's archery

▶ Merlene Ottey (Jamaica, in green), bronze, 200 m

1992 Barcelona 423

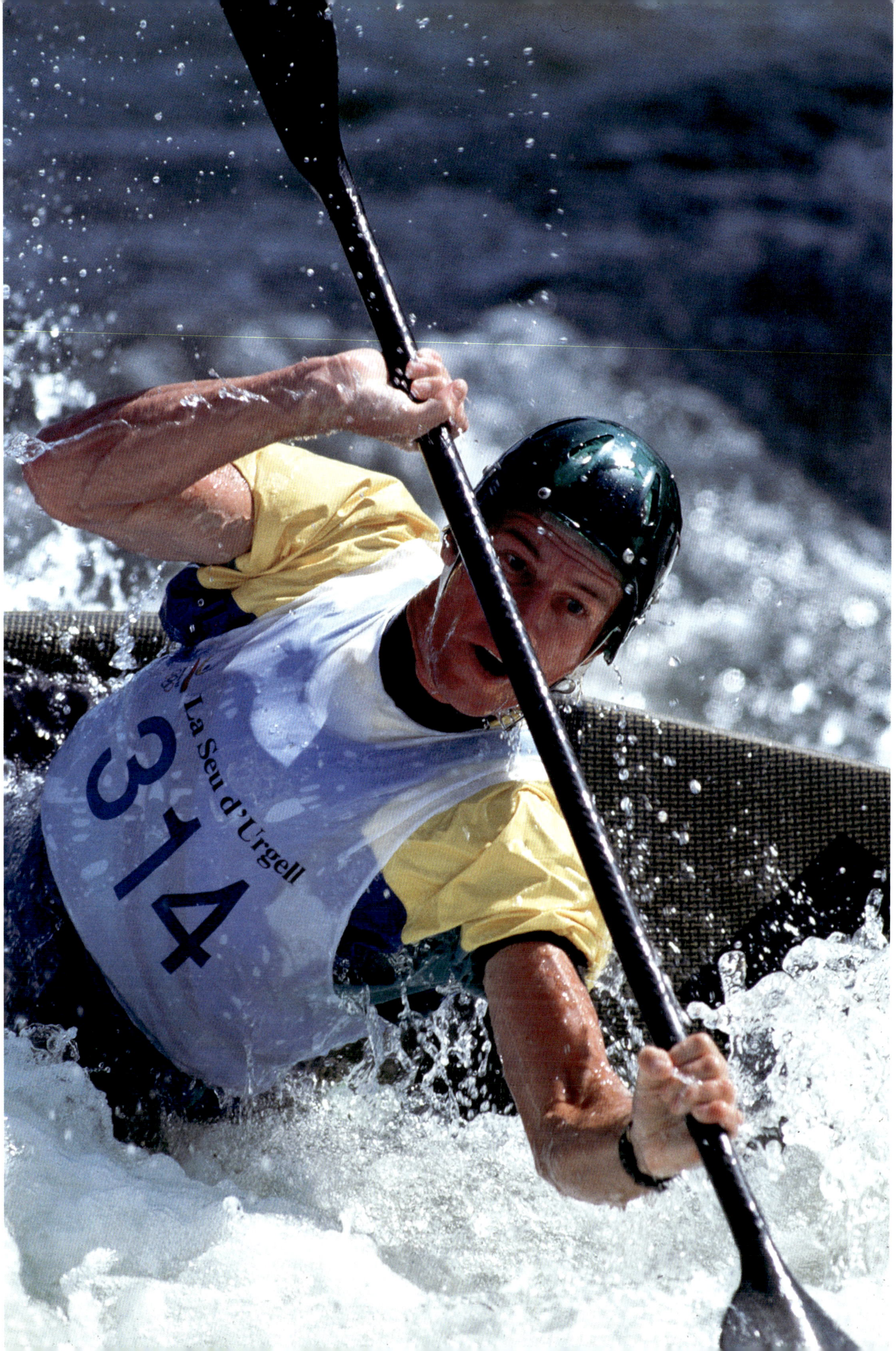
La Seu d'Urgell
314

▲ Vitaly Scherbo (Unified Team), 6 gold, gymnastics
◀ Men's K1 canoeing

Sweden, gold, ice hockey

1994

Lillehammer Norway

XVII Olympic Winter Games

12 – 27 February 1994

61 events ▪ 6 sports

67 competing nations ▪ 1,737 athletes

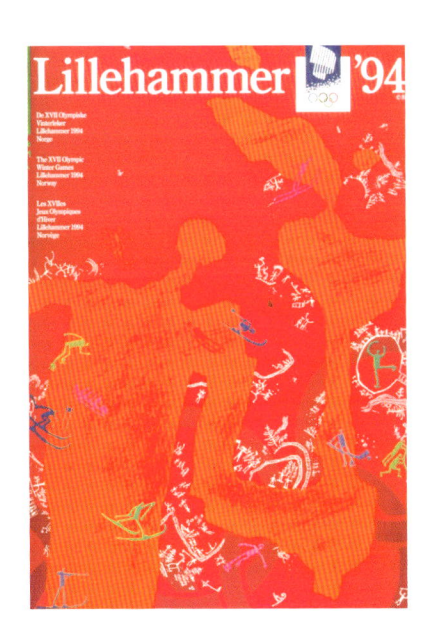

Nelson Mandela, president, South Africa

Nicolas Jean-Prost (France), ski jumping

Surya Bonaly (France), **figure skating**

1994 Lillehammer

Alberto Tomba (Italy), silver, men's slalom

Elizabeth McIntyre (United States), silver, women's moguls

▲ Anna-Lena Fritzon (Sweden), women's 5 km cross-country

▶ Vreni Schneider (Switzerland), gold, women's slalom; silver, combined; bronze, giant slalom

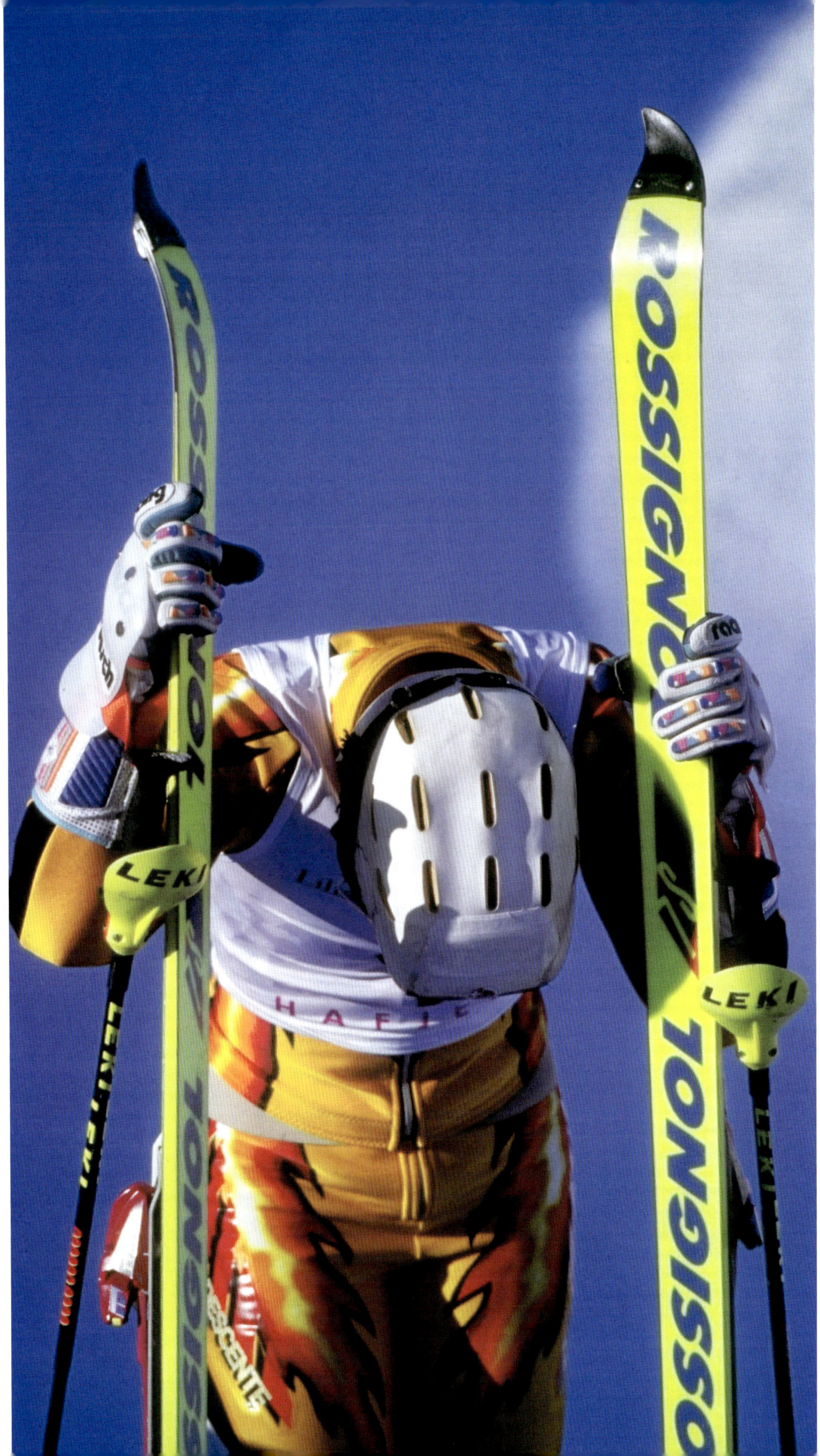
ROSSIGNOL
ROSSIGNOL
LEKI
LEKI

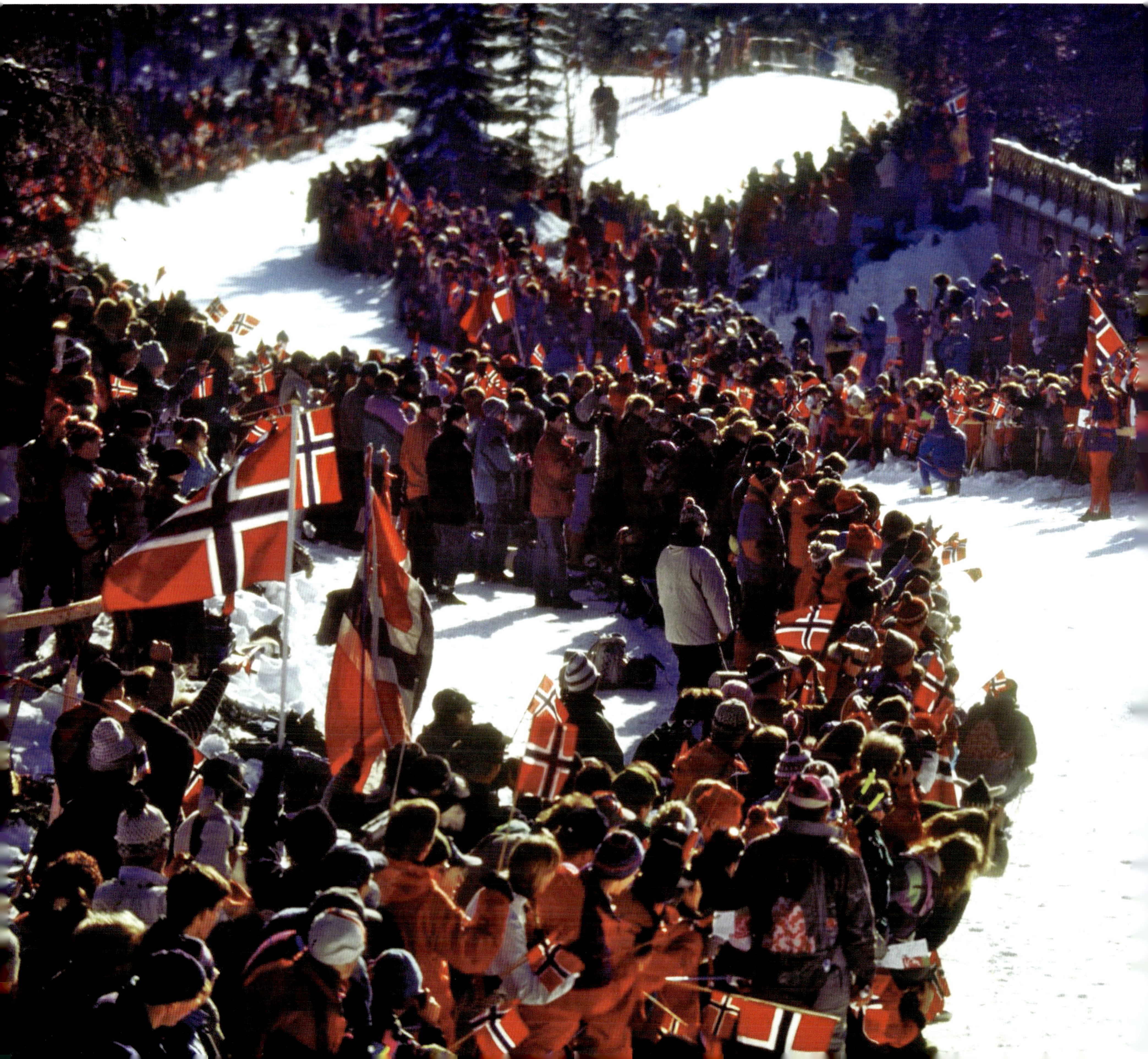

Grant Snow (United States) vs Finland, ice hockey

Bjørn Dæhlie (Norway), gold, men's 10 km cross-country & combined pursuit; silver, 30 km & 4 x 10 km relay

1994 Lillehammer 435

Jean-Luc Brassard (Canada), gold, men's freestyle moguls

Johan Olav Koss (Norway), gold, 1,500 m, 5,000 m & 10,000 m speed skating

470 class, Savannah, Georgia

1996

Atlanta
United States

Games of the XXVI Olympiad

19 July – 4 August 1992

271 events ▪ 26 sports

197 competing nations ▪ 10,318 athletes

Olympic Park bombing

Yuri Melinchenko (Kazakhstan, red), gold, vs Dennis Hall (United States), wrestling

Team France, synchronized swimming

Sandra Pires (Brazil), gold, beach volleyball

Mike Powell (United States), long jump

United States (gold) vs Great Britain (silver), men's doubles tennis

Canada, gold, 4 x 100 m relay

Japan, synchronized swimming

China, silver, women's volleyball

1996 Atlanta **447**

Dominique Monceau (United States), gold, team gymnastics, with her coach

Liu Guoliang (China), gold, singles & doubles table tennis

Randy Barnes (United States), gold, shot put

Michael Johnson (United States), gold, 200 m & 400 m, sets a world 200 m record

Kent Bostick (United States), individual pursuit

Blyth Tait (New Zealand) & Chesterfield, bronze, team three-day event

1996 Atlanta 453

Laura Flessel (France, right), gold, individual épée & team épée

1996 Atlanta 455

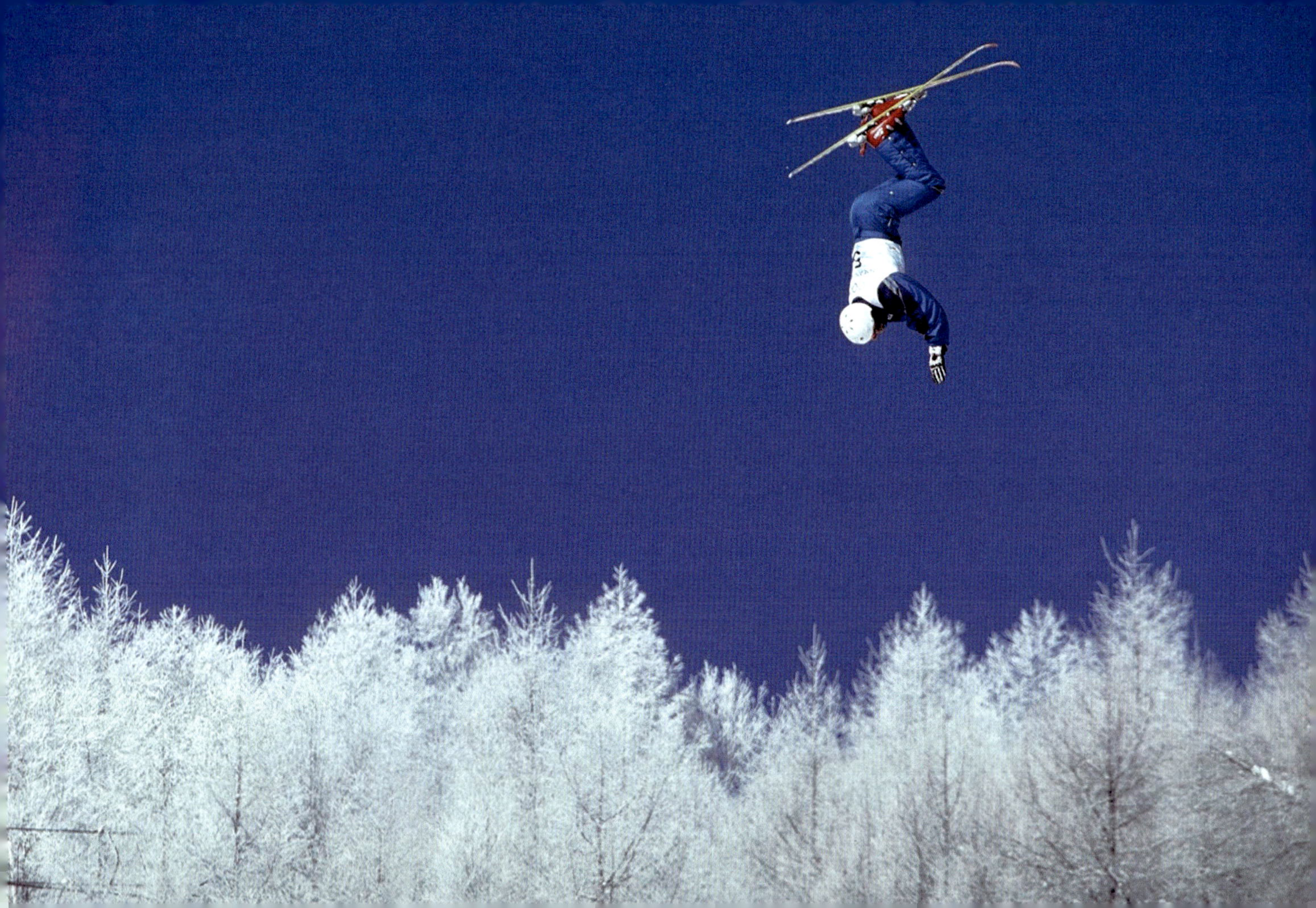

1998

Nagano
Japan

XVIII Olympic Winter Games

7 – 22 February 1998

68 events ▪ 7 sports

72 competing nations ▪ 2,176 athletes

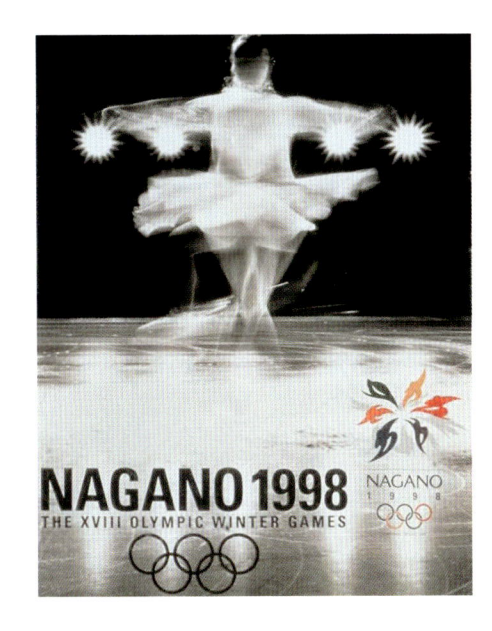

Peace Agreement, Northern Ireland

Men's 1,000 m short-track speed skating

Women's cross-country relay

Skiing billboard

460 1998 Nagano

Gian Simmen (Switzerland), gold, halfpipe snowboarding

Curling

Czech Republic (white) vs Canada, ice hockey semi-final

1998 Nagano 463

Bjørn Dæhlie (Norway), gold, 10 km, 50 km & 4 x 10 km relay cross-country; silver, 10 km & 15 km combined pursuit

Sung-Yeol Jaegal (South Korea), 500 m speed skating

Japanese fan

Tara Lipinski (United States), gold, figure skating

Men's triathlon, Sydney Harbour

2000
Sydney
Australia

Games of the XXVII Olympiad

15 September – 1 October 2000

3000 events ▪ 28 sports

199 competing nations ▪ 10,651 athletes

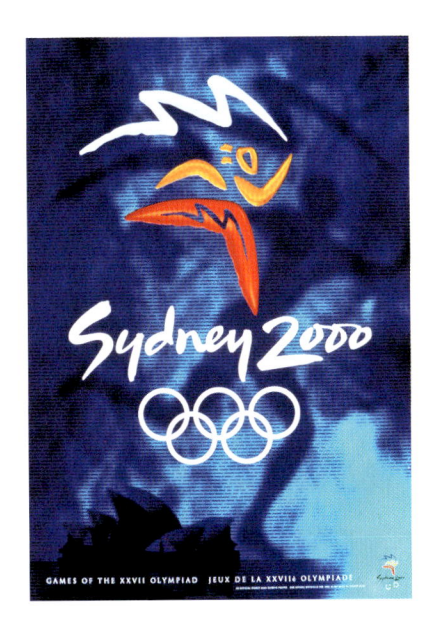

Mad cow disease, Europe

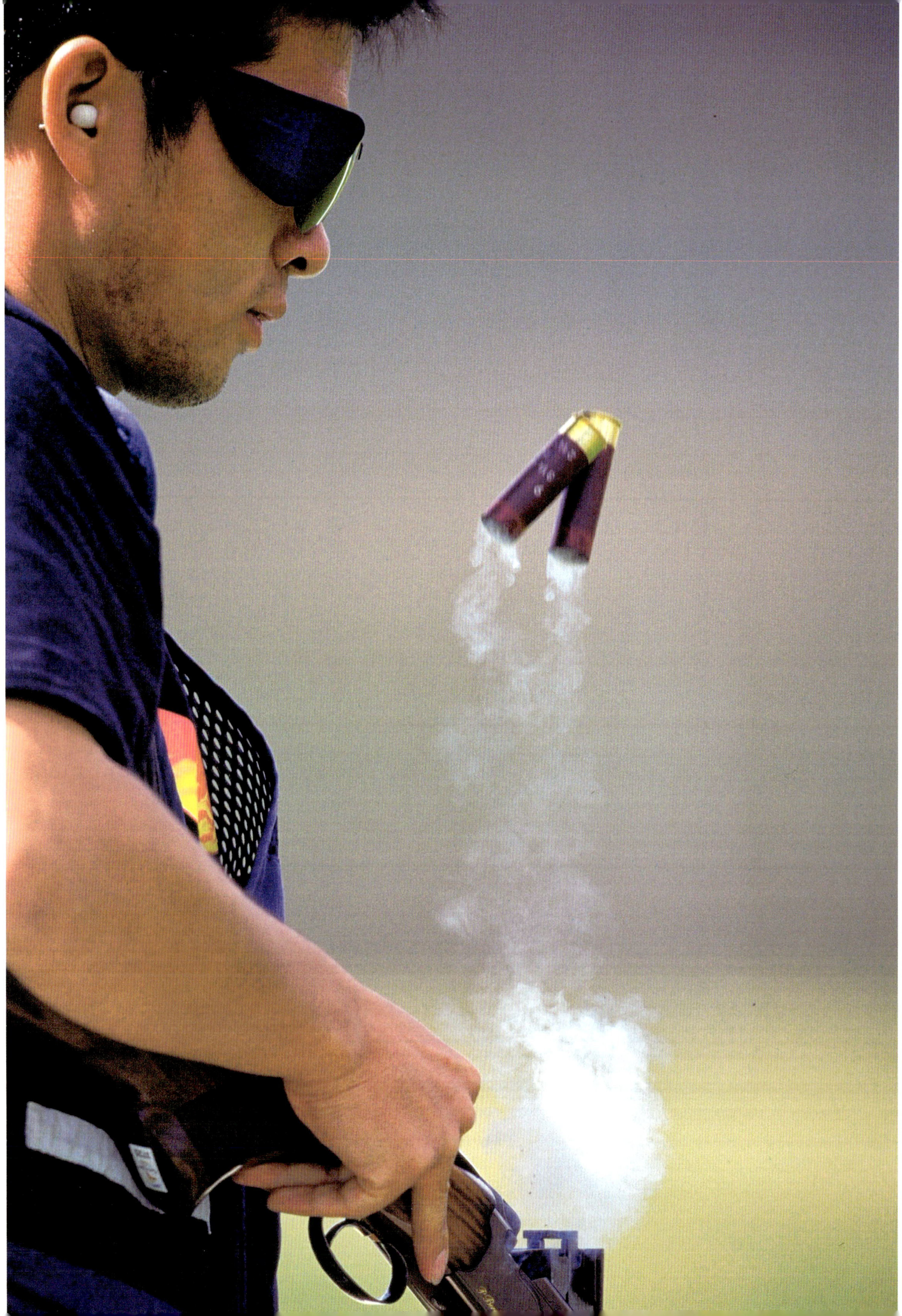

▲ George Roumain (United States), men's volleyball
◀ Di Jin (China), skeet shooting

2000 Sydney 471

Women's balance beam

Team showjumping

2000 Sydney

Felix Savon (Cuba, red), gold, vs Sultan Ibragimov (Soviet Union), silver, heavyweight boxing

Brahim Asloum (France), gold, light flyweight boxing

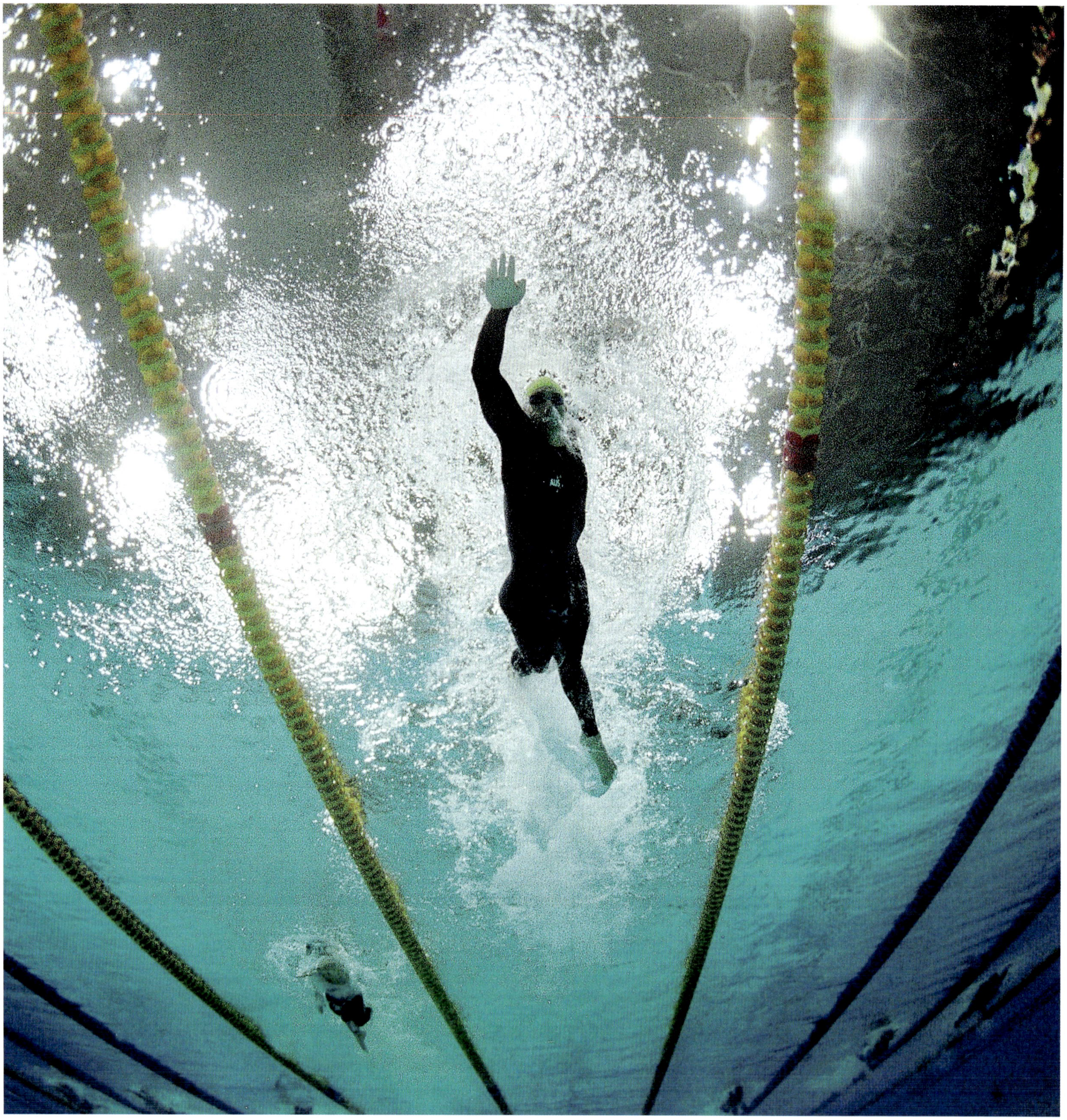

▲ Cathy Freeman (Australia), gold, 400 m
◀ Ian Thorpe (Australia), gold, 400 m freestyle & 4 x 100 m & 4 x 200 m freestyle relays; silver, 200 m freestyle & 4 x 100 m medley

2000 Sydney 477

Anthony Nossiter (Australia), Finn class

Tim Foster, Matthew Pinsent, Steve Redgrave and James Cracknell (Great Britain); gold, coxless fours

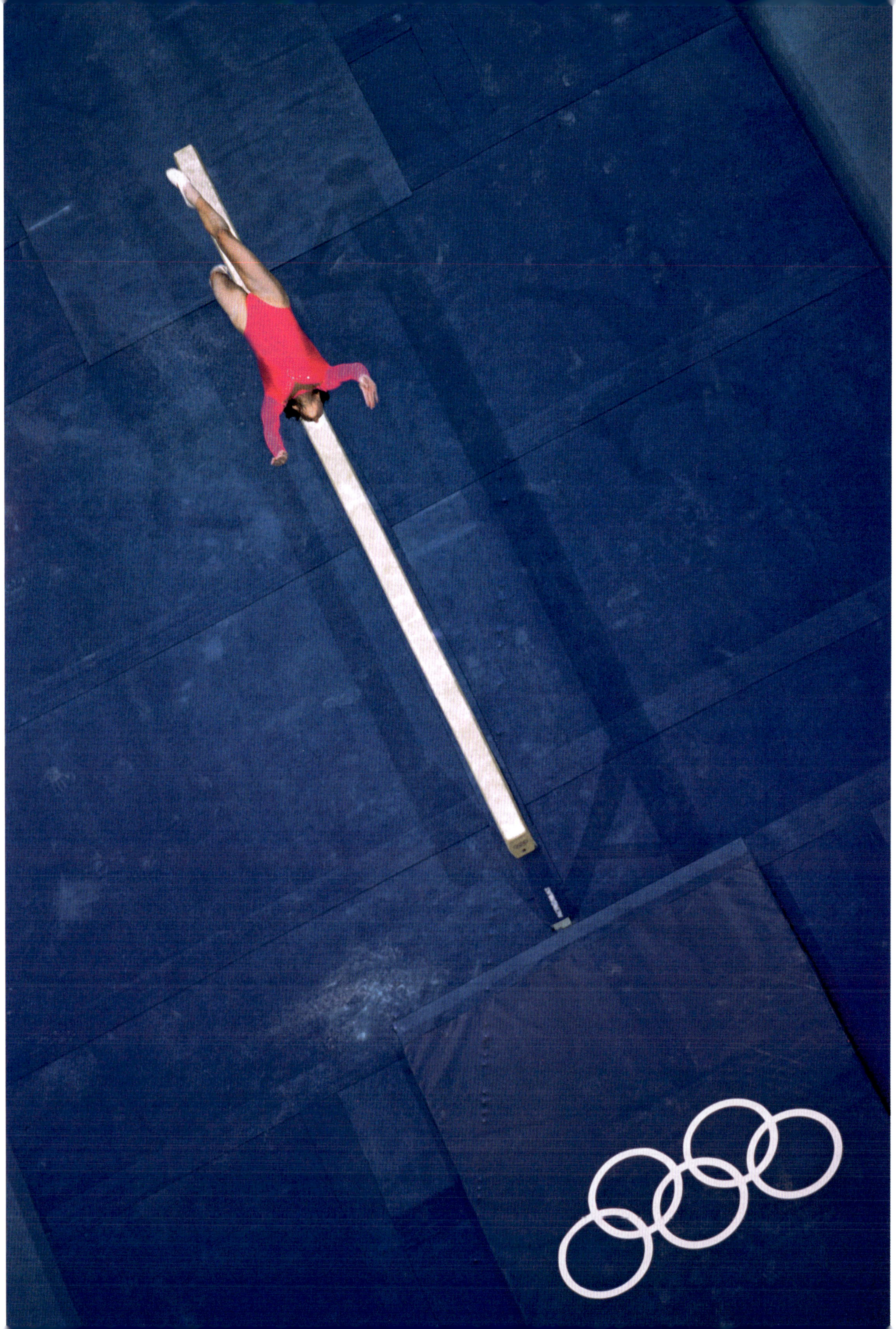

▲ Roger Federer (Switzerland), semi-finals, men's singles tennis
◀ Elise Ray (United States), bronze, team gymnastics

Thrine Kane (United States), 50-m rifle three positions

Svetlana Kazanina (Kazakhstan), javelin, heptathlon

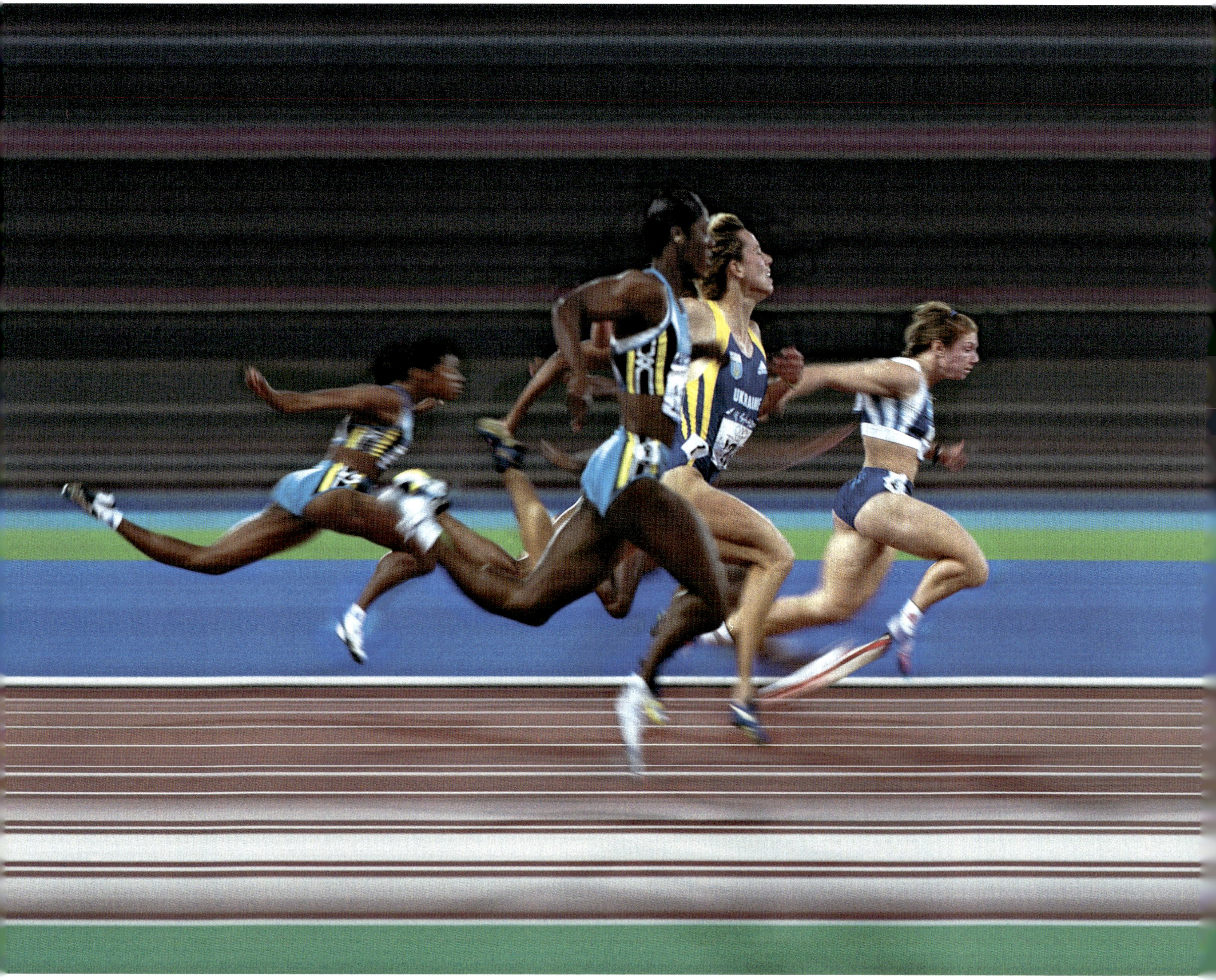

Marion Jones (United States), 100 m; later stripped of medal for drug abuse

Cuba, gold, women's volleyball

Women's beach volleyball

Paavo Puurunen (Finland), 4 x 7.5 km biathlon relay

2002
Salt Lake City United States

XIX Olympic Winter Games

8 – 24 February 2002

78 events ▪ 7 sports

77 competing nations ▪ 2,399 athletes

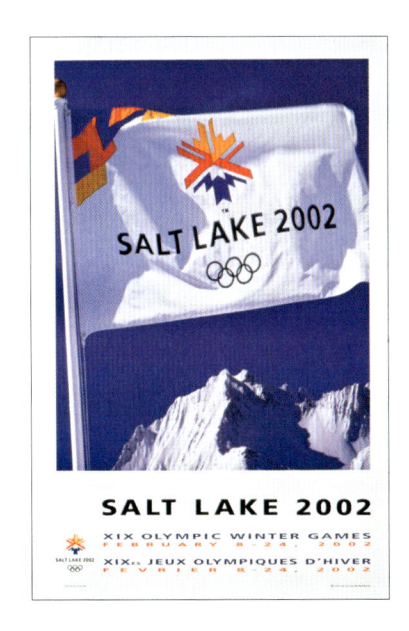

Operation Anaconda, Afghanistan

Great Britain (grey), gold, vs Switzerland, silver, women's curling

Steven Bradbury (Australia, left), gold, 1,000 m short-track speed skating after crash

Gregor Stähli (Switzerland), bronze, men's skeleton

Men's 4 x 7.5 km biathlon relay

Albena Denkova & Maxim Staviyski (Bulgaria), ice dancing

Nicola Franceschina (Italy), silver, men's short track speed skating 5,000 m relay

2002 Salt Lake City 495

Kjetil André Aamodt (Norway), gold, men's combined and super giant slalom

Canada (white) vs United States, 3–2, men's ice hockey final

Philipp Schoch (Switzerland), gold, men's snowboarding parallel giant slalom

SUI-1 (Switzerland), bobsleigh

Blythe Hartley and Émilie Heymans (Canada), bronze, synchronized 10-m platform diving

2004

Athens
Greece

Games of the XXVIII Olympiad

13 – 29 August 2004

301 events ▪ 28 sports

201 competing nations ▪ 11,099 athletes

Tsunami, Indian Ocean

Milorad Cavic (Serbia & Montenegro), 100 m freestyle

Ryuichi Obata & Oliver Q (Japan), show jumping

2004 Athens

Denise Lewis (Great Britain), heptathlon

Great Britain, silver, team pursuit

2004 Athens 505

Irena Pavelkova (Czech Republic), K-1 slalom

Shuying Gao (China), pole vault

United States, synchronized swimming

Germany, coxed eight

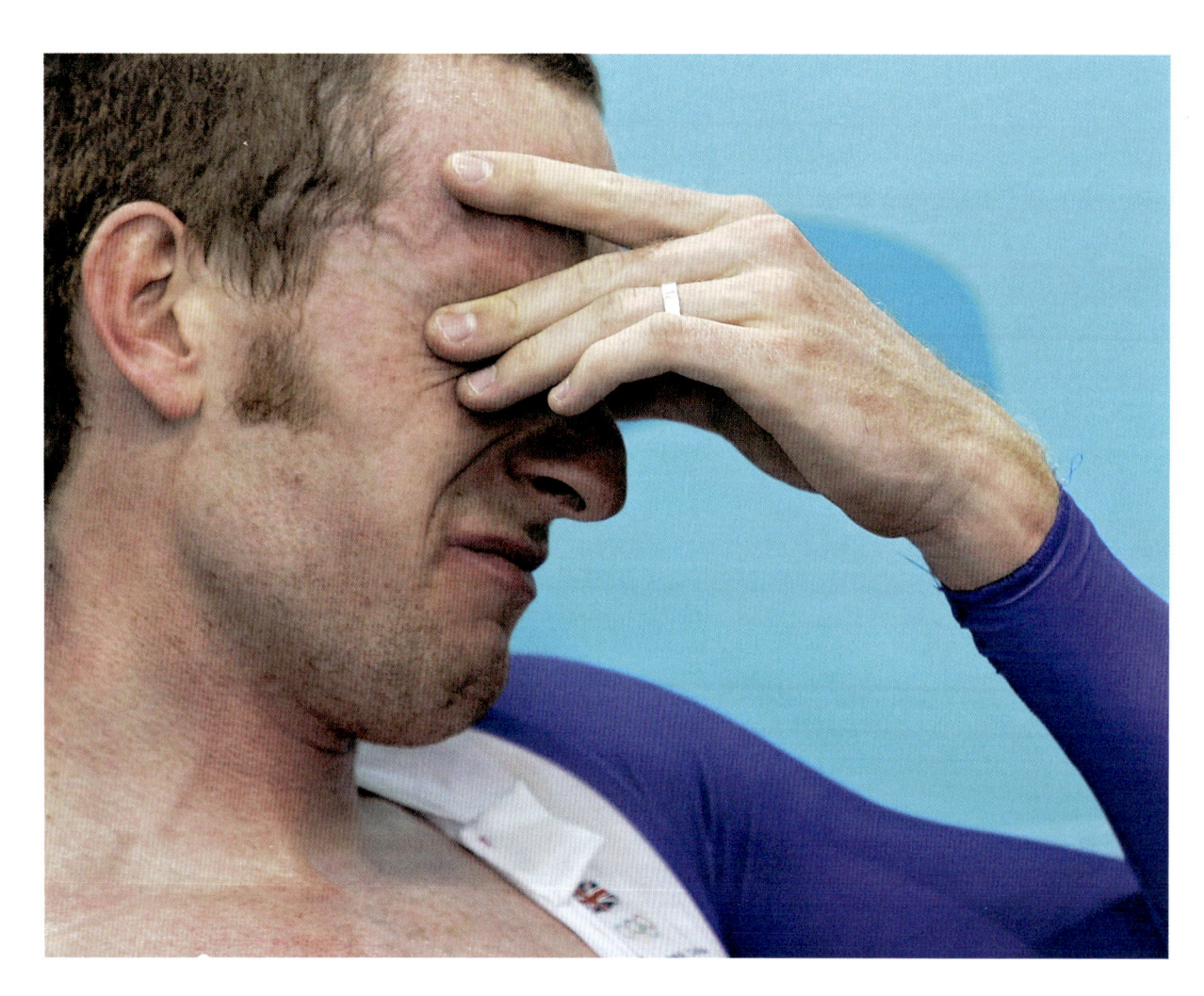

▲ Bradley Wiggins (Great Britain), gold, individual pursuit; silver, team pursuit, cycling
▶ Kelly Holmes (Great Britain, bottom) gold, 1,500 m

2004 Athens 511

Birgit Fischer (Germany), gold, K-4 500 m canoe sprint; silver, K-2 500 m

Hicham El-Guerrouj (Morocco), gold, 1,500 m & 5,000 m

Greece (black) vs United States, men's volleyball

Great Britain (white) vs Argentina, hockey

2004 Athens

▲ Stian Grimseth (Norway), weightlifting

▶ Hao Wang (China, red), silver, vs Seung-Min Ryu (South Korea), gold, table tennis

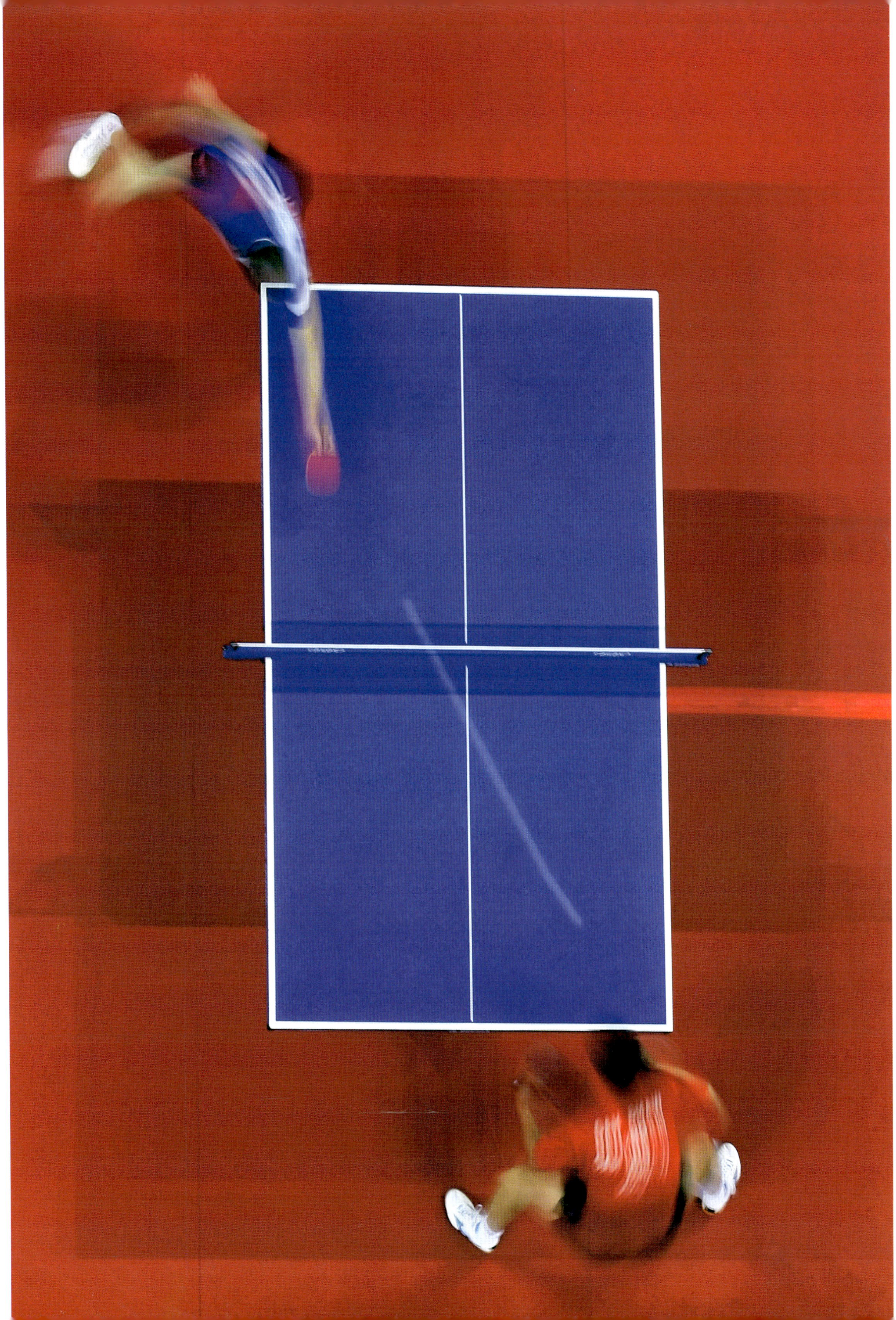

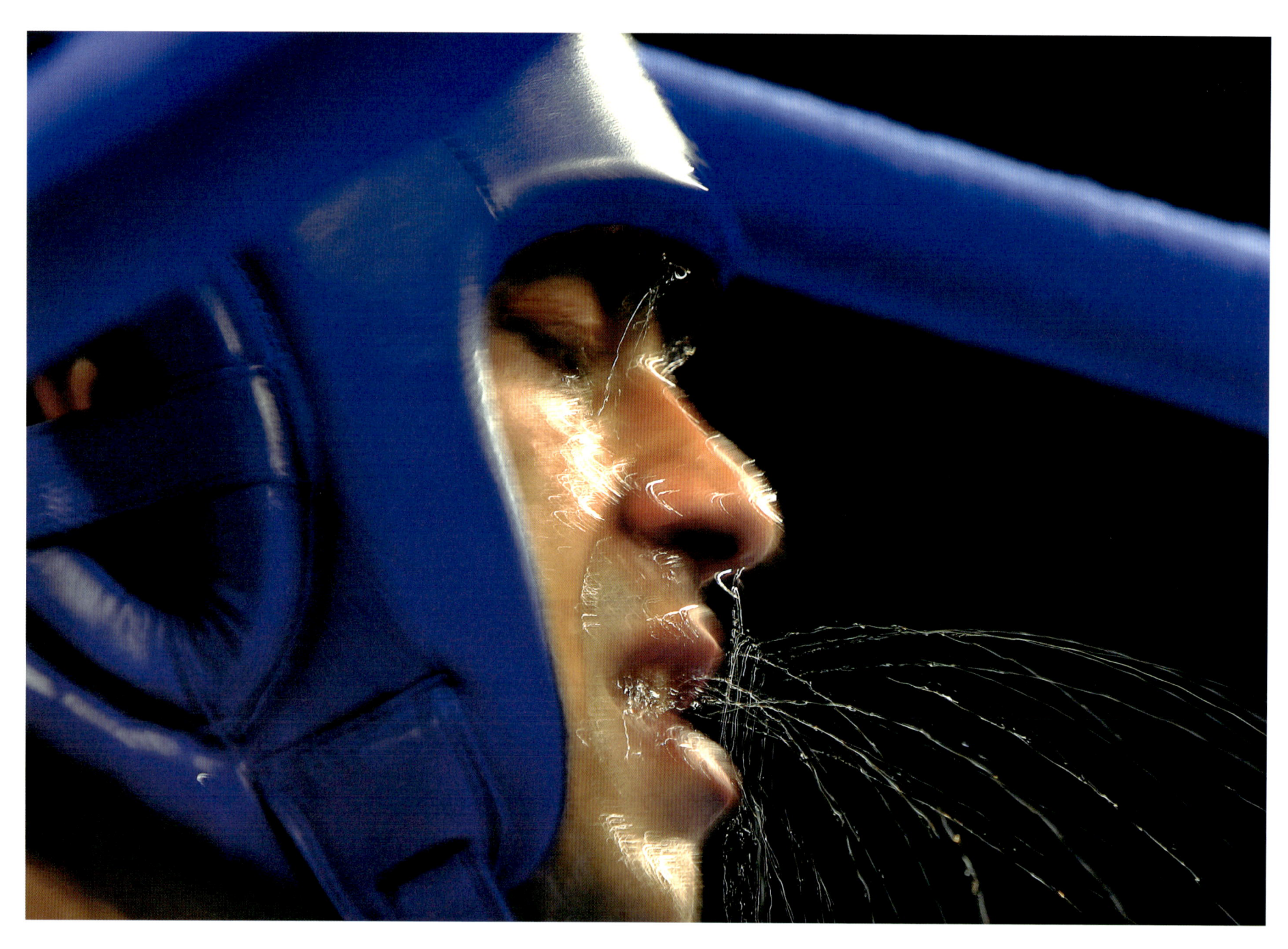

▲ Marian Simion (Romania), boxing

▶ Gennadiy Golovkin (Kazakhstan, red), silver, boxing

519

Dmitri Dashinski (Belarus), silver, freestyle skiing aerials

2006
Turin
Italy

XX Olympic Winter Games

10 – 26 February 2006

84 events ▪ 7 sports

80 competing nations ▪ 2,508 athletes

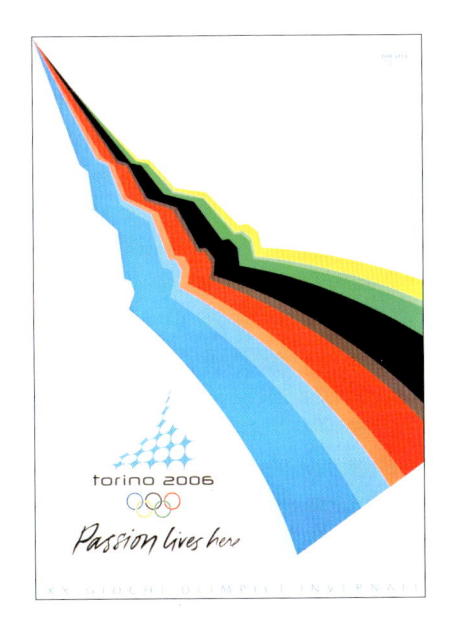

Hamas government, Gaza Strip

Shiuzuka Arakawa (Japan), gold, figure skating

Galit Chait & Sergei Sakhnovski (Israel), ice dancing

Katerina Neumannova (Czech Republic), gold, 30 km cross-country; silver, 15 km pursuit

Janica Kostelic (Croatia), gold, women's combined; silver, super-giant slalom

2006 Turin

United States, bobsleigh

Latvia 2, bobsleigh

2006 Turin

Brothers Philipp (right), gold, and Simon Schloch (Switzerland), silver, men's parallel giant slalom snowboard

2006 Turin

Brigitte Acton (Canada), women's combined

Sasha Cohen (United States), silver, figure skating

Ma Lin (China), gold, table tennis

2008
Beijing China

Games of the XXIX Olympiad

8 – 24 August 2008

302 events ▪ 28 sports

204 competing nations ▪ 11,028 athletes

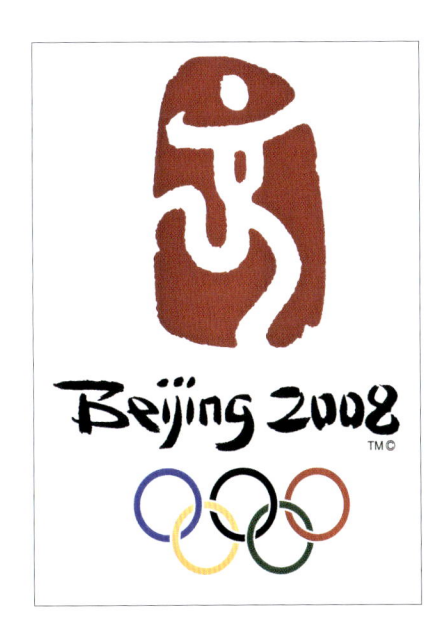

Barack Obama, president, United States

Women's triathlon, Ming emperors' tombs

Men's road race, Tiananmen Square

Mariel Zagunis (United States, right), gold, Becca Ward (United States), bronze, women's sabre

LeBron James (United States), men's basketball

Women's archery

Drew Ginn (Australia), gold, men's coxless pairs

Michael Phelps (United States, right) defeats Milorad Cavic (Serbia) 100 m butterfly; Phelps won 8 golds

Michael Phelps (right) and teammates, gold, 4 x 200 m freestyle relay

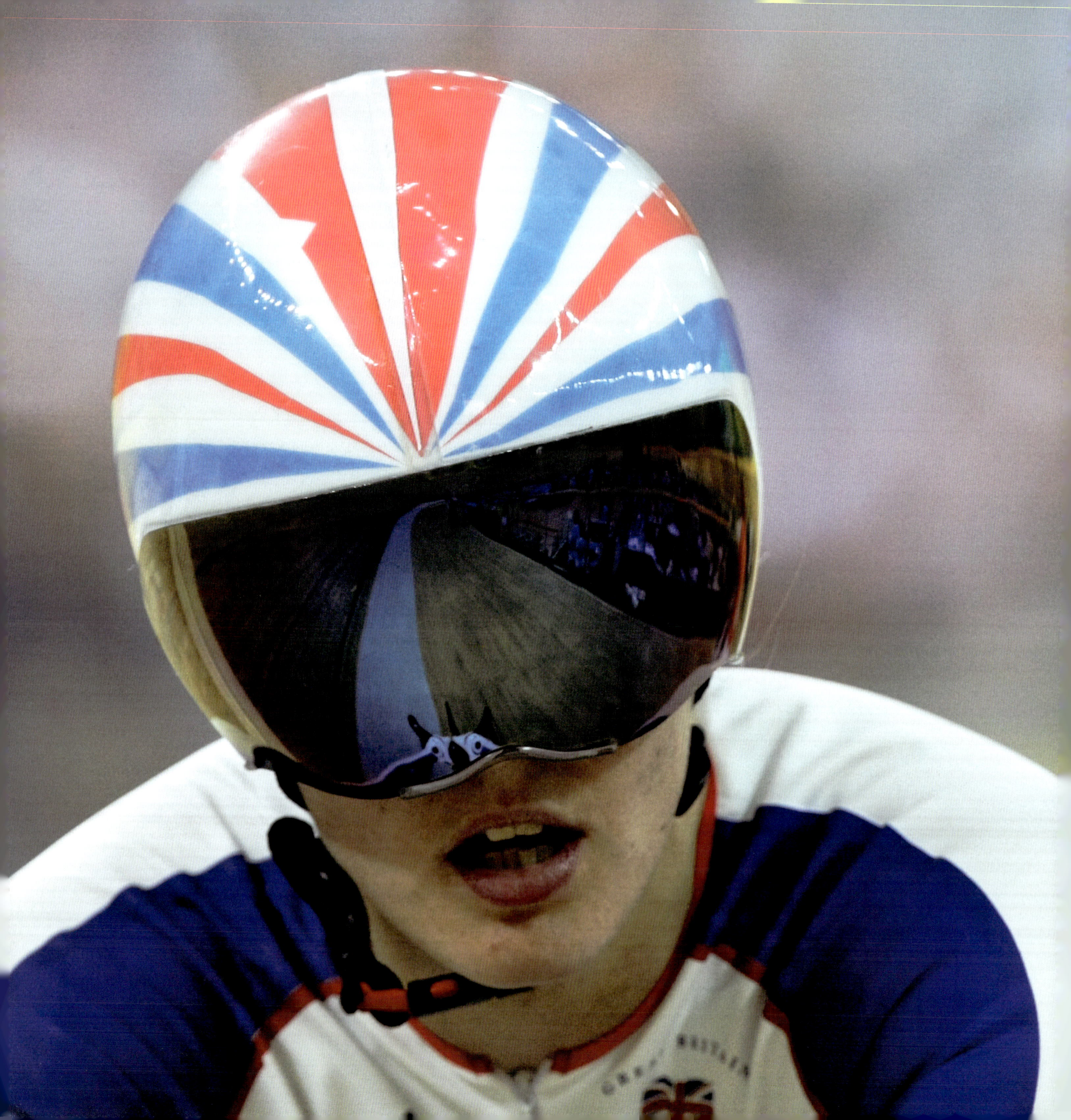

▲ Australia, men's team pursuit
◀ Victoria Pendleton (Great Britain), gold, women's individual sprint

2008 Beijing 543

Chen Yibing (China), gold, team all-around gymnastics & individual rings

1,500 m, men's decathlon

Kobe Bryant (United States), men's basketball

Pole vault, men's decathlon

Usain Bolt (Jamaica), men's 200 m

Usain Bolt (Jamaica), gold, 100 m, 200 m & 4 x 100 m relay

2008 Beijing

▲ Women's steeplechase
▶ Closing ceremony, Bird's Nest Stadium

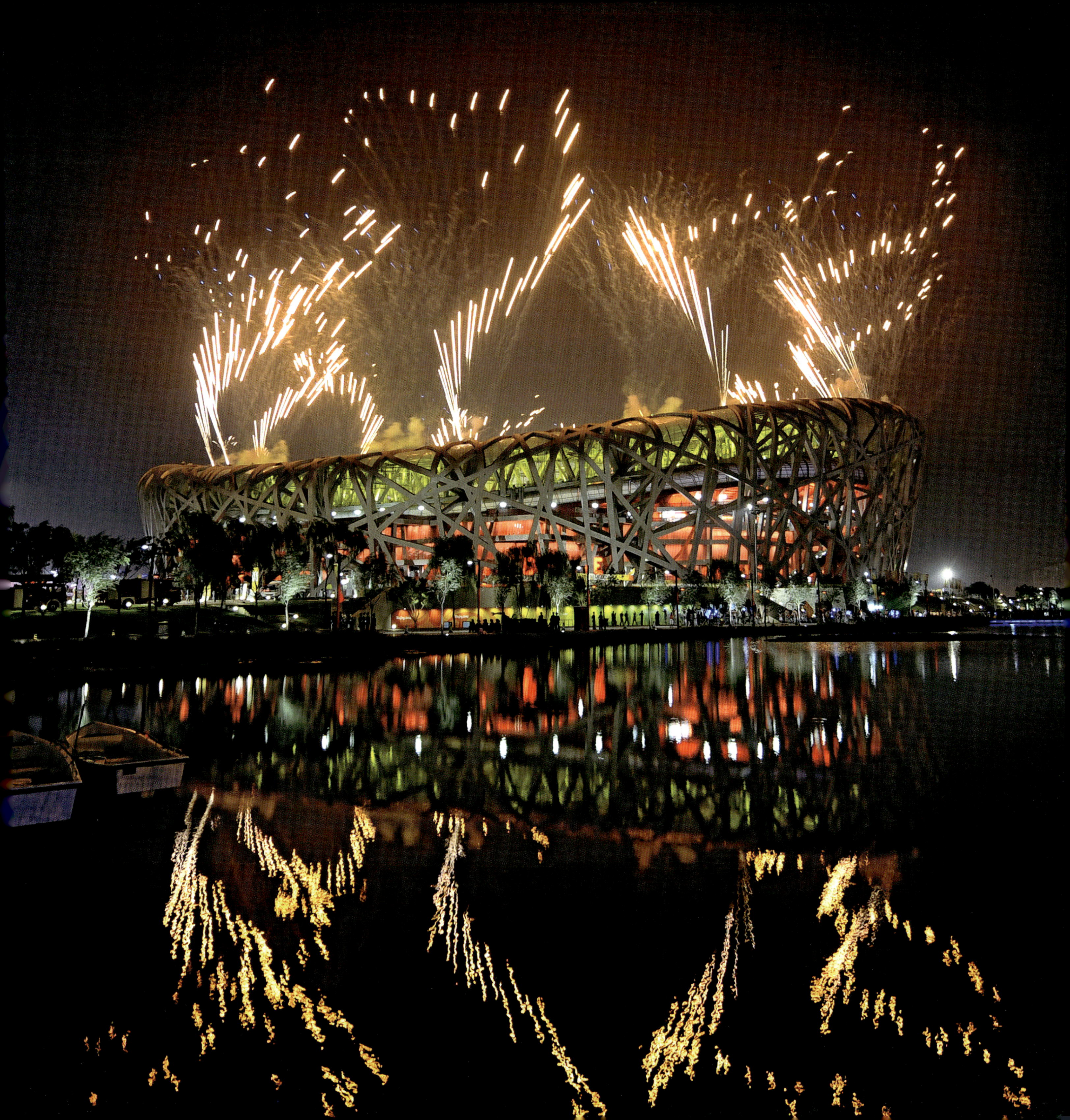

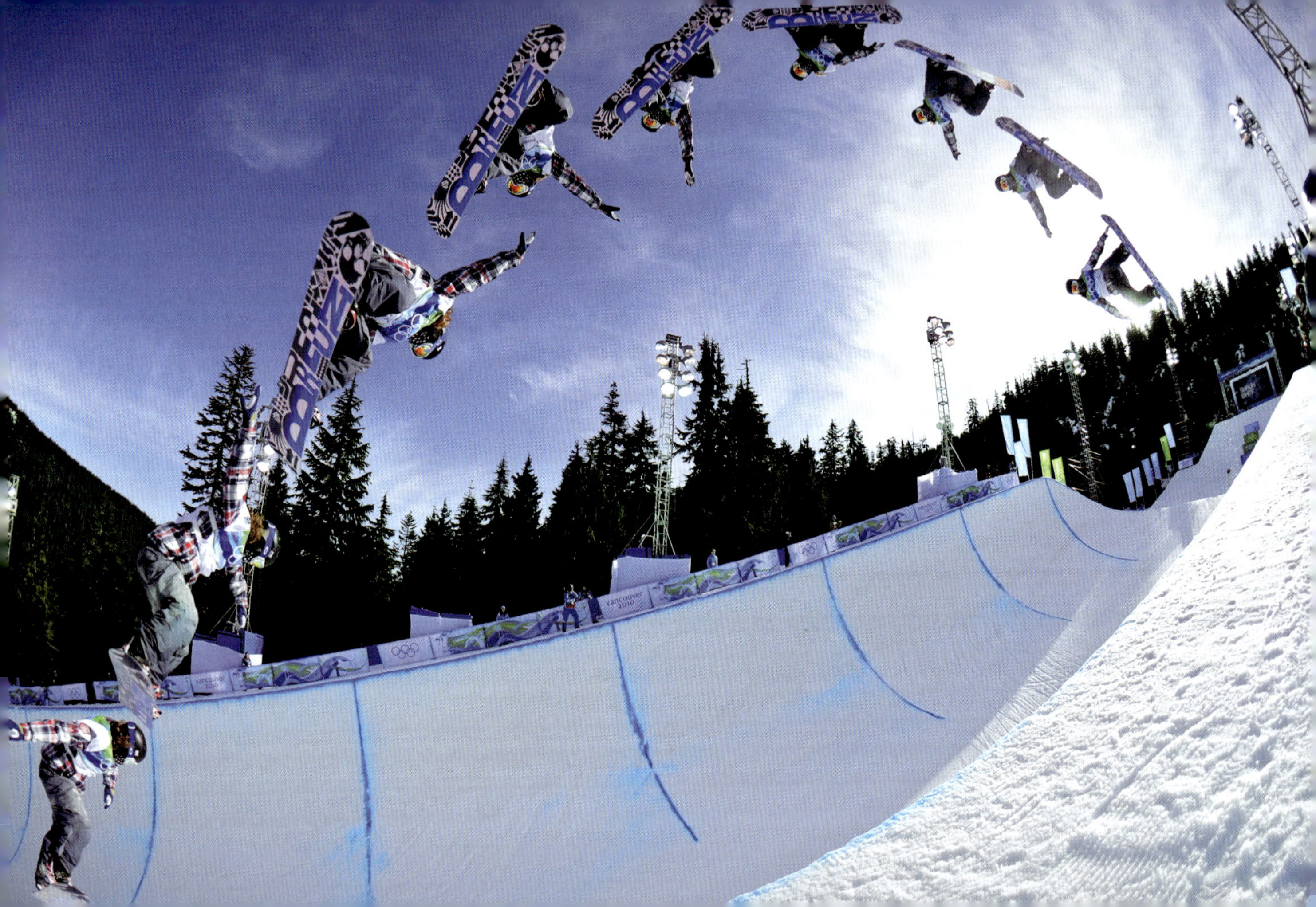
vancouver 2010

2010
Vancouver Canada

XXI Olympic Winter Games

12 – 28 February 2010

86 events ▪ 15 sports

82 competing nations ▪ 2,622 athletes

Aung San Suu Kyi released, Myanmar (Burma)

USA-3, bobsleigh

Nikita Kriukov (Russia, left), gold, & Alexander Panzhinskiy (Russia), cross-country sprint

2010 Vancouver

Collision, men's freestyle ski cross

USA-1, gold, four-man bobsleigh

Canada (white), gold, vs United States, silver, men's ice hockey

Yu-Na Kim (South Korea), gold, figure skating

Czechoslovakia-2, bobsleigh

Julia Mancuso (United States), silver, downhill & super combined

2010 Vancouver 561

Medal Tables

1896 Athens

	Gold	Silver	Bronze	Total
United States (USA)	11	7	2	20
Greece (GRE)	10	17	19	46
Germany (GER)	6	5	2	13
France (FRA) (FRA)	5	4	2	11
Great Britain (GBR)	2	3	2	7
Hungary (HUN)	2	1	3	6
Austria (AUT)	2	1	2	5
Australia (AUS)	2	0	0	2
Denmark (DEN)	1	2	3	6
Switzerland (SUI)	1	2	0	3
Mixed Team (ZZX)	1	1	1	3

1900 Paris

	Gold	Silver	Bronze	Total
France (FRA)	25	41	34	100
United States (USA)	19	14	14	47
Great Britain (GBR)	15	6	9	30
Mixed Team (ZZX)	6	3	3	12
Switzerland (SUI)	6	2	1	9
Belgium (BEL)	5	5	5	15
Germany (GER)	4	2	2	8
Italy (ITA)	2	1	0	3
Australia (AUS)	2	0	3	5
Denmark (DEN)	1	3	2	6
Hungary (HUN)	1	3	2	6
Cuba (CUB)	1	1	0	2
Canada (CAN)	1	0	1	2
Spain (ESP)	1	0	0	1
Luxembourg (LUX)	1	0	0	1
Austria (AUT)	0	3	3	6
Norway (NOR)	0	2	3	5
India (IND)	0	2	0	2
Netherlands (NED)	0	1	3	4
Bohemia (BOH)	0	1	1	2
Mexico (MX)	0	0	1	1
Sweden (SWE)	0	0	1	1

1904 St. Louis

	Gold	Silver	Bronze	Total
United States USA)	77	81	78	236
Germany (GER)	4	4	5	13
Cuba (CUB)	4	2	3	9
Canada (CAN)	4	1	1	6
Hungary (HUN)	2	1	1	4
Great Britain (GBR)	1	1	0	2
Mixed Team (ZZX)	1	1	0	2
Switzerland (SUI)	1	0	1	2
Greece (GRE)	1	0	1	2
Austria (AUT)	0	0	1	1

1908 London

	Gold	Silver	Bronze	Total
Great Britain (GBR)	56	51	39	146
United States (USA)	23	12	12	47
Sweden (SWE)	8	6	11	25
France (FRA)	5	5	9	19
Germany (GER)	3	5	5	13
Hungary (HUN)	3	4	2	9
Canada (CAN)	3	3	10	16
Norway (NOR)	2	3	3	8
Italy (ITA)	2	2	0	4
Belgium (BEL)	1	5	2	8
Australaisa (ANZ)	1	2	2	5
Russia (RUS)	1	2	0	3
Finland (FIN)	1	1	3	5
South Africa (RSA)	1	1	0	2
Greece (GRE)	0	3	0	3
Denmark (DEN)	0	2	3	5
Bohemia (BOH)	0	0	2	2
Netherlands (NED)	0	0	2	2
Austria (AUT)	0	0	1	1

1912 Stockholm

	Gold	Silver	Bronze	Total
United States (USA)	25	19	19	63
Sweden (SWE)	24	24	17	65
Great Britain (GBR)	10	15	16	41
Finland (FNI)	9	8	9	26
France (FRA)	7	4	3	14
Germany (GER)	5	13	7	25
South Africa (RSA)	4	2	0	6
Norway (NOR)	4	1	4	9
Hungary (HUN)	3	2	3	8
Canada (CAN)	3	2	3	8
Italy (ITA)	3	1	2	6
Australasia (ANZ)	2	2	3	7
Belgium (BEL)	2	1	3	6
Denmark (DEN)	1	6	5	12
Greece (GRE)	1	0	1	2
Russia (RUS)	0	2	3	5
Austria (AUT)	0	2	2	4
Netherlands (NED)	0	0	3	3

1920 Antwerp

	Gold	Silver	Bronze	Total
United States (USA)	41	27	27	95
Sweden (SWE)	19	20	25	64
Great Britain (GBR)	16	15	13	44
Finland (FIN)	15	10	9	34
Belgium (BEL)	14	11	11	36
Norway (NOR)	13	9	9	31
Italy (ITA)	13	5	5	23
France (FRA)	9	19	13	41
Netherlands (NED)	4	2	5	11
Denmark (DEN)	3	9	1	13
South Africa (RSA)	3	4	3	10
Canada (CAN)	3	3	3	9
Switzerland (SUI)	2	2	7	11
Estonia (EST)	1	2	0	3
Brazil (BRA)	1	1	1	3
Australia (AUS)	0	2	1	3
Japan (JPN)	0	2	0	2
Spain (ESP)	0	2	0	2
Greece (GRE)	0	1	0	1
Luxembourg (LUX)	0	1	0	1
Czechoslovakia (TCH)	0	0	2	2
New Zealand (NZL)	0	0	1	1

1924 Chamonix

	Gold	Silver	Bronze	Total
Norway (NOR)	4	7	6	17
Finland (FIN)	4	4	3	11
Austria (AUT)	2	1	0	3
Switzerland (SUI)	2	0	1	3
United States (USA)	1	2	1	4
Great Britain (GBR)	1	1	2	4
Sweden (SWE)	1	1	0	2
Canada (CAN)	1	0	0	1
France (FRA)	0	0	3	3
Belgium (BEL)	0	0	1	1

1924 Paris

	Gold	Silver	Bronze	Total
United States (USA)	45	27	27	99
Finland (FIN)	14	13	10	37
France (FRA)	13	15	10	38
Great Britain (GBR)	9	13	12	34
Italy (ITA)	8	3	5	16
Switzerland (SUI)	7	8	10	25
Norway (NOR)	5	2	3	10
Sweden (SWE)	4	13	12	29
Netherlands (NED)	4	1	5	10
Belgium (BEL)	3	7	3	13
Australia (AUS)	3	1	2	6
Denmark (DEN)	2	5	2	9
Hungary (HUN)	2	3	4	9
Yugoslavia (YUG)	2	0	0	2
Czechoslovakia (TCH)	1	4	5	10
Argentina (ARG)	1	3	2	6
Estonia (EST)	1	1	4	6
South Africa (RSA)	1	1	1	3
Uruguay (URU)	1	0	0	1
Austria (AUT)	0	3	1	4
Canada (CAN)	0	3	1	4
Poland (POL)	0	1	1	2
Haiti (HAI)	0	0	1	1
Japan (JPN)	0	0	1	1
New Zealand (NZL)	0	0	1	1
Portugal (POR)	0	0	1	1
Romania (ROU)	0	0	1	1

1928 Amsterdam

	Gold	Silver	Bronze	Total
United States (USA)	22	18	16	56
Germany (GER)	10	7	14	31
Finland (FIN)	8	8	9	25
Sweden (SWE)	7	6	12	25
Italy (ITA)	7	5	7	19
Switzerland (SUI)	7	4	4	15
France (FRA)	6	10	5	21
Netherlands (NED)	6	9	4	19
Hungary (HUN)	4	5	0	9
Canada (CAN)	4	4	7	15
Great Britain (GBR)	3	10	7	20
Argentina (ARG)	3	3	1	7
Denmark (DEN)	3	1	2	6
Czechoslovakia (TCH)	2	5	2	9
Japan (JPN)	2	2	1	5
Estonia (EST)	2	1	2	5
Egypt (EGY)	2	1	1	4
Austria (AUT)	2	0	1	3
Australia (AUS)	1	2	1	4
Norway (NOR)	1	2	1	4
Poland (POL)	1	1	3	5
Yugoslavia (YUG)	1	1	3	5
South Africa (RSA)	1	0	2	3
India (IND)	1	0	0	1
Ireland (IRL)	1	0	0	1
New Zealand (NZL)	1	0	0	1
Spain (ESP)	1	0	0	1
Uruguay (URU)	1	0	0	1
Belgium (BEL)	0	1	2	3
Chile (CHI)	0	1	0	1
Haiti (HAI)	0	1	0	1
Philippines (PHI)	0	0	1	1
Portugal (POR)	0	0	1	1

1928 St Moritz

	Gold	Silver	Bronze	Total
Norway (NOR)	6	4	5	15
United States (USA)	2	2	2	6
Sweden (SWE)	2	2	1	5
Finland (FIN)	2	1	1	4
Canada (CAN)	1	0	0	1
France (FRA)	1	0	0	1
Austria (AUT)	0	3	1	4
Belgium (BEL)	0	0	1	1
Czechoslovakia (TCH)	0	0	1	1
Germany (GER)	0	0	1	1
Great Britain (GBR)	0	0	1	1
Switzerland (SUI)	0	0	1	1

1932 Lake Placid

	Gold	Silver	Bronze	Total
United States (USA)	6	4	3	13
Norway (NOR)	3	4	3	10
Sweden (SWE)	1	2	0	3
Canada (CAN)	1	1	5	7
Finland (FIN)	1	1	1	3
Austria (AUT)	1	1	0	2
France (FRA)	1	0	0	1
Switzerland (SUI)	0	1	0	1
Germany (GER)	0	0	2	2
Hungary (HUN)	0	0	1	1

1932 Los Angeles

	Gold	Silver	Bronze	Total
United States (USA)	41	32	30	103
Italy (ITA)	12	12	12	36
France (FRA)	10	5	4	19
Sweden (SWE)	9	5	9	23
Japan (JPN)	7	7	4	18
Hungary (HUN)	6	4	5	15
Finland (FIN)	5	8	12	25
Great Britain (GBR)	4	7	5	16
Germany (GER)	3	12	5	20
Australia (AUS)	3	1	1	5
Argentina (ARG)	3	1	0	4
Canada (CAN)	2	5	8	15
Netherlands (NED)	2	5	0	7
Poland (POL)	2	1	4	7
South Africa (RSA)	2	0	3	5
Ireland (IRL)	2	0	0	2
Czechoslovakia (TCH)	1	2	1	4
Austria (AUT)	1	1	3	5
India (IND)	1	0	0	1
Denmark (DEN)	0	3	3	6
Mexico (MEX)	0	2	0	2
Latvia (LAT)	0	1	0	1
New Zealand (NZL)	0	1	0	1
Switzerland (SUI)	0	1	0	1
Philippines (PHI)	0	3	3	6
Spain (ESP)	0	0	1	1
Uruguay (URU)	0	0	1	1

1936 Garmisch-Partenkirchen

	Gold	Silver	Bronze	Total
Norway (NOR)	7	5	3	15
Germany (GER)	3	3	0	6
Sweden (SWE)	2	2	3	7
Finland (FIN)	1	2	3	6
Switzerland (SUI)	1	2	0	3
Austria (AUT)	1	1	2	4
Great Britain (GBR)	1	1	1	3
United States (USA)	1	0	3	4
Canada (CAN)	0	1	0	1
France (FRA)	0	0	1	1
Hungary (HUN)	0	0	1	1

1936 Berlin

	Gold	Silver	Bronze	Total
Germany (GER)	33	26	30	89
United States (USA)	24	20	12	56
Hungary (HUN)	10	1	5	16
Italy (ITA)	8	9	5	22
Finland (FIN)	7	6	6	19
France (FRA)	7	6	6	19
Sweden (SWE)	6	5	9	20
Japan (JAP)	6	4	8	18
Netherlands (NED)	6	4	7	17
Great Britain (GBR)	4	7	3	14
Austria (AUT)	4	6	3	13
Czechoslovakia (TCH)	3	5	0	8
Argentina (ARG)	2	2	3	7
Estonia (EST)	2	2	3	7
Egypt (EGY)	2	1	2	5
Switzerland (SUI)	1	9	5	15
Canada (CAN)	1	3	5	9
Norway (NOR)	1	3	2	6
Turkey (TUR)	1	0	1	2
New Zealand (NZL)	1	0	0	1
India (IND)	1	0	0	1
Poland (POL)	0	0	3	3
Denmark (DEN)	0	2	3	5
Latvia (LAT)	0	1	1	2
Romania (ROU)	0	1	0	1
South Africa (RSA)	0	1	0	1
Yugoslavia (YUG)	0	1	0	1
Mexico (MEX)	0	0	3	3
Belgium (BEL)	0	0	2	2
Australia (AUS)	0	0	1	1
Portugal (POR)	0	0	1	1
Philippines (PHI)	0	0	1	1

1948 St Moritz

	Gold	Silver	Bronze	Total
Sweden (SWE)	4	3	3	10
Norway (NOR)	4	3	3	10
Switzerland (SUI)	3	4	3	10
United States (USA)	3	4	2	9
France (FRA)	2	1	2	5
Canada (CAN)	2	0	1	3
Austria (AUT)	1	3	4	8
Finland (FIN)	1	3	2	6
Belgium (BEL)	1	1	0	2
Italy (ITA)	1	0	0	1
Czechoslovakia (TCH)	0	1	0	1
Hungary (HUN)	0	1	0	1
Great Britain (GBR)	0	0	2	2

1948 London

	Gold	Silver	Bronze	Total
United States (USA)	38	27	19	84
Sweden (SWE)	16	11	17	44
France (FRA)	10	6	13	29
Hungary (HUN)	10	5	12	27
Italy (ITA)	8	11	8	27
Finland (FIN)	8	7	5	20
Turkey (TUR)	6	4	2	12
Czechoslovakia (TCH)	6	2	3	11
Switzerland (SUI)	5	10	5	20
Denmark (DEN)	5	7	8	20
Netherlands (NED)	5	2	9	16
Great Britain (GBR)	3	14	6	23
Argentina (ARG)	3	3	1	7
Australia (AUS)	2	6	5	13
Belgium (BEL)	2	2	3	7
Egypt (EGY)	2	2	1	5
Mexico (MEX)	2	1	2	5
South Africa (RSA)	2	1	1	4
Norway (NOR)	1	3	3	7
Jamaica (JAM)	1	2	0	3
Austria (AUT)	1	0	3	4
India (IND)	1	0	0	1
Peru (PER)	1	0	0	1
Yugoslavia (YUG)	0	2	0	2
Canada (CAN)	0	1	2	3
Portugal (POR)	0	1	1	2
Uruguay (URU)	0	1	1	2
Ceylon (CEY)	0	1	0	1
Cuba (CUB)	0	1	0	1
Spain (ESP)	0	1	0	1
Trinidad and Tobago (TRI)	0	1	0	1
Panama (PAN)	0	0	2	2

Continued overleaf

1948 London continued

	Gold	Silver	Bronze	Total
South Korea (KOR)	0	0	2	2
Brazil (BRA)	0	0	1	1
Iran (IRI)	0	0	1	1
Poland (POL)	0	0	1	1
Puerto Rico (PUR)	0	0	1	1

1952 Oslo

	Gold	Silver	Bronze	Total
Norway (NOR)	7	3	6	16
United States (USA)	4	6	1	11
Finland (FIN)	3	4	2	9
Germany (GER)	3	2	2	7
Austria (AUT)	2	4	2	8
Canada (CAN)	1	0	1	2
Italy (ITA)	1	0	1	2
Great Britain (GBR)	1	0	0	1
Netherlands (NED)	0	3	0	3
Sweden (SWE)	0	0	4	4
Switzerland (SUI)	0	0	2	2
France (FRA)	0	0	1	1
Hungary (HUN)	0	0	1	1

1952 Helsinki

	Gold	Silver	Bronze	Total
United States (USA)	40	19	17	76
Soviet Union (URS)	22	30	19	71
Hungary (HUN)	16	10	16	42
Sweden (SWE)	12	13	10	35
Italy (ITA)	8	9	4	21
Czechoslovakia (TCH)	7	3	3	13
France (FRA)	6	6	6	18
Finland (FIN)	6	3	13	22
Australia (AUS)	6	2	3	11
Norway (NOR)	3	2	0	5
Switzerland (SUI)	2	6	6	14
South Africa (RSA)	2	4	4	10
Jamaica (JAM)	2	3	0	5
Belgium (BEL)	2	2	0	4
Denmark (DEN)	2	1	3	6
Turkey (TUR)	2	0	1	3
Japan (JPN)	1	6	2	9
Great Britain (GBR)	1	2	8	11
Argentina (ARG)	1	2	2	5
Poland (POL)	1	2	1	4
Canada (CAN)	1	2	0	3
Yugoslavia (YUG)	1	2	0	3

	Gold	Silver	Bronze	Total
Romania (ROU)	1	1	2	4
New Zealand (NZL)	1	0	2	3
Brazil (BRA)	1	0	2	3
India IND)	1	0	1	2
Luxembourg (LUX)	1	0	0	1
Germany (GER)	0	7	17	24
Netherlands (NED)	0	5	0	5
Iran (IRI)	0	3	4	7
Chile (CHI)	0	2	0	2
Austria (AUT)	0	1	1	2
Lebanon (LIB)	0	1	1	2
Mexico (MEX)	0	1	0	1
Ireland (IRL)	0	1	0	1
Spain (ESP)	0	1	0	1
South Korea (KOR)	0	0	2	2
Trinidad and Tobago (TRI)	0	0	2	2
Uruguay (URU)	0	0	2	2
Venezuela (VEN)	0	0	1	1
Portugal (POR)	0	0	1	1
Bulgaria (BUL)	0	0	1	1
Egypt (EGY)	0	0	1	1

1956 Cortina d'Ampezzo

	Gold	Silver	Bronze	Total
Soviet Union (URS)	7	3	6	16
Austria (AUT)	4	3	4	11
Finland (FIN)	3	3	1	7
Switzerland (SUI)	3	2	1	6
Sweden (SWE)	2	4	4	10
United States (USA)	2	3	2	7
Norway (NOR)	2	1	1	4
Italy (ITA)	1	2	0	3
Germany (EUA)	1	0	1	2
Canada (CAN)	0	1	2	3
Japan (JPN)	0	1	0	1
Hungary (HUN)	0	0	1	1
Poland (POL)	0	0	1	1

1956 Melbourne

	Gold	Silver	Bronze	Total
Soviet Union (URS)	37	29	32	98
United States USA)	32	25	17	74
Australia (AUS)	13	8	14	35
Hungary (HUN)	9	10	7	26
Italy (ITA)	8	8	9	25
Sweden (SWE)	8	5	6	19
Germany (EUA)	6	13	7	26
Great Britain (GBR)	6	7	11	24
Romania (ROU)	5	3	5	13
Japan (JPN)	4	10	5	19
France (FRA)	4	4	6	14
Turkey (TUR)	3	2	2	7
Finland (FIN)	3	1	11	15
Iran (IRI)	2	2	1	5
Canada (CAN)	2	1	3	6
New Zealand (NZL)	2	0	0	2
Poland (POL)	1	4	4	9
Czechoslovakia (TCH)	1	4	1	6
Bulgaria (BUL)	1	3	1	5

1960 Squaw Valley

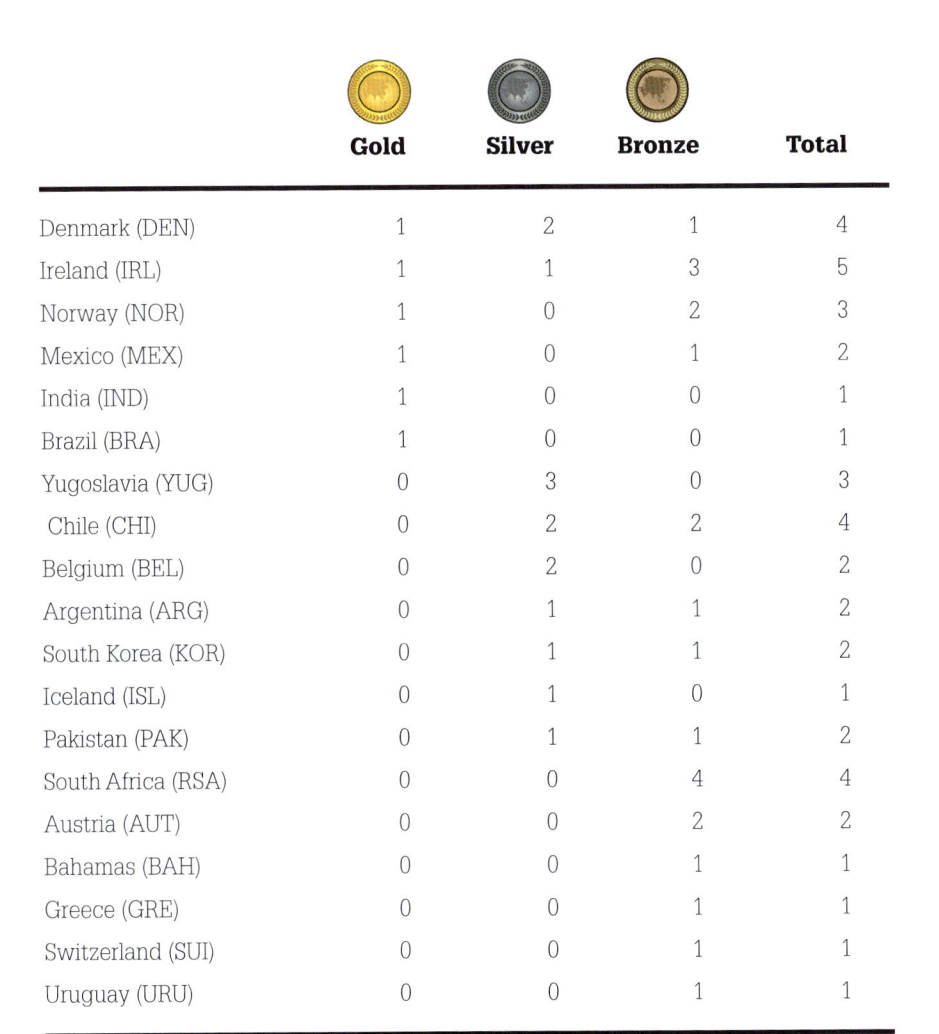

	Gold	Silver	Bronze	Total
Denmark (DEN)	1	2	1	4
Ireland (IRL)	1	1	3	5
Norway (NOR)	1	0	2	3
Mexico (MEX)	1	0	1	2
India (IND)	1	0	0	1
Brazil (BRA)	1	0	0	1
Yugoslavia (YUG)	0	3	0	3
Chile (CHI)	0	2	2	4
Belgium (BEL)	0	2	0	2
Argentina (ARG)	0	1	1	2
South Korea (KOR)	0	1	1	2
Iceland (ISL)	0	1	0	1
Pakistan (PAK)	0	1	1	2
South Africa (RSA)	0	0	4	4
Austria (AUT)	0	0	2	2
Bahamas (BAH)	0	0	1	1
Greece (GRE)	0	0	1	1
Switzerland (SUI)	0	0	1	1
Uruguay (URU)	0	0	1	1

	Gold	Silver	Bronze	Total
Soviet Union (URS)	7	5	9	21
Germany (EUA)	4	3	1	8
United States (USA)	3	4	3	10
Norway (NOR)	3	3	0	6
Sweden (SWE)	3	2	2	7
Finland (FIN)	2	3	3	8
Canada (CAN)	2	1	1	4
Switzerland (SUI)	2	0	0	2
Austria (AUT)	1	2	3	6
France (FRA)	1	0	2	3
Netherlands (NED)	0	1	1	2
Poland (POL)	0	1	1	2
Czechoslovakia (TCH)	0	1	0	1
Italy (ITA)	0	0	1	1

1960 Rome

	Gold	Silver	Bronze	Total
Soviet Union (USR)	43	29	31	103
United States (USA)	34	21	16	71
Italy (ITA)	13	10	13	36
Germany (EUA)	12	19	11	32
Australia (AUS)	8	8	6	22
Turkey (TUR)	7	2	0	9
Hungary (HUN)	6	8	7	21
Japan (JPN)	4	7	7	18
Poland (POL)	4	6	11	21
Czechoslovakia (TCH)	3	2	3	8
Romania (ROU)	3	1	6	10
Great Britain (GBR)	2	6	12	20
Denmark (DEN)	2	3	1	6
New Zealand (NZL)	2	0	1	3
Bulgaria (BUL)	1	3	3	7
Sweden (SWE)	1	2	3	6
Finland (FIN)	1	1	3	5
Austria (AUT)	1	1	0	2
Yugoslavia (YUG)	1	1	0	2
Pakistan (PAK)	1	0	1	2
Norway (NOR)	1	0	0	1
Ethiopia (ETH)	1	0	0	1

	Gold	Silver	Bronze	Total
Greece (GRE)	1	0	0	1
Switzerland (SUI)	0	3	3	6
France (FRA)	0	2	3	5
Belgium (BEL)	0	2	2	4
Iran (IRI)	0	1	3	4
Netherlands (NED)	0	1	2	3
South Africa (RSA)	0	1	2	3
Argentina (ARG)	0	1	1	2
Egypt (EGY)	0	1	1	2
Canada (CAN)	0	1	0	1
Republic of China (ROC)	0	1	0	1
Ghana (GHA)	0	1	0	1
India (IND)	0	1	0	1
Morocco (MAR)	0	1	0	1
Portugal (POR)	0	1	0	1
Singapore (SIN)	0	1	0	1
Brazil (BRA)	0	0	2	2
British West Indies (BWI)	0	0	2	2
Iraq (IRQ)	0	0	1	1
Mexico (MEX)	0	0	1	1
Spain (ESP)	0	0	1	1
Venezuela (VEN)	0	0	1	1

1964 Innsbruck

	Gold	Silver	Bronze	Total
Soviet Union (URS)	11	8	6	25
Austria (AUT)	4	5	3	12
Norway (NOR)	3	6	6	15
Finland (FIN)	3	4	3	10
France (FRA)	3	4	0	7
Germany (EUA)	3	3	3	9
Sweden (SWE)	3	3	1	7
United States (USA)	1	2	3	6
Netherlands (NED)	1	1	0	1
Canada (CAN)	1	0	2	3
Great Britain (GBR)	1	0	0	1
Italy (ITA)	0	1	3	4
North Korea (PRK)	0	1	0	1
Czechoslovakia (TCH)	0	0	1	1

1964 Tokyo

	Gold	Silver	Bronze	Total
United States (USA)	36	26	28	90
Soviet Union (URS)	30	31	35	96
Japan (JPN)	16	5	8	29
Germany (EUA)	10	22	18	50
Italy (ITA)	10	10	7	27
Hungary (HUN)	10	7	5	22
Poland (POL)	7	6	10	23
Australia (AUS)	6	2	10	18
Czechoslovakia (TCH)	5	6	3	14
Great Britain (GBR)	4	12	2	18
Bulgaria (BUL)	3	5	2	10
Finland (FIN)	3	0	2	5
New Zealand (NZL)	3	0	2	5
Romania (ROU)	2	4	6	12
Netherlands	2	4	4	10
Turkey (TUR)	2	3	1	6
Sweden (SWE)	2	2	4	8
Denmark (DEN)	2	1	3	6
Yugoslavia (YUG)	2	1	2	5
Belgium (BEL)	2	0	1	3
France (FRA)	1	8	6	15
Canada (CAN)	1	2	1	4
Switzerland (SUI)	1	2	1	4
Bahamas (BAH)	1	0	0	1
Ethiopia (ETH)	1	0	0	1
India (IND)	1	0	0	1
South Korea (KOR)	0	2	1	3
Trinidad and Tobago (TRI)	0	1	2	3
Tunisia (TUN)	0	1	1	2
Pakistan (PAK)	0	1	0	1
Philippines (PHI)	0	1	0	1
Argentina (ARG)	0	1	0	1

Continued overleaf

1964 Tokyo continued

	Gold	Silver	Bronze	Total
Cuba (CUB)	0	1	0	1
Iran (IRI)	0	0	2	2
Brazil (BRA)	0	0	1	1
Ghana (GHA)	0	0	1	1
Ireland (IRL)	0	0	1	1
Kenya (KEN)	0	0	1	1
Mexico (MEX)	0	0	1	1
Nigeria (NGR)	0	0	1	1
Uruguay (URU)	0	0	1	1

1968 Grenoble

	Gold	Silver	Bronze	Total
Norway (NOR)	6	6	2	14
Soviet Union (URS)	5	5	3	13
France (FRA)	4	3	2	9
Italy (ITA)	4	0	0	4
Austria (AUT)	3	4	4	11
Netherlands (NED)	3	3	3	9
Sweden (SWE)	3	2	3	7
West germany (FRG)	2	2	3	7
United States (USA)	1	5	1	7
East Germany (GDR)	1	2	2	5
Finland (FIN)	1	2	2	5
Czechoslovakia (TCH)	1	2	1	4
Canada (CAN)	1	1	1	3
Switzerland (SUI)	0	2	4	6
Romania (ROU)	0	0	1	1

1968 Mexico City

	Gold	Silver	Bronze	Total
United States (USA)	45	28	34	107
Soviet Union (URS)	29	32	30	91
Japan (JPN)	11	7	7	25
Hungary (HUN)	10	10	12	32
East germany (GDR)	9	9	7	25
France (FRA)	7	3	5	15
Czechoslovakia (TCH)	7	2	4	13
West Germany (FRG)	5	11	10	26
Australia (AUS)	5	7	5	17
Great Britain (GBR)	5	5	3	13
Poland (POL)	5	2	11	18
Romania (ROU)	4	6	5	15
Italy (ITA)	3	4	9	16
Kenya (KEN)	3	4	2	9
Mexico (MEX)	3	3	3	9
Yugoslavia (YUG)	3	3	2	8
Netherlands (NED)	3	3	1	7
Bulgaria (BUL)	2	4	3	9
Iran (IRI)	2	1	2	5
Sweden (SWE)	2	1	1	4
Turkey (TUR)	2	0	0	2
Denmark (DEN)	1	4	3	8

	Gold	Silver	Bronze	Total
Canada (CAN)	1	3	1	5
Finland (FIN)	1	2	1	4
Ethiopia (ETH)	1	1	0	2
Norway (NOR)	1	1	0	2
New Zealand (NZL)	1	0	2	3
Tunisia (TUN)	1	0	1	2
Venezuela (VEN)	1	0	0	1
Pakistan (PAK)	1	0	0	1
Cuba (CUB)	0	4	0	4
Austria (AUT)	0	2	2	4
Switzerland (SUI)	0	1	4	5
Mongolia (MGL)	0	1	3	4
Brazil (BRA)	0	1	2	3
Belgium (BEL)	0	1	1	2
South Korea (KOR)	0	1	1	2
Uganda (UGA)	0	1	1	2
Jamaica (JAM)	0	1	0	1
Cameroon (CMR)	0	1	0	1
Argentina (ARG)	0	0	2	2
Greece (GRE)	0	0	1	1
India (IND)	0	0	1	1
Republic of China (ROC)	0	0	1	1

1972 Sapporo

	Gold	Silver	Bronze	Total
Soviet Union (URS)	8	5	3	16
East Germany (GDR)	4	3	7	14
Switzerland (SUI)	4	3	3	10
Netherlands (NED)	4	3	2	9
United States (USA)	3	2	3	8
West Germany (FRG)	3	1	1	5
Norway (NOR)	2	5	5	12
Italy (ITA)	2	2	1	5
Austria (AUT)	1	2	2	5
Sweden (SWE)	1	1	2	4
Japan (JPN)	1	1	1	3
Czechoslovakia (TCH)	1	0	2	3
Poland (POL)	1	0	0	1
Spain (ESP)	1	0	0	1
Finland (FIN)	0	4	1	5
France (FRA)	0	1	2	3
Canada (CAN)	0	1	0	1

1972 Munich

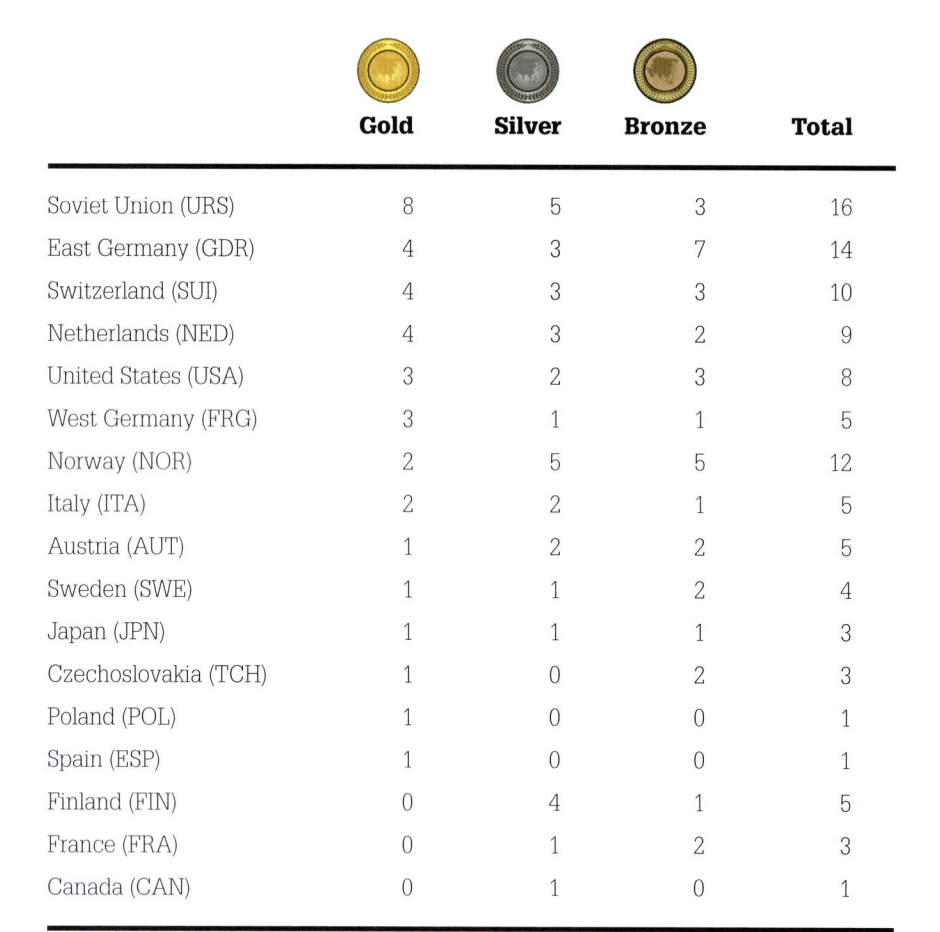

	Gold	Silver	Bronze	Total
Soviet Union (URS)	50	27	22	99
United States (USA)	33	31	30	94
East Germany (GDR)	20	23	23	66
West Germany (FRG)	13	11	16	40
Japan (JPN)	13	8	8	29
Australia (AUS)	8	7	2	17
Poland (POL)	7	5	9	21
Hungary (HUN)	6	13	16	35
Bulgaria (BUL)	6	10	5	21
Italy (ITA)	5	3	10	18
Sweden (SWE)	4	6	6	16
Great Britain (GBR)	4	5	9	18
Romania (ROU)	3	6	7	16
Finland (FIN)	3	1	4	8
Cuba (CUB)	3	1	4	8
Netherlands (NED)	3	1	1	5
France (FRA)	2	4	7	13
Czechoslovakia (TCH)	2	4	2	8
Kenya (KEN)	2	3	4	9
Yugoslavia (YUG)	2	1	2	5
Norway (NOR)	2	1	1	4
North Korea (PRK)	1	1	3	5
New Zealand (NZL)	1	1	1	3
Uganda (UGA)	1	1	0	2

1976 Innsbruck

	Gold	Silver	Bronze	Total
Denmark (DEN)	1	0	0	1
Switzerland (SUI)	0	3	0	3
Canada (CAN)	0	2	3	5
Iran (IRI)	0	2	1	3
Greece (GRE)	0	2	0	2
Belgium (BEL)	0	2	0	2
Austria (AUT)	0	1	2	3
Colombia (COL)	0	1	2	3
Argentina (ARG)	0	1	0	1
South Korea (KOR)	0	1	0	1
Lebanon LIB)	0	1	0	1
Mexico (MEX)	0	1	0	1
Mongolia (MGL)	0	1	0	1
Pakistan (PAK)	0	1	0	1
Tunisia (TUN)	0	1	0	1
Turkey (TUR)	0	1	0	1
Brazil (BRA)	0	0	2	2
Ethiopia (ETH)	0	0	2	2
Ghana (GHA)	0	0	1	1
India (IND)	0	0	1	1
Jamaica (JAM)	0	0	1	1
Niger (NIG)	0	0	1	1
Nigeria (NGR)	0	0	1	1
Spain (ESP)	0	0	1	1

	Gold	Silver	Bronze	Total
Soviet Union (URS)	13	6	8	27
East Germany (GDR)	7	5	7	19
United States (USA)	3	3	4	10
Norway (NOR)	3	3	1	7
West Germany (FRG)	2	5	3	10
Finland (FIN)	2	4	1	7
Austria (AUT)	2	2	2	6
Switzerland (SUI)	1	3	1	5
Netherlands (NED)	1	2	3	6
Italy (ITA)	1	2	1	4
Canada (CAN)	1	1	1	3
Great Britain (GBR)	1	0	0	1
Czechoslovakia (TCH)	0	1	0	1
Liechtenstein (LIE)	0	0	2	2
Sweden (SWE)	0	0	2	2
France (FRA)	0	0	1	1

1976 Montreal

	Gold	Silver	Bronze	Total
Soviet Union (URS)	49	41	35	125
East Germany (GDR)	40	25	25	90
United States (USA)	34	35	25	104
West Germany (FRG)	10	12	17	39
Japan (JPN)	9	6	10	25
Poland (POL)	7	6	13	26
Bulgaria (BUL)	6	9	7	22
Cuba (CUB)	6	4	3	13
Romania (ROU)	4	9	14	27
Hungary (HUN)	4	5	13	22
Finland (FIN)	4	2	0	6
Sweden (SWE)	4	1	0	5
Great Britain (GBR)	3	5	5	13
Italy (ITA)	2	7	4	13
France (FRA)	2	3	4	9
Yugoslavia (YUG)	2	3	3	8
Czechoslovakia (TCH)	2	2	4	8
New Zealand (NZL)	2	1	1	4
South Korea (KOR)	1	1	4	6
Switzerland (SUI)	1	1	2	4
North Korea (PRK)	1	1	0	2

	Gold	Silver	Bronze	Total
Jamaica (JAM)	1	1	0	2
Norway (NOR)	1	1	0	2
Denmark (DEN)	1	0	2	3
Mexico (MEX)	1	0	1	2
Trinidad and Tobago (TRI)	1	0	0	1
Canada (CAN)	0	5	6	11
Belgium (BEL)	0	3	3	6
Netherlands (NED)	0	2	3	5
Portugal (POR)	0	2	0	2
Spain (ESP)	0	2	0	2
Australia (AUS)	0	1	4	5
Iran (IRI)	0	1	1	2
Mongolia (MGL)	0	1	0	1
Venezuela (VEN)	0	1	0	1
Brazil (BRA)	0	0	2	2
Austria (AUT)	0	0	1	1
Bermuda (BER)	0	0	1	1
Pakistan (PAK)	0	0	1	1
Puerto Rico (PUR)	0	0	1	1
Thailand (THA)	0	0	1	1

1980 Lake Placid

	Gold	Silver	Bronze	Total
Soviet Union (URS)	10	6	6	22
East Germany (GDR)	9	7	7	23
United States (USA)	6	4	2	12
Austria (AUT)	3	2	2	7
Sweden (SWE)	3	0	1	4
Liechtenstein (LIE)	2	2	0	4
Finland (FIN)	1	5	3	9
Norway (NOR)	1	3	6	10
Netherlands (NED)	1	2	1	4
Switzerland (SUI)	1	1	3	5
Great Britain (GBR)	1	0	0	1
West germany (FRG)	0	2	3	5
Italy (ITA)	0	2	0	2
Canada (CAN)	0	1	1	2
Hungary (HUN)	0	1	0	1
Japan (JPN)	0	1	0	1
Bulgaria (BUL)	0	0	1	1
Czechoslovakia (TCH)	0	0	1	1
France (FRA	0	0	1	1

1980 Moscow

	Gold	Silver	Bronze	Total
Soviet Union (URS)	80	69	46	195
East Germany (GDR)	47	37	42	126
Bulgaria (BUL)	8	16	17	41
Cuba (CUB)	8	7	5	20
Italy (ITA)	8	3	4	15
Hungary (HUN)	7	10	15	32
Romania (ROU)	6	6	13	25
France (FRA)	6	5	3	14
Great Britain (GBR)	5	7	9	21
Poland (POL)	3	14	15	32
Sweden (SWE)	3	3	6	12
Finland (FIN)	3	1	4	8
Czechoslovakia (TCH)	2	3	9	14
Yugoslavia (YUG)	2	3	4	9
Australia (AUS)	2	2	5	9
Denmark (DEN)	2	1	2	5
Brazil (BRA)	2	0	2	4
Ethiopia (ETH)	2	0	2	4
Switzerland (SUI)	2	0	0	2
Spain (ESP)	1	3	2	6
Austria (AUT)	1	2	1	4
Greece (GRE)	1	0	2	3
Belgium (BEL)	1	0	0	1
India (IND)	1	0	0	1
Zimbabwe (ZIM)	1	0	0	1
North Korea (PRK)	0	3	2	5
Mongolia (MGL)	0	2	2	4
Tanzania (TAN)	0	2	0	2
Mexico (MEX)	0	1	3	4
Netherlands (NED)	0	1	2	3
Ireland (IRL)	0	1	1	2
Uganda (UGA)	0	1	0	1

Continued overleaf

1980 Moscow continued

	Gold	Silver	Bronze	Total
Venezuela (VEN)	0	1	0	1
Jamaica (JAM)	0	0	3	3
Guyana (GUY)	0	0	1	1
Lebanon (LIB)	0	0	1	1

1984 Sarajevo

	Gold	Silver	Bronze	Total
East Germany (GDR)	9	9	6	24
Soviet Union (URS)	6	10	9	25
United States (USA)	4	4	0	8
Finland (FIN)	4	3	6	13
Sweden (SWE)	4	2	2	8
Norway (NOR)	3	2	4	9
Switzerland (SUI)	2	2	1	5
Canada (CAN)	2	1	1	4
West Germany (FRG)	2	1	1	4
Italy (ITA)	2	0	0	2
Great Britain (GBR)	1	0	0	1
Czechoslovakia (TCH)	0	2	4	6
France (FRA)	0	1	2	3
Japan (JPN)	0	1	0	1
Yugoslavia (YUG)	0	1	0	1
Liechtenstein (LIE)	0	0	2	2
Austria (AUT)	0	0	1	1

1984 Los Angeles

	Gold	Silver	Bronze	Total
United States (USA)	83	61	30	174
Romania (ROU)	20	16	17	53
West Germany (FRG)	17	19	23	59
China (CHN)	15	8	9	32
Italy (ITA)	14	6	12	32
Canada (CAN)	10	18	16	44
Japan (JPN)	10	8	14	32
New Zealand (NZL)	8	1	2	13
Yugoslavia YUG)	7	4	7	18
South Korea (KOR)	6	6	7	19
Great Britain (GBR)	5	11	21	37
France (FRA)	5	7	16	28
Netherlands (NED)	5	2	6	13
Australia (AUS)	4	8	12	24
Finland (FIN)	4	2	6	12
Sweden (SWE)	2	11	6	19
Mexico (MEX)	2	3	1	6
Morocco (MAR)	2	0	0	2
Brazil (BRA)	1	5	2	8
Spain (ESP)	1	2	2	5
Belgium (BEL)	1	1	2	4
Austria (AUT)	1	1	1	3
Kenya (KEN)	1	0	2	3
Portugal (POR)	1	0	2	3

	Gold	Silver	Bronze	Total
Pakistan (PAK)	1	0	0	1
Switzerland (SUI)	0	4	4	8
Denmark (DEN)	0	3	3	6
Jamaica (JAM)	0	1	2	3
Norway (NOR)	0	1	2	3
Greece (GRE)	0	1	1	2
Nigeria (NGR)	0	1	1	2
Puerto Rico (PUR)	0	1	1	2
Colombia (COL)	0	1	0	1
Côte d'Ivoire (CIV)	0	1	0	1
Egypt (EGY)	0	1	0	1
Ireland (IRL)	0	1	0	1
Peru (PER)	0	1	0	1
Syria (SYR)	0	1	0	1
Thailand (THA)	0	1	0	1
Turkey (TUR)	0	0	3	3
Venezuela (VEN)	0	0	3	3
Algeria (ALG)	0	0	2	2
Chinese Taipei (TPE)	0	0	1	1
Cameroon (CMR)	0	0	1	1
Dominican Republic (DOM)	0	0	1	1
Iceland (ISL)	0	0	1	1
Zambia (ZAM)	0	0	1	1

1988 Calgary

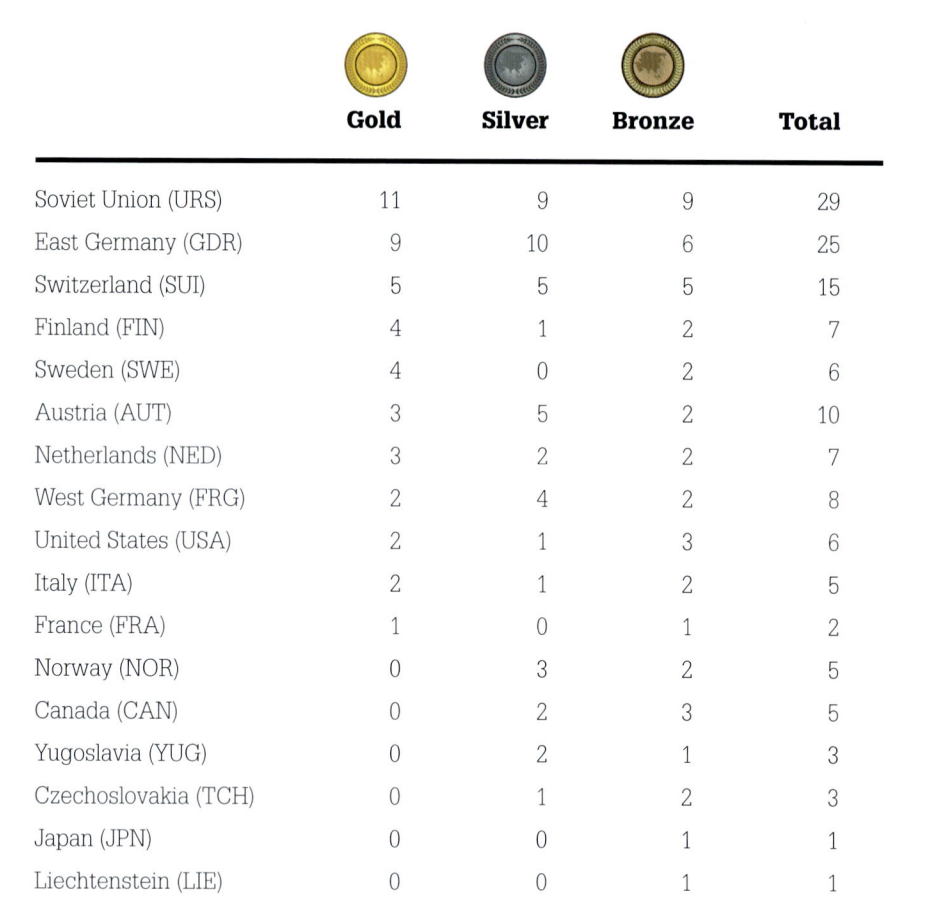

	Gold	Silver	Bronze	Total
Soviet Union (URS)	11	9	9	29
East Germany (GDR)	9	10	6	25
Switzerland (SUI)	5	5	5	15
Finland (FIN)	4	1	2	7
Sweden (SWE)	4	0	2	6
Austria (AUT)	3	5	2	10
Netherlands (NED)	3	2	2	7
West Germany (FRG)	2	4	2	8
United States (USA)	2	1	3	6
Italy (ITA)	2	1	2	5
France (FRA)	1	0	1	2
Norway (NOR)	0	3	2	5
Canada (CAN)	0	2	3	5
Yugoslavia (YUG)	0	2	1	3
Czechoslovakia (TCH)	0	1	2	3
Japan (JPN)	0	0	1	1
Liechtenstein (LIE)	0	0	1	1

1988 Seoul

	Gold	Silver	Bronze	Total
Soviet Union (URS)	55	31	46	132
East germany (GDR)	37	35	30	102
United States (USA)	36	31	27	94
South Korea (KOR)	12	10	11	33
West Germany (FRG)	11	14	15	40
Hungary (HUN)	11	6	6	23
Bulgaria (BUL)	10	12	13	35
Romania (ROU)	7	11	6	24
France (FRA)	6	4	6	16
Italy (ITA)	6	4	4	14
China (CHN)	5	11	12	28
Great Britain (GBR)	5	10	9	24
Kenya (KEN)	5	2	2	9
Japan (JPN)	4	3	7	14
Australia (AUS)	3	6	5	14
Yugoslavia (YUG)	3	4	5	12
Czechoslovakia (TCH)	3	3	2	8
New Zealand (NZL)	3	2	8	13
Canada (CAN)	3	2	5	10
Poland (POL)	2	5	9	16
Norway (NOR)	2	3	0	5
Netherlands (NED)	2	2	5	9
Denmark (DEN)	2	1	0	3
Brazil (BRA)	1	2	3	6
Spain (ESP)	1	1	2	4
Finland (FIN)	1	1	2	4

1992 Albertville

	Gold	Silver	Bronze	Total
Turkey (TUR)	1	1	0	2
Morocco (MAR)	1	0	2	3
Austria (AUT)	1	0	0	1
Suriname (SUR)	1	0	0	1
Portugal (POR)	1	0	0	1
Sweden (SWE)	0	4	7	11
Switzerland (SUI)	0	2	2	4
Jamaica (JAM)	0	2	0	2
Argentina (ARG)	0	1	1	2
Chile (CHI)	0	1	0	1
Costa Rica (CRC)	0	1	0	1
Indonesia (INA)	0	1	0	1
Iran (IRI)	0	1	0	1
Netherlands Antilles (AHO)	0	1	0	1
Peru (PER)	0	1	0	1
Senegal (SEN)	0	1	0	1
Virgin Islands (ISV)	0	1	0	1
Belgium (BEL)	0	0	2	2
Mexico (MEX)	0	0	2	2
Colombia (COL)	0	0	1	1
Djibouti (DJI)	0	0	1	1
Greece (GRE)	0	0	1	1
Mongolia (MGL)	0	0	1	1
Pakistan (PAK)	0	0	1	1
Phillippines (PHI)	0	0	1	1
Thailand (THA)	0	0	1	1

	Gold	Silver	Bronze	Total
Germany (GER)	10	10	6	26
Uniified Team (EUN)	9	6	8	23
Norway (NOR)	9	6	5	20
Austria (AUT)	6	7	8	21
United States (USA)	5	4	2	11
Italy (ITA)	4	6	4	14
France (FRA)	3	5	1	9
Finland (FIN)	3	1	3	7
Canada (CAN)	2	3	2	7
South Korea (KOR)	2	1	1	4
Japan (JPN)	1	2	4	7
Netherlands (NED)	1	1	2	4
Sweden (SWE)	1	0	3	4
Switzerland (SUI)	1	0	2	3
China (CHN)	0	3	0	3
Luxembourg (LUX)	0	2	0	2
New Zealand (NZL)	0	1	0	1
Czechoslovakia (TCH)	0	0	3	3
North Korea (PRK)	0	0	1	1
Spain (ESP)	0	0	1	1

1992 Barcelona

	Gold	Silver	Bronze	Total
Unified Team (EUN)	45	38	29	112
United States (USA)	37	34	37	108
Germany (GER)	33	21	28	82
China (CHN)	16	22	16	54
Cuba (CUB)	14	6	11	31
Spain (ESP)	13	7	2	22
South Korea (KOR)	12	5	12	19
Hungary (HUN)	11	12	7	30
France (FRA)	8	5	16	29
Australia (AUS)	7	9	11	27
Canada (CAN)	7	4	7	18
Italy (ITA)	6	5	8	19
Great Britain (GBR)	5	3	12	20
Romania (ROU)	4	6	8	18
Czechoslovakia (TCH)	4	2	1	7
North Korea (PRK)	4	0	5	9
Japan (JPN)	3	8	11	22
Bulgaria (BUL)	3	7	6	16
Poland (POL)	3	6	10	19
Netherlands (NED)	2	6	7	15
Kenya (KEN)	2	4	2	8
Norway (NOR)	2	4	1	7
Turkey (TUR)	2	2	2	6
Indonesia (INA)	2	2	1	5
Brazil (BRA)	2	1	0	3
Greece (GRE)	2	0	0	2
Sweden (SWE)	1	7	4	12
New Zealand (NZL)	1	4	5	10
Finland (FIN)	1	2	2	5
Denmark (DEN)	1	1	4	6
Morocco (MAR)	1	1	1	3
Ireland (IRL)	1	1	0	2

	Gold	Silver	Bronze	Total
Ethiopia (ETH)	1	0	2	3
Algeria (ALG)	1	0	1	2
Estonia (EST)	1	0	1	2
Lithuania (LTU)	1	0	1	2
Switzerland (SUI)	1	0	0	1
Jamaica (JAM)	0	3	1	4
Nigeria (NGR)	0	3	1	4
Latvia (LAT)	0	2	1	3
Austria (AUT)	0	2	0	2
Namibia (NAM)	0	2	0	2
South Africa (RSA)	0	2	0	2
Belgium (BEL)	0	1	2	3
Croatia (CRO)	0	1	2	3
Independent Participants (IOP)	0	1	2	3
Iran (IRI)	0	1	2	3
Israel (ISR)	0	1	1	2
Chinese Taipei (TPE)	0	1	0	1
Mexico (MEX)	0	1	0	1
Peru (PER)	0	1	0	1
Mongolia (MGL)	0	0	2	2
Slovenia (SLO)	0	0	2	2
Argentina (ARG)	0	0	1	1
Bahamas (BAH)	0	0	1	1
Colombia (COL)	0	0	1	1
Ghana (GHA)	0	0	1	1
Malaysia (MAS)	0	0	1	1
Pakistan (PAK)	0	0	1	1
Philippines (PHI)	0	0	1	1
Puerto Rico (PUR)	0	0	1	1
Qatar (QAT)	0	0	1	1
Suriname (SUR)	0	0	1	1
Thailand (THA)	0	0	1	1

1994 Lillehammer

	Gold	Silver	Bronze	Total
Russia (RUS)	11	8	4	23
Norway (NOR)	10	11	5	26
Germany (GER)	9	7	8	24
Italy (ITA)	7	5	8	20
United States (USA)	6	5	2	13
South Korea (KOR)	4	1	1	6
Canada (CAN)	3	6	4	13
Switzerland (SUI)	3	4	2	9
Austria (AUT)	2	3	4	9
Sweden (SWE)	2	1	0	3
Japan (JPN)	1	2	2	5
Kazakhstan (KAZ)	1	2	0	3
Ukraine (UKR)	1	0	1	2
Uzbekistan (UZB)	1	0	0	1
Belarus (BLR)	0	2	0	2
Finland (FIN)	0	1	5	6
France (FRA)	0	1	4	5
Netherlands (NED)	0	1	3	4
China (CHN)	0	1	2	3
Lovenia (SLO)	0	0	3	3
Great Britain (GBR)	0	0	2	2
Australia (AUS)	0	0	1	1

1996 Atlanta

	Gold	Silver	Bronze	Total
United States (USA)	44	32	25	101
Russian Federation (RUS)	26	21	16	63
Germany (GER)	20	18	27	65
China (CHN)	16	22	12	50
France (FRA)	15	7	15	37
Italy (ITA)	13	10	12	35
Australia (AUS)	9	9	23	41
Cuba (CUB)	9	8	8	25
Ukraine (UKR)	9	2	12	23
South Korea (KOR)	7	15	5	27
Poland (POL)	7	5	5	17
Hungary (HUN)	7	4	10	21
Spain (ESP)	5	6	6	17
Romania (ROU)	4	7	9	20
Netherlands (NED)	4	5	10	29
Greece (GRE)	4	4	0	8
Czech Republic (CZE)	4	3	4	11
Switzerland (SUI)	4	3	0	7
Denmark (DEN)	4	1	1	6
Turkey (TUR)	4	1	1	6
Canada (CAN)	3	11	8	22
Bulgaria (BUL)	3	7	5	15
Japan (JPN)	3	6	5	14
Kazakhstan (KAZ)	3	4	4	11
Brazil (BRA)	3	3	9	15
New Zealand (NZL)	3	2	1	6
South Africa (RSA)	3	1	1	5
Ireland (IRL)	3	0	1	5
Sweden (SWE)	2	4	2	8
Norway (NOR)	2	2	3	7
Belgium (BEL)	2	2	2	6
Nigeria (NGR)	2	1	3	6

Continued overleaf

1996 Atlanta continued

	Gold	Silver	Bronze	Total
North Korea (PRK)	2	1	2	5
Algeria (ALG)	2	0	1	3
Ethiopia (ETH)	2	0	1	3
Great Britain (GBR)	1	8	6	15
Belarus (BLR)	1	6	8	15
Kenya (KEN)	1	4	3	8
Jamaica (JAM)	1	3	2	6
Finland (FIN)	1	2	1	4
Indonesia (INA)	1	1	2	4
Yugoslavia (YUG)	1	1	2	4
Iran (IRI)	1	1	1	3
Slovakia (SVK)	1	1	1	3
Armenia (ARM)	1	1	0	2
Croatia (CRO)	1	1	0	2
Portugal (POR)	1	0	1	2
Thailand (THA)	1	0	1	2
Burundi (BDI)	1	0	0	1
Costa Rica (CRC)	1	0	0	1
Ecuador (ECU)	1	0	0	1
Hong-Kong (HKG)	1	0	0	1
Syria (SYR)	1	0	0	1
Argentina (ARG)	0	2	1	3
Namibia (NAM)	0	2	0	2
Slovenia (SLO)	0	2	0	2

	Gold	Silver	Bronze	Total
Austria (AUT)	0	1	2	3
Malaysia (MAS)	0	1	1	2
Moldova (MDA)	0	1	1	2
Uzbekistan (UZB)	0	1	1	2
Azerbaijan (AZE)	0	1	0	1
Bahamas (BAH)	0	1	0	1
Chinese Taipei (TPE)	0	1	0	1
Latvia (LAT)	0	1	0	1
Philippines (PHI)	0	1	0	1
Tonga (TGA)	0	1	0	1
Zambia (ZAM)	0	1	0	1
Georgia (GEO)	0	0	2	2
Morocco (AMR)	0	0	2	2
Trinidad and Tobago (TRI)	0	0	2	2
India (IND)	0	0	1	1
Israel (ISR)	0	0	1	1
Lithuania (LTU)	0	0	1	1
Mexico (MEX)	0	0	1	1
Mongolia (MGL)	0	0	1	1
Mozambique (MOZ)	0	0	1	1
Puerto Rico (PUR)	0	0	1	1
Tunisia (TUN)	0	0	1	1
Uganda (UGA)	0	0	1	1

1998 Nagano

	Gold	Silver	Bronze	Total
Germany (GER)	12	9	8	29
Norway (NOR)	10	10	5	25
Russia (RUS)	9	6	3	18
Canada (CAN)	6	5	4	15
United States (USA)	6	3	4	13
Netherlands (NED)	5	4	2	13
Japan (JPN)	5	1	4	10
Austria (AUT)	3	5	9	17
South Korea (KOR)	3	1	2	6
Italy (ITA)	2	6	2	10
Finland (FIN)	2	4	6	12
Switzerland (SUI)	2	2	3	7
France (FRA)	2	1	5	8
Czech Republic (CZE)	1	1	1	3
Bulgaria (BUL)	1	0	0	1
China (CHN)	0	6	2	8
Sweden (SWE)	0	2	1	3
Denmark (DEN)	0	1	0	1
Ukraine (UKR)	0	1	0	1
Belarus (BLR)	0	0	2	2
Kazakhstan (KAZ)	0	0	2	2
Australia (AUS)	0	0	1	1
Belgium (BEL)	0	0	1	1
Great Britain (GBR)	0	0	1	1

2000 Sydney

	Gold	Silver	Bronze	Total
United States (USA)	40	24	33	97
Russian Federation (RUS)	32	28	28	88
China (CHN)	28	16	15	59
Australia (AUS)	16	25	17	58
Germany (GER)	13	17	26	56
France (FRA)	13	14	11	38
Italy (ITA)	13	8	13	34
Netherlands (NED)	12	9	4	25
Cuba (CUB)	11	11	7	29
Great Britain (GBR)	11	10	7	29
Romania (ROU)	11	6	8	25
South Korea (KOR)	8	10	10	28
Hungary (HUN)	8	6	3	17
Poland (POL)	6	5	3	14
Japan (JPN)	5	8	5	18
Bulgaria (BUL)	5	6	2	13
Greece (GRE)	4	6	3	13
Sweden (SWE)	4	5	3	12
Norway (NOR)	4	3	3	10
Ethiopia (ETH)	4	1	3	8
Ukraine (UKR)	3	10	10	23
Kazakhstan (KAZ)	3	4	0	7
Belarus (BLR)	3	3	11	17
Canada (CAN)	3	3	8	14
Spain (ESP)	3	3	5	11
Turkey (TUR)	3	0	2	5
Iran (IRI)	3	0	1	4
Czech Republic (CZE)	2	3	3	8
Kenya (KEN)	2	3	2	7
Denmark (DEN)	2	3	1	6
Finland (FIN)	2	1	1	4
Austria (AUT)	2	1	0	3

Continued overleaf

2000 Sydney continued

	Gold	Silver	Bronze	Total
Lithuania (LTU)	2	0	3	5
Azerbaijan (AZE)	2	0	1	3
Slovenia (SLO)	2	0	0	2
Switzerland (SUI)	1	6	2	9
Indonesia (INA)	1	3	2	6
Slovakia (SVK)	1	3	1	5
Mexico (MEX)	1	2	3	6
Algeria (ALG)	1	1	3	5
Uzbekistan (UZB)	1	1	2	4
Latvia (LAT)	1	1	1	3
Yugoslavia (YUG)	1	1	1	3
Bahamas (BAH)	1	1	0	2
New Zealand (NZL)	1	1	3	5
Estonia (EST)	1	0	2	3
Thailand (THA)	1	0	2	3
Croatia (CRO)	1	0	1	2
Cameroon (CMR)	1	0	0	1
Colombia (COL)	1	0	0	1
Mozambique (MOZ)	1	0	0	1
Brazil (BRA)	0	6	6	12
Jamaica (JAM)	0	5	4	9
Nigeria (NGR)	0	3	0	3
South Africa (RSA)	0	2	3	5
Belgium (BEL)	0	2	3	5

	Gold	Silver	Bronze	Total
Argentina (ARG)	0	2	0	2
Chinese Taipei (TPE)	0	1	4	5
Morocco (MAR)	0	1	4	5
North Korea (PRK)	0	1	3	4
Moldova (MDA)	0	1	1	2
Saudi Arabia (KSA)	0	1	1	2
Trinidad and Tobago (TRI)	0	1	1	2
Ireland (IRL)	0	1	0	1
Uruguay (URU)	0	1	0	1
Vietnam (VIE)	0	1	0	1
Sri Lanka (SRI)	0	1	0	1
Georgia (GEO)	0	0	6	6
Costa Rica (CRC)	0	0	2	2
Portugal (POR)	0	0	2	2
Armenia (ARM)	0	0	1	1
Barbados (BAR)	0	0	1	1
Chile (CHI)	0	0	1	1
Iceland (ISL)	0	0	1	1
India (IND)	0	0	1	1
Israel (IRS)	0	0	1	1
Kuwait (KUW)	0	0	1	1
Kyrgyzstan (KGZ)	0	0	1	1
Macedonia (MKD)	0	0	1	1
Qatar (QAT)	0	0	1	1

2002 Salt Lake City

	Gold	Silver	Bronze	Total
Norway (NOR)	13	5	7	25
Germany (GER)	12	16	8	36
United States (USA)	10	13	11	34
Canada (CAN)	7	3	7	17
Russia (RUS)	5	4	4	13
France (FRA)	4	5	2	11
Italy (ITA)	4	4	5	13
Finland (FIN)	4	2	1	7
Netherlands (NED)	3	5	0	8
Austria (AUT)	3	4	10	17
Switzerland (SUI)	3	2	6	11
Croatia (CRO)	3	1	0	4
China (CHN)	2	2	4	8
South Korea (KOR)	2	2	0	4
Australia (AUS)	2	0	0	2
Czech Republic (CZE)	1	2	0	3
Estonia (EST)	1	1	1	3
Great Britain (GBR)	1	0	1	2
Sweden (SWE)	0	2	5	7
Bulgaria (BUL)	0	1	2	3
Japan (JPN)	0	1	1	2
Poland (POL)	0	1	1	2
Belarus (BLR)	0	0	1	1
Slovenia (SLO)	0	0	1	1

2004 Athens

	Gold	Silver	Bronze	Total
United States (USA)	35	39	29	103
China (CHN)	32	17	14	63
Russia (RUS)	27	27	38	92
Australia (AUS)	17	16	16	49
Japan (JPN)	16	9	12	37
Germany (GER)	14	16	18	48
France (FRA)	11	9	13	33
Italy (ITA)	10	11	11	32
South Korea (KOR)	9	12	9	30
Great Britain (GBR)	9	9	12	30
Cuba (CUB)	9	7	11	27
Ukraine (UKR)	9	5	9	23
Hungary (HUN)	8	6	3	17
Romania (ROU)	8	5	6	19
Greece (GRE)	6	6	4	16
Brazil (BRA)	5	2	3	10
Norway (NOR)	5	0	1	6
Netherlands (NED)	4	9	9	22
Sweden (SWE)	4	1	2	7
Spain (ESP)	3	11	5	19
Canada (CAN)	3	6	3	12
Turkey (TUR)	3	3	4	10
Poland (POL)	3	2	5	10
New Zealand (NZL)	3	2	0	5
Thailand (THA)	3	1	4	8
Belarus (BLR)	2	6	7	15
Austria (AUT)	2	4	1	7
Ethiopia (ETH)	2	3	2	7
Iran (IRI)	2	2	2	6
Slovakia (SVK)	2	2	2	6
Taiwan (TPE)	2	2	1	5
Georgia (GEO)	2	2	0	4

Continued overleaf

2004 Athens continued

	Gold	Silver	Bronze	Total
Bulgaria (BUL)	2	1	9	12
Jamaica (JAM)	2	1	2	5
Uzbekistan (UZB)	2	1	2	5
Morocco (MAR)	2	1	0	3
Denmark (DEN)	2	0	6	8
Argentina (ARG)	2	0	4	6
Chile (CHI)	2	0	1	3
Kazakhstan (KAZ)	1	4	3	8
Kenya (KEN)	1	4	2	7
Czech Republic (CZE)	1	3	4	8
South Africa (RSA)	1	3	2	6
Croatia (CRO)	1	2	2	5
Lithuania (LTU)	1	2	0	3
Egypt (EGY)	1	1	3	5
Switzerland (SUI)	1	1	3	5
Indonesia (INA)	1	1	2	4
Zimbabwe (ZIM)	1	1	1	3
Azerbaijan (AZE)	1	0	4	5
Belgium (BEL)	1	0	2	3
Bahamas (BAH)	1	0	1	2
Israel (ISR)	1	0	1	2
Cameroon (CMR)	1	0	0	1

	Gold	Silver	Bronze	Total
Dominican Republic (DOM)	1	0	0	1
Ireland (IRL)	1	0	0	1
United Arab Emirates (UAE)	1	0	0	1
North Korea (PRK)	0	4	1	5
Latvia (LAT)	0	4	0	4
Mexico (MEX)	0	3	1	4
Portugal (POR)	0	2	1	3
Finland (FIN)	0	2	0	2
Serbia and Montenegro (SCG)	0	2	0	2
Slovenia (SLO)	0	1	3	4
Estonia (EST)	0	1	2	3
Hong Kong (HKG)	0	1	0	1
India (IND)	0	1	0	1
Paraguay (PAR)	0	1	0	1
Colombia (COL)	0	0	1	1
Nigeria (NGR)	0	0	2	2
Venezuela (VEN)	0	0	2	2
Eritrea (ERI)	0	0	1	1
Mongolia (MGL)	0	0	1	1
Syria (SYR)	0	0	1	1
Trinidad and Tobago (TRI)	0	0	1	1

2006 Turin

	Gold	Silver	Bronze	Total
Germany (GER)	11	12	6	29
United States (USA)	9	9	7	25
Austria (AUT)	9	7	7	23
Russia (RUS)	8	6	8	22
Canada (CAN)	7	10	7	24
Sweden (SWE)	7	2	5	14
South Korea (KOR)	6	3	2	11
Switzerland (SUI)	5	4	5	14
Italy (ITA)	5	0	6	11
France (FRA)	3	2	4	9
Netherlands (NED)	3	2	4	9
Estonia (EST)	3	0	0	3
Norway (NOR)	2	8	9	19
China (CHN)	2	4	5	11
Czech Republic (CZE)	1	2	1	4
Croatia (CRO)	1	2	0	3
Australia (AUS)	1	0	1	2
Japan (JPN)	1	0	0	1
Finland (FIN)	0	6	3	9
Poland (POL)	0	1	1	2
Belarus (BLR)	0	1	0	1
Bulgaria (BUL)	0	1	0	1
Great Britain (GBR)	0	1	0	1
Slovakia (SVK)	0	1	0	1
Ukraine (UKR)	0	0	2	2
Latvia (LAT)	0	0	1	1

2008 Beijing

	Gold	Silver	Bronze	Total
China (CHN)	51	21	28	100
United States (USA)	36	38	36	110
Russia (RUS)	23	21	28	72
Great Britain (GBR)	19	13	15	47
Germany (GER)	16	19	15	41
Australia (AUS)	14	15	17	46
South Korea (KOR)	13	10	8	31
Japan (JPN)	9	6	10	25
Italy (ITA)	8	9	10	27
France (FRA)	7	16	18	41
Ukraine (UKR)	7	5	4	16
Netherlands (NED)	7	5	4	16
Kenya (KEN)	6	4	4	14
Jamaica (JAM)	6	3	2	11
Spain (ESP)	5	10	3	18
Belarus (BLR)	4	5	10	19
Romania (ROU)	4	1	3	8
Ethiopia (ETH)	4	1	2	7
Canada (CAN)	3	9	6	18
Hungary (HUN)	3	5	2	10
Poland (POL)	3	6	1	10
Norway (NOR)	3	5	1	9
Brazil (BRA)	3	4	8	15
Czech Republic (CZE)	3	3	0	6
New Zealand (NZL)	3	2	4	9
Slovakia (SVK)	3	2	1	6
Georgia (GEO)	3	0	3	6
Cuba (CUB)	2	11	11	24
Kazakhstan (KAZ)	2	4	7	13
Denmark (DEN)	2	2	3	7
Mongolia (MGL)	2	2	0	4
Thailand (THA)	2	2	0	4

Continued overleaf

2008 Beijing continued

	Gold	Silver	Bronze	Total
North Korea (PRK)	2	1	3	6
Switzerland (SUI)	2	0	5	7
Argentina (ARG)	2	0	4	6
Mexico (MEX)	2	0	1	3
Turkey (TUR)	1	4	3	8
Zimbabwe (ZIM)	1	3	0	4
Azerbaijan (AZE)	1	2	4	7
Uzbekistan (UZB)	1	2	3	6
Slovenia (SLO)	1	2	2	5
Bulgaria (BUL)	1	1	3	5
Indonesia (INA)	1	1	3	5
Finland (FIN)	1	1	2	4
Latvia (LAT)	1	1	1	3
Belgium (BEL)	1	1	0	2
Dominican Republic (DOM)	1	1	0	2
Estonia (EST)	1	1	0	2
Portugal (POR)	1	1	0	2
India (IND)	1	0	2	3
Serbia (SRB)	1	0	2	3
Iran (IRI)	1	0	1	2
Cameroon (CMR)	1	0	0	1
Panama (PAN)	1	0	0	1
Tunisia (TUN)	1	0	0	1
Sweden (SWE)	0	4	1	5
Croatia (CRO)	0	2	3	5
Lithuania (LTU)	0	2	3	5
Greece (GRE)	0	2	2	4

	Gold	Silver	Bronze	Total
Trinidad & Tobago (TRI)	0	2	0	2
Nigeria (NGR)	0	1	3	4
Austria (AUT)	0	1	2	3
Ireland (IRL)	0	1	2	3
Algeria (ALG)	0	1	1	2
Bahamas (BAH)	0	1	1	2
Colombia (COL)	0	1	1	2
Kyrgyzstan (KGZ)	0	1	1	2
Morocco (MAR)	0	1	1	2
Tajikistan (TJK)	0	1	1	2
Chile (CHI)	0	1	0	1
Ecuador (ECU)	0	1	0	1
Iceland (ISL)	0	1	0	1
Malaysia (MAS)	0	1	0	1
South Africa (RSA)	0	1	0	1
Singapore (SIN)	0	1	0	1
Sudan (SUD)	0	1	0	1
Vietnam (VIE)	0	1	0	1
Armenia (ARM)	0	0	6	6
Chinese Taipei (TPE)	0	0	4	4
Afghanistan (AFG)	0	0	1	1
Egypt (EGY)	0	0	1	1
Israel (ISR)	0	0	1	1
Moldova (MDA)	0	0	1	1
Mauritius (MRI)	0	0	1	1
Togo (TOG)	0	0	1	1
Venezuela (VEN)	0	0	1	1

2010 Vancouver

	Gold	Silver	Bronze	Total
Canada (CAN)	14	7	5	26
Germany (GER)	10	13	7	30
United States (USA)	9	15	13	37
Norway (NOR)	9	8	6	23
South Korea (KOR)	6	6	2	14
Switzerland (SUI)	6	0	3	9
China (CHN)	5	2	4	11
Sweden (SWE)	5	2	4	11
Austria (AUT)	4	6	6	16
Netherlands (NED)	4	1	3	8
Russia (RUS)	3	5	7	15
France (FRA)	2	3	6	11
Australia (AUS)	2	1	0	3
Czech Republic (CZE)	2	0	4	6
Poland (POL)	1	3	2	6
Italy (ITA)	1	1	3	5
Belarus (BLR)	1	1	1	3
Slovakia (SVK)	1	1	1	3
Great Britain (GBR)	1	0	0	1
Japan (JPN)	0	3	2	5
Croatia (CRO)	0	2	1	3
Slovenia (SLO)	0	2	1	3
Latvia (LAT)	0	2	0	2
Finland (FIN)	0	1	4	5
Estonia (EST)	0	1	0	1
Kazakhstan (KAZ)	0	1	0	1

EVENTS	DISZIPLINEN	ÉPREUVES	ONDERDELEN
SUMMER	**SOMMER**	**ÉTÉ**	**ZOMER**
Archery	Bogenschießen	Tir à l'arc	Boogschieten
Athletics	Leichtathletik	Athlétisme	Atletiek
100 m	100 m	100 m	100 m
200 m	200 m	200 m	200 m
400 m	400 m	400 m	400 m
800 m	800 m	800 m	800 m
1500 m	1500 m	1500 m	1500 m
5000 m	5000 m	5000 m	5000 m
10,000 m	10,000 m	10000 m	10.000 m
Marathon	Marathon	Marathon	Marathon
110 m hurdles	110 m Hürden	110 m haies	110 m horden
400 m hurdles	400 m Hürden	400 m haies	400 m horden
3000 m steeplechase	3000 m Hindernis	3000 m steeple	3000 m steeplechase
Cross-country	Cross-Country	Cross-country	Crosscountry
4 x 100 m relay	4 x 100 m Staffellauf	4 x 100 m relais	4 x 100 m estafette
4 x 400 m relay	4 x 400 m Staffellauf	4 x 400 m relais	4 x 400 m estafette
20 km walk	20 km Gehen	20 km marche	20 km snelwandelen
50 km walk	50 km Gehen	50 km marche	50 km snelwandelen
High jump	Hochsprung	Saut en hauteur	Hoogspringen
Pole vault	Stabhochsprung	Saut à la perche	Polsstokhoogspringen
Long jump	Weitsprung	Saut en longueur	Verspringen
Triple jump	Dreisprung	Triple saut	Hink-stap-springen
Shot put	Kugelstoßen	Lancer du poids	Kogelstoten
Discus throw	Diskuswerfen	Lancer du disque	Discuswerpen
Hammer throw	Hammerwerfen	Lancer du marteau	Kogelslingeren
Javelin throw	Speerwurf	Lancer du javelot	Speerwerpen
Decathlon	Zehnkampf	Décathlon	Tienkamp
Heptathlon	Siebenkampf	Heptathlon	Zevenkamp
Badminton	Badminton	Badminton	Badminton
Baseball	Baseball	Baseball	Honkbal
Basketball	Basketball	Basketball	Basketbal
Boxing	Boxen	Boxe	Boksen
Canoe/kayak – sprint	Kanu/Kajak – Sprint	Canoë/kayak – course en ligne	Kano/kajakvaren – vlakwaterraces
Canoe/kayak – slalom	Kanu/Kajak – Slalom	Canoë/kayak – slalom	Kano/kajakvaren – wildwaterslalom
Cycling – BMX	Radsport – BMX	Cyclisme – BMX	Wielersport – BMX
Cycling – Mountain biking	Radsport – Mountainbike	Cyclisme – VTT	Wielersport – Mountainbiken
Cycling – Road cycling	Radsport – Straßenrennen	Cyclisme – Route	Wielersport – Wegwielrennen
Time trial	Zeitfahren	Course contre-la-montre	Tijdrit
Cycling – Track cycling	Radsport – Bahnradrennen	Cyclisme – Sur piste	Wielersport – Baanwielrennen
Individual pursuit	Einzelverfolgung	Poursuite individuelle	Achtervolging, individueel
Tandem	Tandem	Tandem	Tandem
Team pursuit	Mannschaftsverfolgung	Poursuite par équipes	Achtervolging, team
Fencing	Fechten	Escrime	Schermen
Epée	Degen	Epée	Degen
Foil	Florett	Fleuret	Floret
Sabre	Säbel	Sabre	Sabel
Field hockey	Hockey	Hockey sur gazon	Hockey
Football	Fußball	Football	Voetbal
Golf	Golf	Golf	Golf
Gymnastics – Artistic	Turnen – Kunstturnen	Gymnastique – Artistique	Gymnastiek – Turnen
All-around	Mehrkampf	Concours général	Allround
Balance beam	Schwebebalken	Poutre	Evenwichtsbalk
Floor	Boden	Sol	Vloer
Horizontal bar	Reck	Barre fixe	Paard
Parallel bars	Barren	Barres parallèles	Brug met gelijke opleggers
Rings	Ringe	Anneaux	Ringen
Uneven bars	Stufenbarren	Barres asymétriques	Brug met ongelijke opleggers
Gymnastics – Rhythmic	Turnen – Rhythmische Sportgymnastik	Gymnastique – Rythmique	Gymnastiek – Ritmisch
Gymnastics – Trampoline	Turnen – Trampolin	Gymnastique – Trampoline	Gymnastiek – Trampolinespringen
Handball	Handball	Handball	Handbal
Horse-riding – Dressage	Reiten – Dressur	Equitation – Dressage	Paardensport – Dressuur
Horse-riding – Eventing	Reiten – Military	Equitation – Concours complet	Paardensport – Eventing
Horse-riding – Jumping	Reiten – Springen	Equitation – Saut d'obstacles	Paardensport – Springen
Judo	Judo	Judo	Judo
Modern pentathlon	Moderner Fünfkampf	Pentathlon moderne	Moderne vijfkamp
Polo	Polo	Polo	Polo

DISCIPLINAS	**DISCIPLINE**	**PROVAS**
VERANO	**ESTATE**	**VERÃO**
Tiro con arco	Tiro con l'arco	Tiro com arco
Atletismo	Atletica leggera	Atletismo
100 m	100 m	100 m
200 m	200 m	200 m
400 m	400 m	400 m
800 m	800 m	800 m
1500 m	1500 m	1500 m
5000 m	5000 m	5000 m
10.000 m	10.000 m	10 000 m
Maratón	Maratona	Maratona
110 m vallas	110 m ad ostacoli	110 m barreiras
400 m vallas	400 m ad ostacoli	400 m barreiras
3000 m obstáculos	3000 m siepi	3000 m obstáculos
Campo a través	Corsa campestre	Corta-mato
4 x 100 m relevos	Staffetta 4 x 100 m	4 x 100 m estafetas
4 x 400 m relevos	Staffetta 4 x 400 m	4 x 400 m estafetas
20 km marcha	Marcia 20 km	20 km marcha
50 km marcha	Marcia 50 km	50 km marcha
Salto de altura	Salto in alto	Salto em altura
Salto con pértiga	Salto con l'asta	Salto à vara
Salto de longitud	Salto in lungo	Salto em comprimento
Triple salto	Salto triplo	Triplo salto
Lanzamiento de peso	Lancio del peso	Lançamento do peso
Lanzamiento de disco	Lancio del disco	Lançamento do disco
Lanzamiento de martillo	Lancio del martello	Lançamento do martelo
Lanzamiento de jabalina	Lancio del giavellotto	Lançamento do dardo
Decatlón	Decathlon	Decatlo
Heptatlón	Eptathlon	Heptatlo
Bádminton	Badminton	Badminton
Béisbol	Baseball	Basebol
Baloncesto	Pallacanestro	Basquetebol
Boxeo	Pugilato	Boxe
Canoa/kayak – Sprint	Canoa/kayak – Slalom	Canoa/caiaque – sprint
Canoa/kayak – Eslalon	Canoa/kayak – Velocità	Canoa/caiaque – slalom
Ciclismo – BMX	Ciclismo – BMX	Ciclismo – BMX
Ciclismo de montaña	Ciclismo – Mountain bike	Ciclismo – Ciclismo de montanha
Ciclismo en ruta	Ciclismo – Strada	Ciclismo – Ciclismo de estrada
Contrarreloj	Cronometro	Contra-relógio
Ciclismo de pista	Ciclismo – Pista	Ciclismo – Ciclismo de pista
Persecución individual	Inseguimento individuale	Perseguição individual
Tándem	Tandem	Tandem
Persecución por equipos	Inseguimento a squadre	Perseguição por equipas
Esgrima	Scherma	Esgrima
Espada	Spada	Espada
Florete	Fioretto	Florete
Sable	Sciabola	Sabre
Hockey sobre hierba	Hockey su prato	Hóquei em campo
Fútbol	Calcio	Futebol
Golf	Golf	Golfe
Gimnasia – Artística	Ginnastica – Artistica	Ginástica – Artística
Completo	Concorso generale	Todas as modalidades
Potro	Trave di equilibrio	Trave olímpica
Suelo	Corpo libero	Solo
Barra fija	Sbarra	Barra fixa
Paralelas	Parallele	Barras paralelas
Anillas	Anelli	Argolas
Barras asimétricas	Parallele asimmetriche	Barras assimétricas
Gimnasia – Rítmica	Ginnastica – Ritmica	Ginástica – Rítmica
Gimnasia – Cama elástica	Ginnastica – Trampolino	Ginástica – Trampolim
Balonmano	Pallamano	Andebol
Hípica – Doma	Equitazione – Dressage	Hipismo – Dressage
Hípica – Concurso completo	Equitazione – Completo	Hipismo – Concurso completo de equitação
Hípica – Saltos	Equitazione – Salto	Hipismo – Salto
Judo	Judo	Judo
Pentatlón moderno	Pentathlon moderno	Pentatlo moderno
Polo	Polo	Pólo

English	German	French	Dutch
Rowing	Rudern	Aviron	Roeien
Coxed eights	Achter mit Steuermann	Huit	Acht
Coxless fours	Vierer ohne Steuermann	Quatre sans barreur	Vier zonder
Coxless pairs	Zweier ohne Steuermann	Deux sans barreur	Twee zonder
Sculls	Skull	Skiff	Skiff
Rugby union	Rugby	Rugby	Rugby
Sailing	Segeln	Voile	Zeilen
Finn	Finn	Finn	Finn
470 Class	470er Klasse	Classe des 470	470 klasse
Flying Dutchman Class	Flying Dutchman	Classe Flying Dutchman	Flying Dutchman
Shooting	Schießen	Tir	Schietsport
Miniature rifle	Pistole	Carabine	Pistool
Pigeon	Tontaube	Tir au pigeon	Kleiduivenschieten
Skeet	Skeet	Tir au skeet	Skeet
Small bore	Kleinkaliber	Pistolet	Kleinkalibergeweer
Three-position rifle	Dreistellung	Carabine 3 positions	Vrij geweer, drie houdingen
Swimming – Diving	Schwimmen – Wasserspringen	Natation – Plongeon	Zwemmen – Schoonspringen
Platform	Turmspringen	Haut vol	Toren
Springboard	Sprungbrett	Tremplin	Plank
Synchronized	Synchronspringen	Plongeon synchronisé	Synchroon
Swimming – Swimming	Schwimmen – Schwimmen	Natation – Natation	Zwemmen – Zwemmen
Backstroke	Rücken	Dos crawlé	Rugslag
Breaststroke	Brust	Brasse	Schoolslag
Butterfly	Butterfly	Papillon	Vlinderslag
Freestyle	Freistil	Nage libre	Vrije slag
Medley	Lagen	4 nages	Wisselslag
Swimming – Synchronized	Synchronschwimmen	Natation – Synchronisée	Zwemmen – Synchroonzwemmen
Swimming – Water polo	Schwimmen – Wasserball	Natation – Water polo	Zwemmen – Waterpolo
Table tennis	Tischtennis	Tennis de table	Tafeltennis
Taekwondo	Taekwondo	Taekwondo	Taekwondo
Tennis	Tennis	Tennis	Tennis
Singles	Einzel	Simple	Enkelspel
Doubles	Doppel	Double	Dubbelspel
Mixed doubles	Mixed Doppel	Double mixte	Gemengd dubbelspel
Triathlon	Triathlon	Triathlon	Triatlon
Tug-of-war	Tauziehen	Tir à la corde	Touwtrekken
Volleyball – beach	Volleyball – Beach	Volleyball – plage	Volleybal – Beachvolleybal
Volleyball – indoor	Volleyball – Halle	Volleyball – en salle	Volleybal – Zaalvolleybal
Weightlifting	Gewichtheben	Haltérophilie	Gewichtheffen
Wrestling – Freestyle	Ringen – Freistil	Lutte – Libre	Worstelen – Vrije stijl
Wrestling – Greco-Roman	Ringen – Griechisch-Römisch	Lutte – Gréco-romaine	Worstelen – Grieks-Romeins
WINTER	**WINTER**	**HIVER**	**WINTER**
Alpine skiing	Ski Alpin	Ski alpin	Alpineskiën
Combined	Kombination	Combiné	Combinatie
Downhill	Abfahrt	Descente	Afdaling
Giant slalom	Riesenslalom	Slalom géant	Reuzenslalom
Slalom	Slalom	Slalom	Slalom
Super-G	Super-G	Super-G	Super-g
Biathlon	Biathlon	Biathlon	Biatlon
Bobsleigh	Bobfahren	Bobsleigh	Bobsleeën
Cross country skiing	Langlauf	Ski de fond	Langlaufen
Curling	Curling	Curling	Curling
Dog-sled racing	Schlittenhunderennen	Course de chiens de traineaux	Sledehondenrennen
Figure skating	Eiskunstlaufen	Patinage artistique	Kunstrijden
Freestyle skiing	Freestyle-Skiing	Ski acrobatique	Freestyleskiën
Aerials	Springen	Saut	Aerials
Cross	Skicross	Ski cross	Skicross
Moguls	Buckelpiste	Bosses	Moguls
Horse racing	Pferderennen	Course de chevaux	Paardenrennen
Ice dancing	Eistanzen	Patinage artistique - Danse	IJsdansen
Ice hockey	Eishockey	Hockey sur glace	IJshockey
Luge	Rennrodeln	Luge	Rodelen
Nordic combined	Nordische Kombination	Combiné nordique	Noordse combinatie
Short track speed skating	Eislaufen – Shorttrack	Patinage de vitesse sur piste courte	Short track schaatsen
Skeleton	Skeleton	Skeleton	Skeleton
Skijoring	Skijöring	Ski joëring	Skijöring
Ski jumping	Skispringen	Saut à ski	Schansspringen
Snowboarding	Snowboard	Snowboard	Snowboarden
Halfpipe	Halfpipe	Halfpipe	Halfpipe
Parallel Giant Slalom	Parallel-Riesentorlauf	Slalom géant parallèle	Parallelreuzenslalom
Speed skating	Eisschnelllauf	Patinage de vitesse	Langebaanschaatsen

Remo	Canottaggio	Remo
Ocho con timonel	Otto con timoniere	Oito com timoneiro
Cuatro sin timonel	Quattro senza timoniere	Quatro sem timoneiro
Dos sin timonel	Due senza timoniere	Dois sem timoneiro
Scull	Singolo	Sculls
Rugby unión	Rugby	Râguebi
Vela	Vela	Vela
Finn	Finn	Finn
Clase 470	470	Classe 470
Clase Flying Dutchman	Flying Dutchman	Classe Flying Dutchman
Tiro	Tiro	Tiro
Rifle pequeño	Pistola	Carabina miniatura
Blanco móvil	Piccione	Tiro aos pombos
Al plato	Piattello	Skeet
Carabina pequeña	Piccolo calibro	Pequeno calibre
Carabina en tres posiciones	Carabina 3 posizioni	Carabina de três posições
Natación – Saltos	Nuoto – Tuffi	Natação – Mergulho
Plataforma	Piattaforma	Plataforma
Trampolín	Trampolino	Trampolim
Sincronizados	Sincronizzato	Sincronizada
Natación – Natación	Nuoto – Nuoto	Natação – Natação
Espalda	Dorso	Costas
Braza	Rana	Bruços
Mariposa	Farfalla	Mariposa
Estilo libre	Stile libero	Estilo livre
Relevos de estilos	Misti	Medley
Natación – Sincronizada	Nuoto – Sincronizzato	Natação – Sincronizada
Natación – Waterpolo	Nuoto – Pallanuoto	Natação – Pólo aquático
Tenis de mesa	Tennis tavolo	Ténis de mesa
Taekwondo	Taekwondo	Taekwondo
Tenis	Tennis	Ténis
Individuales	Singolo	Individuais
Dobles	Doppio	Pares
Dobles mixtos	Doppio misto	Pares mistos
Triatlón	Triathlon	Triatlo
Tira y afloja	Tiro alla fune	Luta de tracção com corda
Voleibol – playa	Beach volley	Voleibol – praia
Voleibol – tradicional	Pallavolo	Voleibol – interior
Halterofilia	Sollevamento pesi	Halterofilismo
Lucha – Libre	Lotta libera	Luta – Estilo livre
Lucha – Grecorromana	Lotta greco-romana	Luta – Greco-Romana

INVIERNO	**INVERNO**	**INVERNO**
Esquí alpino	Sci alpino	Esqui alpino
Combinada	Combinata	Combinado
Descenso	Discesa libera	Downhill
Eslalon gigante	Slalom gigante	Slalom gigante
Eslalon	Slalom speciale	Slalom
Súper gigante	Supergigante	Super-G
Biatlón	Biathlon	Biatlo
Bobsleigh	Bob	Bobsleigh
Esquí a campo traviesa	Sci di fondo	Esqui de fundo
Curling	Curling	Curling
Trineo de perros	Sleddog – Cani da slitta	Corrida de cães de trenó
Patinaje artístico	Pattinaggio di figura	Patinagem artística
Esquí estilo libre	Sci acrobatico	Esqui estilo livre
Aerial	Salti	Aérea
Cross	Ski cross	Obstáculos
Mogul	Gobbe	Mogul
Carrera de caballos	Equitazione	Hipismo
Patinaje artístico – danza	Pattinaggio su ghiaccio – Danza	Dança no gelo
Hockey sobre hielo	Hockey su ghiaccio	Hóquei no gelo
Luge	Slittino	Luge
Combinada nórdica	Combinata nordica	Combinado nórdico
Patinaje de velocidad en pista corta	Pattinaggio su ghiaccio – Short track	Patinagem de velocidade de pista curta
Skeleton	Skeleton	Skeleton
Skijoring	Sci trainato da cavalli – Skijoring	Skijoring
Saltos de esquí	Salto con gli sci	Salto de esqui
Snowboard	Snowboard	Snowboard
Halfpipe	Halfpipe	Halfpipe
Eslalon paralelo gigante	Slalom gigante parallelo	Slalom gigante paralelo
Patinaje de velocidad	Pattinaggio su ghiaccio – Velocità	Patinagem de velocidade

PHOTO CREDITS

All images in this book are courtesy of Getty Images, including the following which have additional attributions:

AFP: 2, 57r, 146, 213r, 238, 239, 241, 247, 260, 261, 262, 263, 264, 625, 289, 292, 293, 297r, 303, 310, 313r, 316, 320, 323, 330-1, 334, 338-9, 341r, 342, 344, 346, 348-9, 351, 361, 365, 372, 409r, 420-1, 425, 457, 469l, 487, 492, 494-5, 501r, 512, 520, 521r, 522-3, 525, 528, 530, 533, 542, 546, 548-9, 551, 553l, 554, 556, 558, 559, 560, 562; **American Stock Archive:** 71r; **Apic:** 105r; **Archive Holdings Inc.:** 41r; **Nathan Bilow:** 433, 449; **Bongarts:** 389, 445, 451, 456, 460-1, 462, 472-3, 513, 526, 539, 547, 555; **Bloomberg:** 133l; **Chicago History Museum:** 31; **Steven Clevenger:** 353r; **Focus on Sport:** 318; **Ernst Haas:** 188, 192, 196, 197, 314; **Haynes Archive:** 102, 103; **Gamma Keystone:** 77, 116, 117, 121, 122, 154, 160, 163, 215, 229, 230, 242, 243, 290; **Imagno:** 92, 93, 107; **IOC Olympic Museum:** 10, 11l, 12, 13, 17l, 23, 25l, 33r, 41l, 47, 49l, 57l, 63l, 64, 68, 73, 74, 78, 79l, 80, 81, 82, 83, 84, 87l, 88, 91, 94, 101, 105l, 111, 113l, 125l, 145l, 153l, 164, 165l, 170, 175l, 189l, 199l, 213l, 221l, 235l, 236, 245l, 259l, 269l, 285l, 297l, 313l, 325l, 341l, 353l, 369l, 381l, 397l, 409l, 427l, 439l, 489l, 501l, 521l; **John Kelly:** 315, 317, 431; **Daniel Leah/Mexsport:** 440; **David Madison:** 347; **Gilles Mingasson:** 439r; **Ronald Modra:** 380; **NBAE:** 414; **National Geographic:** 212; **New York Daily News Archive:** 86, 89, 506; **New York Times Co.:** 79; **Paramount Pictures:** 199r; **Per-Anders Pettersson:** 427r; **Popperfoto:** 14, 16, 18, 19, 020, 21, 22, 24, 26, 27, 28, 29, 30, 37, 42, 46, 48, 50, 52, 53, 55, 58, 62, 66, 69, 70, 71l, 76, 90, 95l, 98, 99, 100, 113, 115, 119, 120, 123, 139, 145r, 147, 162, 179, 189r, 246, 252, 255, 294, 324; **Robert Riger:** 4, 217, 345; **Sankei Archive:** 220, 224; **Science & Society Picture Library:** 17r; **Sean Sexton:** 97; **Chris Smith:** 343, 375; **Sports Illustrated:** 177, 178, 186, 198, 201, 205, 209, 210, 219, 226, 231, 240, 244, 249, 250, 254, 256, 268, 271, 273, 281, 282, 288, 296, 298-9, 300-1, 302, 304-5, 306-7, 308-9, 311, 319, 321, 326-7, 329, 332, 340, 356, 364, 366-7, 371, 373, 385, 387, 390-1, 393, 394, 407, 416, 418, 441, 463, 476, 479, 485, 532, 534-5, 537, 538, 540-1, 545, 550, 552, 557, 561, 563; **Terry O'Neill:** 7; **Tom Stoddart:** 369r; **Bob Thomas:** 43, 51, 65, 336, 354, 376, 384, 424, 458, 465; **Time & Life Pictures:** 132, 141, 142, 143, 152, 155, 156, 157, 158, 159, 161, 165r, 167, 168, 169, 171, 173, 174, 175r, 176, 180, 181, 183, 184, 185, 187, 191, 194, 195, 200, 203, 204, 206, 207, 208, 209, 221r, 222, 223, 234, 235r, 245r, 248, 251, 257, 258, 266, 267, 272, 274, 275, 277, 278, 279, 280, 283, 381r; **Transcendental Graphics:** 40, 112; **Tony Vaccaro:** 125.

DATE DUE

SEP 20 2014	
NOV 18 2014	
OCT 05 2016	
OCT 12 2017	
WITHDRAWN	

BRODART, CO. — Cat. No. 23-221

Killaloe & District Public Library